AUTHORITY

AND

ESTRANGEMENT

Richard Moran

AUTHORITY
AND
ESTRANGEMENT

An Essay on Self-Knowledge

PRINCETON UNIVERSITY PRESS

PRINCETON AND OXFORD

COPYRIGHT © 2001 BY PRINCETON UNIVERSITY PRESS

PUBLISHED BY PRINCETON UNIVERSITY PRESS, 41 WILLIAM STREET,

PRINCETON, NEW JERSEY 08540

IN THE UNITED KINGDOM: PRINCETON UNIVERSITY PRESS, 3 MARKET PLACE,

WOODSTOCK, OXFORDSHIRE OX20 1SY

LIBRARY OF CONGRESS CATALOGING-IN-PUBLICATION DATA

MORAN, RICHARD

AUTHORITY AND ESTRANGEMENT : AN ESSAY ON SELF-KNOWLEDGE /

RICHARD MORAN

P. CM

INCLUDES BIBLIOGRAPHICAL REFERENCES AND INDEX.

ISBN 0-691-08944-2 (CLOTH : ALK. PAPER)—(ISBN 0-691-08945-0 (PBK. : ALK. PAPER)

1. SELF-KNOWLEDGE, THEORY OF. I. TITLE

BD438.5.M67 2001

126—DC21   2001021157

THIS BOOK HAS BEEN COMPOSED IN ITC GARAMOND

PRINTED ON ACID-FREE PAPER. ∞

WWW.PUP.PRINCETON.EDU

PRINTED IN THE UNITED STATES OF AMERICA

1   3   5   7   9   10   8   6   4   2

1   3   5   7   9   10   8   6   4   2

(PBK.)

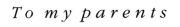

To my parents

Contents

Outline of the Chapters

CHAPTER ONE The Image of Self-Knowledge

1.1 THE FORTUNES OF SELF-CONSCIOUSNESS: DESCARTES, FREUD, AND COGNITIVE SCIENCE

The need to circumscribe the kind of knowledge of oneself that is relevant to philosophical reflection; the relevant sort of self-knowledge seen as specific in both content and in level of description. It is only with respect to *some* contents, and when identified by ordinary "personal level" concepts, that knowledge of oneself is either especially important to the life of the person or different in kind from the knowledge of others.

Asymmetries between first-person and third-person perspectives on mental life. The Perceptual Model of self-knowledge and difficulties in capturing a specifically first-person perspective.

Opposing Cartesianism without either denying the substantiality of
self-knowledge or its differences from the knowledge of others;
different in both the authority of its reports and in the basis on
which they are made.

First-person awareness as "immediate," not based on the observation
of the person's sayings and doings. Immediacy as distinct from
either certainty or infallibility.

1.2 THE POSSIBILITY OF SELF-KNOWLEDGE: INTROSPECTION, PERCEPTION, AND DEFLATION

The question of how self-knowledge, understood in terms of immediacy and authority, should be so much as possible. Fleeing the
"inner eye": various ways of "deflating" the appearance of first-
person reports as genuine reports, expressive of genuine cognitive commitment.

Skepticism about self-knowledge suggested either by functionalism in
theory of mind, or "externalism" about mental content, or Wittgenstein's "rule-following considerations."

In particular, the skepticism inspired by Content-Externalism seen as
presuming a perceptual picture of ordinary knowledge of what
one is thinking.

1.3 CONSTITUTIVE RELATIONS AND DETECTION

Does the immediacy and authority of first-person reports have, in part,
an a priori basis, or is it purely a matter of capacities people happen to have? The suggestion that a conceptual requirement here
would be incompatible with the idea of genuine detection or cognitive achievement, making the "authority" of the first-person a
matter of social concessions.

Conceptual connections and "response-dispositional" concepts; the
example of color and the class of "extension-determining" judgments.

This case does not, however, support "deflationism" about self-knowledge, nor does the biconditional analysis account for any asymmetry between first-person and third-person judgments of mental
life, which is the phenomenon we began trying to account for.
First-person authority as a demand on others as much as a concession
to them.

CHAPTER TWO Making Up Your Mind:
Self-Interpretation and Self-Constitution

2.1 SELF-INTERPRETATION, OBJECTIVITY, AND INDEPENDENCE

Ordinary "realism" about the mental suggests a relation of logical independence between the description of some feature of mental life (e.g., a thought or emotional response) and the feature or state itself. But in the case of the *self*-interpretation of various aspects of psychological and social life, some philosophers have argued that this independence does not obtain. The hermeneutic tradition and Taylor's Constitutive Claim.

We want to understand why this idea of a constitutive relation between interpretation and object is restricted to "intentionally characterized" phenomena, and why within these it is restricted to their *first-person* interpretation.

Distinguishing the Constitutive Claim from the idea that certain conceptual capacities are necessary for the possibility of certain emotional responses.

2.2 SELF-FULFILLMENT AND ITS DISCONTENTS

To say that a person's self-interpretation "constitutes its object," even partially, suggests that, in those cases, the new interpretation *suffices* for a new description to be true of it (perhaps a description conforming to the new interpretation itself). Sometimes taking oneself to be a certain way (e.g., uncomfortable, ambivalent) is sufficient for being truly characterized in those terms. The negative character of such "compromising" self-descriptions, and the self-fulfilling logic of contamination. The appeal of the Constitutive Claim may draw strength from such cases, but they cannot be said to characterize psychological life generally.

2.3 THE WHOLE PERSON'S DISCRETE STATES

The privilege accorded to a person's own interpretation of his state need not be restricted to those cases where the constitutive relation involves the state's *conforming* to the person's interpretation of it. Even an interpretation which we, on the outside, can see as importantly *mistaken* may nonetheless have a claim to defining his state overall, in a way that is not shared by an outsider's interpretation of it. Seeing one's own pride as sinful constitutes it as importantly different from what it would otherwise be, since conditions like pride are orientations of the person and not atomistic particulars.

2.4 BELIEF AND THE ACTIVITY OF INTERPRETING

Verbs such as "interpreting" and "describing" can denote ordinary activities that can be performed at will, but in that sense the activity of "merely describing" one's state a certain way will not be expected to constitute it as different, any more than mere describing makes a constitutive difference to other things in the world. Rather, the examples that make the best sense of the Constitutive Claim concern the self-interpretation of one's emotional state where "interpreting" it a certain way means actually taking it to *be* that way. This involves cognitive commitment which, like belief, is not something that can be undertaken at will. And this begins to clarify why reflection on one's own intentional states should be linked to the transformation of their character.

2.5 THE PROCESS OF SELF-CREATION: THEORETICAL AND DELIBERATIVE QUESTIONS

Sometimes reflection on one's state of mind is a purely theoretical matter, where the question is how some feature of one's mental life is to be correctly identified. But often one's reflection is more "deliberative" in spirit and seeks to bring one's state of mind to some kind of resolution. This sort of uncertainty is answered by something more like a decision than a discovery. The difference between "I don't know what to feel here" and "I don't know what it is that I do feel here."

The situation of deliberative, rather than theoretical, reflection on one's state helps to account for why it should be *self*-interpretation alone that is said to "help shape the emotion itself," and why, even on a commonsense "realism" about mental life, we should *expect* self-interpretation to play this special role.

2.6 RELATIONS OF TRANSPARENCY

It is sometimes claimed that, from the first-person point of view, the question "Do I believe that P?" is *transparent to* a corresponding question "Is P true?," a question which involves no essential reference to oneself at all. "Transparency" here means not reduction, but that the former question is answered in the same way as the latter. But what is the basis for such transparency, when it obtains?

There do seem to be situations where the person can or must answer the psychological question of what his attitude *is* in a way that is *not* "transparent" in the relevant sense. Rather than being guaranteed by logic, the claim of transparency is grounded in the deferral of theoretical reflection on one's state to deliberative reflection about it. Conforming to transparency as a normative demand.

Both the "transforming" character of self-interpretation and the "transparency" of one's present thinking are grounded in the interaction between theoretical and deliberative reflection on one's state of mind and the primacy of the deliberative stance within the first-person.

CHAPTER THREE Self-Knowledge as Discovery and as Resolution

3.1 WITTGENSTEIN AND MOORE'S PARADOX

Why ordinary self-knowledge should be "nonevidential" rather than a matter of theoretical attribution to oneself, and why this difference matters. Moore's Paradox as a way of describing situations where one's attribution of an attitude to oneself does not match the attitude one would explicitly express or endorse (hence, where the Transparency Condition is violated).

What is paradoxical in Moore's Paradox is not restricted to situations
of speech or the pragmatics of assertion.

The Presentational View, whereby the first-person present-tense of
'believe' does not have any psychological reference, but only
serves to "present" the embedded statement (e.g., saying "I *believe* it's going to rain" as expressing uncertainty about *the rain*).
Rejection of this view, and its attribution to Wittgenstein.

First-person authority and first-person subjection; blindspots.

How is transparency consistent with the fact of the different subject
matters of the two questions (a state of mind, a state of the
weather)? Belief as empirical psychological fact about a person,
and belief as commitment to a state of affairs beyond the self.
Inferring from someone's having some belief to the truth of that
belief, versus the categorical relation between belief and "taking
to be true" in the first-person.

3.2 SARTRE, SELF-CONSCIOUSNESS, AND THE LIMITS OF THE EMPIRICAL

The "self-as-facticity" (seeing belief as a psychological fact about oneself) and the "self-as-transcendence" (seeing belief as a commitment of oneself). The case of the gambler as illustrating conflict
between these two perspectives, neither of whose claims is avoidable. One type of "bad faith" as the exploitation of the purely
theoretical perspective on oneself; another type as the empty transcendental assertion of one's freedom and clean slate.

For the first-person, the sense of the primacy of the practical, deliberative question over the predictive, theoretical question.

3.3 AVOWAL AND ATTRIBUTION

"Transparency" as a normative requirement on rational agency.

Reporting one's state of mind, where this is an evidence-based attribution, in the service of psychological explanation, versus expressing or avowing one's attitude, where this is a matter of one's de-
clared commitment. The description of forms of psychic conflict

such as self-deception and *akrasia* requires an account of the clash between attitudes of the *same* basic type, otherwise "reporting" and "expressing" could simply go their separate ways, as in Moore's Paradox.

Anscombe and the sense of "I'm going to bed at midnight." The first-person statement of intention commits itself both practically and empirically.

If we reject the Presentational View and claim that psychological terms like 'believe' can be univocal across first- and third-person contexts, describing the same state of affairs, then the avowal of one's attitude and the explanatory attribution of that attitude can be seen as different routes to knowledge of the same thing. Hence the language of "stances" as applied to deliberative and theoretical questions. This poses the question: For self-knowledge of one's belief or other attitude, why should it matter that this knowledge is arrived at by one route rather than another? What is the importance (both philosophical and psychological) of the specific route of avowability to self-knowledge?

Consideration of an "ideal symptomatic stance" toward oneself to show that the importance of avowability cannot be a matter of either spontaneity, greater certainty, or reliability.

Wittgenstein and Sartre against the purely theoretical picture of self-knowledge; mind-reading as applied to oneself.

The two aspects of the first-person perspective on one's attitudes: "immediacy," in the sense of the report's not basing itself on behavioral evidence; and "endorsement," that the expression of the attitude normally counts as a claim of some sort about its *object*.

The loss of the authority to speak for one's attitudes or feelings is not made up for by any amount of improved theoretical access to them.

3.4 BINDING AND UNBINDING

Deliberation aims to settle the question of what I think or feel, or what I'm going to do. It represents a failure of deliberation when it issues, not in a settled belief or intention, but instead either in the attempt to exert some influence over one's belief or will, or in some state of mind which is then treated as evidence for what one believes or intends.

Not further evidence about oneself, but only the authority of one's commitment, can make for the link between one's present deliberative thinking and one's actual future belief or action. Similarly for the emerging from a purely attributive ("therapeutic") relation to some repressed attitude into the ability to avow it.

The example of settling some question by flipping a coin, and then flipping it again "to make sure." The ability to bind oneself and the recognition that one can always *un*bind oneself. The significance of the behavior of the coin, like the significance of the thought that concludes my deliberation or expresses my conviction, cannot be for me a matter of *discovery*. "Making sure" and the alibi of the appeal to "further evidence," which undoes one's self-knowledge.

Wittgenstein and "I believe I hope you'll come." The retreat from avowal: suspending self-expression and the limitations of truthful attribution.

CHAPTER FOUR The Authority of Self-Consciousness

4.1 EXPRESSING, REPORTING, AND AVOWING

If an avowal is a first-person belief-statement that obeys the Transparency Condition, how can it be thought to retain the status of a *report* with reference to a particular person? Expressivism as the denial that first-person present-tense "psychological" utterances function descriptively, hence a fortiori the denial that such utterances can be statements expressive of self-*knowledge*.

Rejection of expressivism generally, and specifically with respect to avowals.

4.2 RATIONALITY, AWARENESS, AND CONTROL:
A LOOK INSIDE

If avowability is what makes for the difference between "merely attributional" knowledge of oneself and genuine first-person awareness, what is the importance of this difference for the rationality and health of the person? One explanation of this importance is given by the argument that self-knowledge is a requirement for the rational control of beliefs and other attitudes. But the rationality of belief does not generally require monitoring and intervention; and, at the same time, such a requirement would not account for the need for specifically first-person awareness of one's beliefs. The importance of "immediacy."

4.3 FROM SUPERVISION TO AUTHORITY:
AGENCY AND THE ATTITUDES

Authority, responsibility, and the "motivated" or "judgment-sensitive" attitudes.

Two ways of being "active" with respect to one's desires; for example, pinching oneself, on the one hand, and orienting or committing oneself, on the other.

Reasoning, deliberating, versus aiming to produce some belief in oneself. Assuming authority for one's attitudes (seeing them as "up to me") versus exerting control over them.

4.4 THE RETREAT TO EVIDENCE

If the "authority" of "first-person authority" were purely a matter of epistemic access, then the abrogation or replacement of this authority by some other type of access might be conceivable. But the suspension of first-person authority on an occasion does not support the coherence of the idea of its suspension across the board. Even taking the person's own thoughts and words as being only of symptomatic or evidential significance for what his

state of mind actually is must rely at some point on his authority
to speak his mind.

4.5 FIRST-PERSON IMMEDIACY AND AUTHORITY

Once more, the relation of rational authority to the special "immediacy"
of first-person awareness. Why should the particular avenue of
awareness matter? Comparison with Anscombe's Condition on
intentional action.

From the agent's point of view, the primacy of Justifying reasons over
Explanatory reasons for his action.

The two faces of immediacy; epistemic and practical.

The "subject" use of 'I'. This requirement on first-person awareness can
now be seen in terms of the requirement of "immediacy" and the
priority of Justifying reasons over Explanatory ones. Answering
the question of my belief from the Deliberative stance, I do not
refer to myself as falling under any particular description.

4.6 INTROSPECTION AND THE DELIBERATIVE POINT OF VIEW

Further discussion of how the account of deliberation remains part
of the theory of *self-knowledge*. The stance of deliberation as
central to any account of self-knowledge that seeks to account for
three features of the general form of self-knowledge which is of
specifically philosophical interest: Immediacy, Authority, and the
special importance of such self-knowledge to ordinary psychic
health.

4.7 REFLECTION AND THE DEMANDS OF AUTHORITY: APPREHENSION, ARREST, AND CONVICTION

The relation of self-consciousness to rational freedom in Kantian and
post-Kantian traditions of thought (the "Tradition of Reflection").
Why should *this* faculty of awareness have any deeper relation
to freedom or rationality than any other one (e.g., various modes
of perception)?

sophical importance and are more fundamental than any skeptical consequences that may be drawn from them.

Further, the description of the asymmetries themselves does not itself privilege *either* point of view. Neither perspective need be interpreted as *aspiring* to the position or possibilities of the other, and even the authority of the first-person is related to its blind-spots, and the possibilities of "counter-privacy."

5.2 THE PARTIALITY OF THE IMPERSONAL STANCE

Egoism, solipsism, and the imperative of impersonality in Nagel. The Impersonal Principle as expressing "a conception of oneself as simply a person among others, all of whom are included in a single world."

Avoiding an interpretation of the Impersonal Principle which ultimately asserts the dominance of the "external point of view," denying either the distinctiveness or the legitimacy of the demands of the first-person perspective.

In this way we can see that each perspective has a legitimate claim upon us, and neither can do the work of the other. Nonetheless, they can clash, and when they do, neither side has an exclusive claim to dictate the terms of a resolution. For the conflict is between perspectives and not within either one of them, each of which may in such a case be perfectly consistent within itself and reasonable in its own demands. One perspective only "leaves something out" from the perspective of the other one.

Sartre's gambler once again, and the competing demands of being empirically realistic about oneself, and being answerable for one's thought and action. From within either of the two perspectives, the demands of the other one can be described as characteristic forms of evasion.

Impersonality in ethics and its existentialist critique.

Attitudes and relations that are grounded in their "other-directed" application, and which can be adopted toward oneself only under some degree of psychological and conceptual tension.

5.3 SELF-EFFACEMENT AND THIRD-PERSON PRIVILEGE

The possibility of "self-effacing" moral theories and the "appraising function" of terms for certain virtues of character. Williams and the idea of limits to the scope of moral self-consciousness.

Traits of character and the deliberative point of view. When aiming at the manifestation of some trait undermines the claim to possess it.

Pity versus Self-Pity, etc.; avoiding both "first-person exceptionalism" and the *dis*privileging of the first-person.

Instabilities in applying certain terms of moral appraisal to oneself.

5.4 PARADOXES OF SELF-CENSURE

Dr. Johnson and self-censure as "showing what one can spare"; availing oneself of an outside perspective for purposes of both judging and sparing oneself. Self-blame as covert exoneration.

In these examples of forms of self-criticism that either undermine themselves or involve "taking oneself as an object" in some illegitimate way, the diagnosis of what is wrong here still seems misdescribed. A more detailed case is needed to examine just how something deserving the name of "self-objectification" contributes to the undermining of the state objectified.

The "tremendous rakehell"; "feeling bad about feeling good about feeling bad."

Taking one's psychological state as a fact about oneself, and reflecting on it for its expressive import.

Exploiting the difference between "straight" beliefs and other attitudes. Shame as not simply an attitude toward a proposition, but an attitude involving characteristic patterns of attention and experience. The importance of these experiential and temporal dimensions in the moral estimation of a person's attitudes and responses.

But while these very differences between beliefs and other attitudes (e.g., shame) may save the rakehell from straight inconsistency, at the same time they make it harder for him to reach any redeeming interpretation of his response. For the "credit" in question depended on the aspect of shame as experience and orientation of the person, and it is this aspect that his reflections are undoing (even while he retains the straight belief).

5.5 INCORPORATION AND THE EXPRESSIVE READING

Impersonality as evenhandedness. The rakehell's defense in terms of his right and obligation to the "total evidence" of the case. But does this epistemic principle earn him the right to the results of an expressive interpretation of his shame?

The conflicting requirements of the Impersonal Principle.

Incorporating his shame into the total evidence, which can seem epistemically unobjectionable, requires that there is some point here in appealing to evidence to settle some question. But the expressive conclusion he is trying to reach depends on the degree to which he is already settled in his response, the response of shame itself.

Hence, availing himself of the expressive interpretation of his response means reopening the question of what his response is, which will necessarily make a difference to whatever expressive conclusions may be drawn from it. For he is seeking credit for a settled response of his while in the very act of unsettling it, and thus suspending or diminishing its expressive import.

5.6 "NOT FIRST-PERSONAL ENOUGH?"

First-person moral reflection versus appraising oneself from the point of view of an imagined Other. George Eliot and the evasions of responsibility through egocentric guilt, the internalization of a moral observer.

Williams and the first-person cultivation of the virtues as not self-directed enough, or not in the right way. The stance of agency versus the stance of prediction or appraisal.

Sartre on "unrealizables"; the limited truth in his thought that "character has distinct existence only in the capacity of an object of knowledge for the Other."

Reconciling the claims of impersonality with the distinct demands of the first- and third-person perspectives.

Preface

In recent years, several different currents of thought have at times urged that the very idea of the distinctiveness of the "first-person perspective," perhaps especially as this idea centers around questions of self-knowledge, is a piece of metaphysics we must learn to do without. Sometimes this thought is taken to be one of the lessons of Wittgenstein, sometimes the idea hails from somewhere in the discourse of the Death of the Subject, and sometimes it is taken to be a consequence of a broad Naturalism in the philosophy of mind (particularly in the several strategies of decomposition of the person into various subpersonal components), or of a more direct reductionism about personal identity. Indeed, it can often seem as if the only point of convergence between various warring factions in contemporary discourses about the mind is in agreement over some version of the idea that the Self, at least as we have come to know it, has got to go.

"Cartesianism" is one recurrent name for the problematic concept in question, and its irresistibility and longevity as a figure for dismantling is in good part due to its being a complex package of views, combining a metaphysics of the Self with a picture of its special powers and place in the natural world, as well as giving vivid expression to a cluster of epistemological concerns about the knowability of this entity, both to itself and by others of its kind. So it remains an attractive target in good part because it presents so many different facets to aim at. And, indeed, a philosopher might well find himself obliged to be skeptical about any entity that is described as being immaterial, immortal, autonomous, unique and self-identifying, transparent to itself (in being both infallible and complete in its awareness of itself); not to mention being the locus of rationality, responsibility and moral value, and the bestower of meaning on an otherwise featureless universe. And at the same time nothing invested with powers as godlike as *these* can be expected to go away quietly. Small wonder, then, that the Death of the Subject would remain the kind of persistent but forever unfinished business that is familiar in the case of the slaying of other icons.

Some intellectual contexts suggest that, more than any metaphysical extravagances of the Cartesian picture, it is the basic idea of there being anything distinctive or irreducible about the perspective of the first-person that is found objectionable or dispensable—the very idea that the person's own access and relation to his own mental life must be different in its possibilities and limitations from anyone else's. For reasons both philosophical and otherwise, this general idea of unbridgeable differences between the situations of self and other can appear both unmotivated and unwelcome, long before anything like a full-blown "egocentric predicament" may come to seem realistic or philosophically compelling. If there are indeed persons with lives and experiences to be known and explained, one general thought goes, then the facts in question should be as open and indifferent to the limitations of any individual perspective as are the phenomena of any other object of study; otherwise there's simply nothing there to be known, by anyone.

But while we still retain anything like our concepts of persons, minds, and actions, there will be, it seems, basic differences in the logic and consequences of first-person and third-person attitudes. This book seeks to explore some of them, focusing primarily on questions of self-knowledge, and trying to use that case as a kind of point of orientation for considering some of the wider asymmetries between relations to oneself and relations to others. With respect to the specific question of self-knowledge, it seems clear that at least *some* of the strands of the broadly Cartesian picture can be separated from one another, and some of the grander claims for the self's perfect access to itself can be set aside, while still leaving us with the question of how and why attitudes toward oneself (including that of knowing) should exhibit *any* systematic differences from their third-person analogues.

One basic such difference, the defense and articulation of which threads its way throughout the following discussion, is that, while a person may learn of someone else's beliefs or other attitudes from what she says and does, he may arrive at knowledge of his own attitudes in a way that is *not* based on evidence or observation of himself. In this sense, a person may know his own mind "immediately," yet nonetheless declare his belief with an authority that is lacking in anyone else's observation-based description of him. In common philosophical language, a person may know his own belief by *avowing* it, and not only by attributing it to himself on the basis of the same sort of considerations that would be available to others. This is a familiar idea in philosophical discussion, though not one immune to controversy and certainly a striking claim in its own right. But at the same time it is a considerably more modest claim than much of what is built into the classic Metaphysics of the Subject. This basic thought of immediacy does not claim, for instance, that the mind's access to itself is infallible, or complete, or can't be corrected by others or by external evidence. (It is fully compatible, for example, with the picture of the various characteristic failures of self-knowledge in psychoanalytic writing, and later chapters here try to say something about why the restoration of this particular *form* of knowledge of oneself—that is, avowal—should matter at all to the health of the person.) Further, it is not argued here that *all* of a person's awareness of his mental life is achievable in this "immediate" way; much of the hard-won knowledge of oneself will be based on the same kinds of considerations available to others and fraught with the same possibilities for error and misinterpretation.

Nonetheless, the "immediacy" of self-knowledge remains a provocative idea, both as the assertion of a particular capacity we have (i.e., what is it for *any* mental life to be known by me in this way?), and as a characterization of a form of awareness with this specially restricted application (i.e., why is it only *this* mental life that I can know in this way?). And while this form of awareness does not exhaust what a person may know of himself, and while its authority is not absolute, it is argued here that this is a fundamental form of self-apprehension, that a person does not just happen to have this remarkable capacity, but that it belongs to the concept of a person that he should be able to achieve knowledge of his attitudes in this way. These privileges and these restrictions remain to be understood after the Cartesian subject has given way to something less perfectly unified, something more subject to the contingencies of its placement in the world and often willfully blind to itself.

In developing this account, I'm trying to do justice to a certain tension in our thinking about the possibilities of self-knowledge and the distinctiveness of the first-person perspective more generally. On the one hand, it seems undeniable that we can and do bear a host of attitudes and relations toward ourselves that are of the same type, or called by the same names, as many of the attitudes we bear toward other people. After all, among the people we take a certain interest in and entertain thoughts about will be the particular people we are, and even the most selfless among us are not barred by logic from doing so. But, on the other hand, it is also natural to feel that, in many cases at least, these attitudes *cannot* be the same sort of thing in their self-directed and other-directed versions, and in some cases the first-person version of some otherwise unproblematic stance is no more a coherent possibility than being taller than oneself or keeping oneself waiting. "Knowing" is certainly one such attitude whose philosophical discussion embodies just this sort of tension. There are several contexts where speaking of knowing oneself, or knowing one's mind, is natural and unavoidable. We don't want to say that, although we sometimes achieve knowledge of another person's hopes and fears, the very idea of such "knowledge" as applied to oneself makes no sense. I am one person among others in the world, and at the very least the particular ways I have of knowing about *others* should provide me with comparable access to myself. And it may seem that both common sense and the counsel to objectivity about oneself (including "seeing oneself as others do") suggest that this parity should obtain across the attitudes generally.

But at the same time, it is equally natural, and I think unavoidable, to think that, for a range of central cases, whatever knowledge of *oneself* may be, it is a very different thing from the knowledge of others, categorically different in kind and manner, different in consequences, and with its own distinguishing and constraining possibilities for success and failure. It is not necessary to say that the mind of another person is "essentially hidden" from me, in order to acknowledge that this person knows, and comes to know, his own thoughts and experiences in ways that are categorically different from how I may come to know them. And these differences have sometimes seemed so deep and so fundamental to the very idea of the self as to suggest that we cannot be talking about the same thing, the same kind of cognitive attitude, when we speak of "knowledge of self" and "knowledge of others," even though we recognize it is the same kind of creature being apprehended in both cases. This sense of difference can gain expression in the insistence that one cannot ever be "an object" to oneself in thought, or that the phrase "I know" cannot (except perhaps as a joke) be attached to a first-person statement of pain or other sensations, or that the mind's very act of apprehension of itself must alter the facts of the case, or in some other way render the 'I' systematically elusive to genuine knowledge by itself. Although each of these ideas comes in for some criticism here, the discussion is at least as much concerned to understand and take seriously the considerations that have made them seem attractive or unavoidable (sometimes offering a kind of vindication).

In addition, the appeal of such ideas is related to homelier asymmetries, more often encountered in moral psychology than in the metaphysics of mind, where an ordinary stance toward others either means something quite different in its reflexive form, or has only some paradoxical application to oneself. Self-respect and the respect of others are essentially different in their forms and demands, and not only in their objects (think of "respecting someone's wishes" in the two cases); and, notoriously, self-pity is not simply pity directed at the person who is oneself. Self-deception is famously thought to be both a widespread failing and perhaps not a genuinely coherent possibility after all, despite how common and unproblematic the deception of others is, in both theory and practice. And, with self-deception as with other cases, resolving the philosophical problem of coherence in our descriptions does not annul the asymmetry or the special features of the first-person case, but rather places them in a light where different questions can be asked (e.g., why should 'self-deception', whatever it turns out to be, have any special suggestion of irrationality, given that the deception of another need not be irrational on the part of the deceiver, nor need it produce irrationality in the person deceived?). Understanding how the specific attitudes of believing and knowing are subject to special demands and constraints in the first-person case should help us understand these wider asymmetries of self and other. There are, in addition, a host of other stances and attitudes (possibly: excuse and forgiveness, gratitude, deference, certain forms of trust) that can seem reserved for relations with others and that may only be adopted toward oneself through some usurpation of a role proper to some person other than oneself. The hope is that the understanding of first-person authority, as a kind of paradigm asymmetry, will contribute to the understanding of a less worked-over set of questions concerning why some relations necessarily take two, and why others may admit of a self-directed form, but only under some strain, both conceptual and psychological. So, the course of the discussion here traces a path from the more purely epistemological questions about self-knowledge and first-person authority to an interest in certain pathologies of self-concern, and, more generally, the idea of limits on modeling some of the relations to oneself on the possibilities of relations to others.

It will be apparent that the account of first-person authority presented here is partial as well as just sketched-out in places, incomplete even within its restricted range. And there are several related issues, some of them receiving a good bit of attention in recent years, which are hardly considered here at all. The discussion here centers around the knowledge a person may have of his own attitudes: beliefs, desires, intentions, and various emotional states. There are, of course, different things to be said about these cases, and when they matter to the particular turn of argument I try to bring them out. But I make no attempt here to catalog such differences, and some things said about the case of belief will not generalize, or only with some more or less serious adjustment, to other attitudes, other ways in which a person may know his own mind. Further, the discussion here only occasionally touches on either the question of "mental content" (and, e.g., whether externalism poses any special problem for the assumption that a person generally knows what he's thinking of) or questions surrounding the idea of phenomenal or "qualitative consciousness" (and, e.g., whether a person can be said to *know* his qualitative sensations in a way that is essentially unavailable to another person and if so, how such "knowing" is to be understood). My own view is that there are very different things to be said about these questions, and that the diverse phenomena of self-knowledge do not submit to a uniform account, but to argue for that explicitly would deflect the discussion too far from the sorts of questions I want to raise here. In briefest terms, those questions concern the difficulties in getting the proper alignment of the self as agent to the self as spectator, as these perspectives interact, sometimes clashing, in the context of some problem for self-knowledge. Such a clash of perspectives is one thing given expression in the theme of the "diseases of self-consciousness" (Dostoyevsky) as it occurs in the literature and philosophy of romanticism, modernism, and beyond; in the idea that, in the realm of reflection, becoming "visible" to oneself is a matter of becoming divided from oneself. Nothing here is meant to further the idea that self-knowledge (of the special varieties that have attracted the attention of philosophers) simply *is* a form of alienation, but I do mean to show how the conditions that make for the assumption of first-person authority also provide the standing possibilities for certain characteristic forms of alienation.

The discussion to follow makes repeated but sporadic reference to the later Wittgenstein and to the account of self-consciousness and "bad faith" in Sartre's *Being and Nothingness*. This may seem an odd alliance, and I make no special claim for its originality, nor can the discussion that follows count as any kind of extended reading of their work. I do, however, believe that their investigations of the first-person apprehension of oneself are complementary in several ways that are worth pursuing. I see both of them as committed to a complex sense of the irreducible distinctiveness of the first-person position, combined with a rejection of the tenacious picturing of this difference in terms of inner and outer realms. This interpretation itself already puts me at odds with some readers of Wittgenstein (and presumably some readers of Sartre as well) who take the rejection of the picture of inner space to be equivalent to a rejection of self-other asymmetries themselves. In addition, I see them both as beginning (and in some ways ending) with a sense of certain such asymmetries as *basic*, and by this I mean chiefly two things. First, such differences between self and other, while irreducible, are prior to and not in any way equivalent to the skeptical consequences that are sometimes drawn from them. Hence, the differences themselves have a claim on philosophical attention that is independent of such canonical questions. And second, the differences themselves are seen by them as basic in the sense that a proper account of them does not begin by privileging *either* perspective, whether first-

or third-person; and, hence, a proper account of the peculiarities of the first-person position will display that position as defined by its characteristic *dis*advantages as part of its very privilege (and similarly for the third-person). Increasingly, I see the importance and distinctiveness of their writings on the self in terms of making the sheer fact of such differences available as a philosophical topic in its own right. I don't offer anything like an extended defense of this interpretation of either writer, and I don't know that I could, although I do hope its convincingness emerges over the course of the book.

I want to mention three other books at the outset, since each has been crucial for grounding my sense of the philosophical problems of self-knowledge as bound up with such wider questions. They are *Self-Knowledge and Self-Identity* by Sydney Shoemaker, *Freedom of the Individual* by Stuart Hampshire, and *The Claim of Reason* by Stanley Cavell. I did not encounter the Hampshire book until I was well into the project, but its relevance to the argument (especially Chapter Two) will be clear to anyone who knows it. The writings of Shoemaker and Cavell, on the other hand, were inspirational for my original interest in philosophical questions about the first-person and have remained so ever since. I draw attention to these books here because their importance to the framing of the questions I'm pursuing is way out of proportion to the frequency of their explicit appearances in the text. This is hardly the only way in which philosophical writings that have helped define the issues for me over the years fail to come up for explicit discussion in these pages. In recent years there has been a remarkable amount of diverse philosophical interest in the first-person, much of which has helped guide the thinking presented here. In this book I have a somewhat complex story to tell, whose outlines I try to keep reasonably compact and clear, and it seemed best not to risk obscuring that outline further with notes and discussions that may derive from concerns at one remove or another from the ones prompting the discussion here.

Acknowledgments

In the years it took me to complete this book, I was granted leave time from Princeton University and from Harvard University, for which I am very grateful. In addition, I was fortunate to be a Fellow at the National Humanities Center in 1994–95, and at the Princeton University Center for Human Values in 1998–99. I thank both places for the time and the setting thus provided, and for the group of other Fellows with whom I spent the year.

Various people encouraged me in this project in many different ways, sometimes with specific comments and corrections, sometimes in seminars, and sometimes over the course of a continuous conversation spanning many years. I can't begin to sort out what I owe to various people, and in some cases the debt goes back very far indeed. But I want to thank Cynthia Baughman, Marcia Cavell, Stanley Cavell, Jennifer Church, John Cooper, Garrett Deckel, Luca Ferrero, William

Flesch, Juliet Floyd, Harry Frankfurt, Margaret Gilbert, Timothy Gould, Randall Havas, Pamela Hieronymi, Mark Johnston, Christine Korsgaard, Adam Leite, Beatrice Longuenesse, Ed Minar, Alexander Nehamas, Fred Neuhouser, Jeff Nunokawa, George Pitcher, Jim Pryor, Laura Quinney, Joseph Raz, Tom Reinert, Amelie Rorty, T. M. Scanlon, Sydney Shoemaker, Angie Smith, Michael Stocker, Barry Stroud, Susan Sugarman, David Velleman, Jonathan Vogel, and Steven Yalowitz. And thanks, of course, to Borgna Brunner for being there at the final stages.

I'm deeply grateful to Jonathan Lear, Mary Mothersill, Martin Stone, Jennifer Whiting, and George Wilson for reading the completed manuscript. Their responses were crucial in enabling me to bring it to some kind of finish and let it go.

Ann Wald and Ian Malcolm of Princeton University Press have been unfailingly supportive throughout the whole long haul and I thank them.

Thanks to Oliver Carling for help with final copyediting.

PERMISSIONS

Material from the following publications has been incorporated into the present work and is reproduced here with permission from the original publishers: "Making Up Your Mind: Self-Interpretation and Self-Constitution," *Ratio*, December 1988, copyright: Basil Blackwell Publishers, Ltd.; "Impersonality, Character, and Moral Expressivism," *Journal of Philosophy*, November 1993; "Interpretation Theory and the First-Person," *Philosophical Quarterly*, April 1994, copyright: The Editors of the Philosophical Quarterly, Basil Blackwell, Ltd.; "Self-Knowledge: Discovery, Resolution, and Undoing," *European Journal of Philosophy*, 1997, copyright: Basil Blackwell Publishers, Ltd.; "The Authority of Self-Consciousness," *Philosophical Topics*, 1999–2000; "Frankfurt on Identification: Ambiguities of Activity in Mental Life," in *Contours of Agency: Essays for Harry Frankfurt*, edited by Sarah Buss and Lee Overton (MIT Press, 2001), copyright: MIT Press.

CHAPTER ONE

The Image of Self-Knowledge

The question of the nature of first-person relations has not suffered from philosophical neglect in recent years. Perhaps unsurprisingly, attention has tended to concentrate on the particular relation of *knowledge*; and even more particularly, on the specifically first-person awareness we normally take ourselves to have of our own mental life. This chapter attempts to reorient some of our thinking about self-knowledge and place the more familiar epistemological questions in the context of wider self-other asymmetries which, when they receive attention at all, are normally discussed outside the context of the issues concerning self-knowledge. This task is really the concern of the book as a whole, but this first chapter seeks to establish three related points.

The first is simply the proper characterization of the basic difference between how a person may know his own mind and how he may know the mind of another. In one guise or another, this is a familiar idea, and not only in philosophical discussion. However, the various services it has been pressed into, especially in the history of epistemology, have obscured the basic asymmetry and its rationale and freighted the idea of self-knowledge with a host of extraneous philosophical assumptions. For a long time, the problem of distinctively first-person awareness has led a kind of stepchild existence in philosophy, much less often investigated for its own sake than in the context of other problems, either concerning epistemological foundationalism and materialism, or, more recently, externalism about mental content and skepticism about meaning and its determinacy. This has contributed not only to a narrow view of the range and variety of first-person knowledge, but also to a distorting emphasis on various extreme and contentious claims about its nature and extent, which has deflected attention away from the basic differences that remain between knowledge of oneself and knowledge of others, even after the abandonment of anything resembling "introspective infallibility." The wider view of self-other asymmetries, however, within which any such specific claims of first-person authority must take their bearings, obliges us to ground the discussion as much in moral psychology as in epistemology.

A second concern will be to inquire how it is that philosophical accounts of self-knowledge often fail to account for (or sometimes even to describe) a specifically first-person phenomenon. Put somewhat less paradoxically, prominent accounts of self-knowledge often end up either describing something that could just as well be a third-person phenomenon, or transposing an essentially third-person situation to some kind of mental interior. The "internal theater" of Descartes (and Locke and Hume) and the long legacy of treating self-consciousness as a kind of inner perception is probably the most graphic expression of this approach, but the general tendency is broader than this.[1]

---

[1] The most continuous and consistent case against the Perceptual Model generally has been made by Sydney Shoemaker, beginning with *Self-Knowledge and Self-Identity* in 1963, and in a series of papers in the decades since then. See especially (1986),

Nothing especially first-personal is captured by transferring the situation of a spectator from the outside to the inside, nor by construing the person as having any kind of especially good theoretical access to his own mind. A theme throughout the book will be that the difficulties in properly characterizing the first-person position are not merely epistemological ones, and later chapters will take up the theme of characterizing first-person relations that are not based on third-person models and do not involve essentially alienated relations to the self.

A final purpose of this chapter is to show how the lingering influence of a Cartesian picture of introspection creates unwarranted skepticism about the very possibility of self-knowledge. For current purposes, we can see the "Cartesian picture" as combining a radical epistemological claim of infallibility with a characterization of this particular *mode* of awareness as a kind of internal perception. Hence the picture of the "inner eye," incapable of error. Both aspects of this picture have been subject to a good deal of criticism in the past century, but often against the background assumption that introspective access must be something that conforms to this picture if it is to be anything distinctive at all. Hence the fate of Cartesianism has been taken to be decisive for the very notion of first-person awareness, and recent philosophical work has been very creative in developing ways of describing the surface phenomena of first-person discourse that are deliberately deflationary of the claims of that discourse to be reporting any kind of genuine awareness. By contrast, I wish to defend a view of first-person awareness that sees it as both substantial, representing a genuine cognitive achievement, but which nonetheless breaks decisively with the Cartesian and empiricist legacy. As subsequent chapters will show, this entails not only rejection of the "inner eye" as applied to the mechanism of introspection, but an account of the general distortions of the purely theoretical or spectator's stance toward the self (both as expressed in philosophical accounts of introspection, and in the life of

---

(1988), (1990), (1991), and (1994). I have not tried to relate in detail the story I tell here to this body of work, but anyone familiar with it will know what I owe to it.

the self). Being the person whose mental life is brought to self-consciousness involves a stance of agency beyond that of being a kind of expert witness. Thus the discussion taken up here moves from the epistemology of introspection to a set of issues in the moral psychology of the first-person.

1.1 THE FORTUNES OF SELF-CONSCIOUSNESS: DESCARTES, FREUD, AND COGNITIVE SCIENCE

The legacy of Cartesianism has been decisive in the philosophy of mind not only in the positive influence it exerted in the centuries immediately following Descartes, but just as much in the force of its repudiation in the twentieth century. Nowhere is this clearer than in the question of the mind's access to itself and its operations. Recent philosophy typically rejects the picture of the mind as immediately transparent to itself, and then tacitly takes this rejection to be equivalent to rejecting the very idea of introspective access, thereby ceding the very concept of first-person awareness to its Cartesian interpretation. In this first section, I mean to trace some of the main outlines of this story, with the aim of disentangling the basic idea of first-person access from the Cartesian picture. One striking fact about this story is that although largely Cartesian assumptions about the mind's access to itself dominated both epistemology and philosophy of mind since the seventeenth century, it wasn't until the twentieth century that the problem of the person's "privileged access" to his own mental life was treated as a philosophical issue in its own right. Earlier, major figures within both empiricist and rationalist traditions could take for granted that there is nothing in the mind of which the person is not conscious, and that a person's knowledge of his own current mental states is both certain and infallible; in short, that the mind is "transparent" to itself. In the centuries since Descartes, the identification of the mental with consciousness was more often treated as a guiding assumption than as a positive thesis in philosophy, something only occasionally given explicit formulation and defense.[2] And even when, in the twentieth century, the nature of "first-person authority" was identified as a philosophical issue of its own, the primary interest was not so much to investigate or defend the assumption itself as, rather, to give an account of *how* such privileged access was possible, and to find ways to accommodate certain assumptions of infallibility within the logic of first-person discourse.

As a result, it is often assumed today that the idea of philosophically important differences between self-knowledge and knowledge of others depends on maintaining a thesis of introspective infallibility in some form or other. And indeed, the contemporary rejection of this thesis has led various philosophers to reject the idea that there is anything philosophically distinctive about self-knowledge as a type of awareness.[3] This attitude is often supported by appeal either to psychoanalytic theory or, more commonly these days, to various results of experimental psychology and contemporary cognitive science, which seem to show that people's reports about their own reasoning processes are often unreliable and that various aspects of information processing are in principle inaccessible to consciousness.[4]

This development is in turn part of a curious and radical swing exhibited by recent philosophical thought about the mind. In this past century, philosophers have gone from thinking of the mind as totally open to introspection to doubting not just the reliability but the very reality of introspection. Early in the century, for instance, Freud often complained of the opposition he encountered to the very idea of unconscious mental processes from philosophers who simply *identified*

[2] This is not to suggest that the idea of the mind's perfect access to itself was entirely without its dissenters throughout this period. For the explicit denial of this claim, one need go no further than Arnauld's objections to the Meditations (Objections IV, Haldane and Ross, p. 92). See also Objections VI, p. 235.

[3] Chapter 4 of Churchland (1984) is guided by this assumption. See also Rorty (1982) for the claim that "our knowledge of what we are like on the inside is no more 'direct' or 'intuitive' than our knowledge of what things are like in the 'external world'" (pp. 330–31).

[4] See, for example, Nisbett and Wilson (1977), and Nisbett and Ross (1980).

"mental event" with "that which is immediately present to conscious-ness" (Freud 1915). Such an identification was part of philosophical common sense on both sides of the Atlantic for a long time. Nowadays, however, philosophers are apt to express doubt whether *anything* of psychological significance is an object of introspective awareness. Daniel Dennett once expressed this thought in the following terms: "The control of reflexes in man is subconscious, as are the stages of perceptual analysis, and in fact all information *processing*. We are not aware of the processes at all (as one might, with suitable incisions and mirrors, be aware of one's digestive processes). . . . As Lashley says, 'No activity of mind is ever conscious." (1969, p. 128)

Clearly, *some* kind of reconception of the mind and its access to itself is represented in this development, but to take the apparent scientific opposition at face value would be to miss what is distinctive about first-person access. That is, it would be a mistake to see this theoretical development in terms of a single, stable conception of the mind, with respect to which philosophers and psychologists have somehow gone from seeing all its activities as transparent to itself to seeing virtually none of its activities as belonging to consciousness at all. It is not the same sense of 'mental event' that was once thought to be intrinsically conscious and is now seen to be no more conscious than the break-down of sugar in the body. In particular, it matters that the unconscious thoughts Freud postulated were understood by him to be the very sort of thing that could, in principle, be brought to consciousness: the famil-iar states of mind of belief, emotion, and desire. By contrast, with re-spect to psychological processes identified at the "subpersonal" or "computational" level of description, it is doubtful that we have any sense of what could even *count* as introspective awareness. For this reason, Dennett's comparison with observing the processes of diges-tion actually *under*states how "introspectively unavailable" the "activi-ties of the mind" would have to be on the computational model as-sumed in this passage. For with respect to digestion we would at least have some *idea* of what the scene might look like "on the inside," whereas activities subpersonally described provide no such idea, and hence no idea of a *failure* of such access, either.[5] Whatever introspective access is, our understanding of it will have to make sense of its conceptual dependence on the level of commonsense psychological description. For the object of first-person awareness (on *any* account of it) is not all of psychological life, but primarily the states of mind identified under the categories of what is sometimes called "folk psychology": the hopes and fears, pains and experiences we relate to each other in daily life, and not states or processes defined either neurologically or computationally.[6]

This conceptual difference in the *kinds* of states of mind in question (and the level of description appropriate to them) is closely related to a difference in the ordinary *importance* of the availability to consciousness of various psychological phenomena. Here the distance between Freud and Lashley is as great as that between Freud and his earlier philosophical opponents. For in his practice, Freud was concerned to restore something to consciousness, which was an ordinary, if incomplete and insecure, possession of people, and one that was understood to be crucial to the conduct of life. Blindness or ignorance *here*, unlike, say, with regard to the facts about the internal processing of visual stimuli, was understood to be disturbing and debilitating. By contrast, ignorance of the psychological facts of the sort alluded to by Dennett is the normal case for all of us, and those who do know something here do not know it in anything like the way ordinary people take

[5] Recently, John Searle (1992) has taken the inaccessibility to consciousness to be a reason to deny that such subpersonal states and processes posited by cognitive science have any right to be considered *psychological* in any serious sense. While I agree that the distinction of levels of description is extremely important, I don't think our concept of the mental is as rigidly defined as Searle's denial would seem to require.

[6] Christopher Peacocke has emphasized the importance of this distinction for any account of self-knowledge, and in "Conscious Attitudes and Self-Knowledge," he means to reject "the position of someone who says that there is never a personal-level, causal, reason-giving explanation of why a thinker has the belief that he has a certain belief, in normal cases" (1998, p. 77). In my own account, the relation between self-knowledge, the personal-level, and reason-giving will be elaborated in later chapters.

themselves to know about their own thoughts and feelings. Thus, another task for understanding introspective availability is to understand why it should have any importance to ordinary rationality and personhood. It's natural to take the normal importance of self-consciousness for granted and to assume we understand *what* its importance is, but it should not be so obvious once we reflect that mental phenomena may be identified in many different ways (neurologically, computationally, in everyday terms), and that many perfectly rational and adaptive processes neither require nor tolerate self-conscious monitoring for their proper functioning. The normal importance of self-knowledge in a person's life will have to be understood as dependent on the level of description provided by the concepts of ordinary "folkish" psychological discourse.

The problematics of self-knowledge for both commonsense and Freudian thought employ a conception of the mental that is distinct from both the Cartesian picture and that of contemporary cognitive science, as different as these models are from each other. Freud argued against the philosophical identification of the mental with the immediate presentations of consciousness, but he did not deny that there *is* such a thing as ordinary introspective awareness. And he took it to be important to mental health that a person's beliefs and so on should normally be available to him in this way. His claims about the incompleteness and fallibility of this mode of awareness are thus in sharper opposition to the radical Cartesian claims of the mind's transparency to itself than they are to much of the commonsense understanding of self-knowledge (a discourse that allows for the possibility of *difficulty* and failure here, and doesn't contain terms like 'introspective infallibility'). This is not to suggest that there is *no* conflict between Freud and commonsense views of the mental, but it is important to see that the Cartesian picture is something theoretically distinct from either of them. For Descartes' picture assimilates a great range of psychological phenomena to something like the status of episodes of consciousness [*cogitatio*], thus classifying even the operations of will and judgment together with sensations, mental images, and passing thoughts.[7] In this way, grounding the general category of the mental in the paradigm of the experiential and the episodic lends a misleading plausibility to the characteristic Cartesian claims of introspective infallibility and self-intimation. For while it is indeed difficult to conceive of the possibility of, for example, intense pain of which one is utterly unaware (a possibility which even Freud himself, for instance, never countenanced), this is so for reasons quite specific to the special case of pain and does not carry over to motives, moods, beliefs, and the rest of what we commonly think of as belonging to the psychological. The general Cartesian category of the inner is something with a particular philosophical motivation, and indeed a good part of this motivation lies in the effort to identify an epistemological foundation that is precisely *not* prone to the sorts of gaps and errors that belong to our judgments about the external world.

The dependence of the Cartesian picture on such specific epistemological motivation provides all the more reason not to identify it with the general problematics of self-knowledge. For independent of this picture there remains a set of basic asymmetries between self-knowledge and the knowledge of others, which point to a different set of philosophical questions concerning how self-relations necessarily differ from relations with others. There are two basic categories of psychological state to which the ordinary assumption of "privileged access" is meant to apply: occurrent states such as sensations and passing thoughts, and various standing attitudes of the person, such as beliefs, emotional attitudes, and intentions. (I will have comparatively little to

---

[7] This claim of the revisionary distinctiveness of the Cartesian category of the mental and its distance from "common sense," is not itself free from controversy; but in support of such a view, see, for example, Kenny (1968). Such an assimilation of diverse psychological kinds is not unique to Descartes, of course. The doctrine of "ideas" in Modern Philosophy generally did not make our contemporary philosophical distinction between, e.g., images and thoughts, and this made it easier to think of all mental life as immediately present to consciousness.

say here about the case of sensations, which I believe raises issues for self-knowledge quite different from the case of attitudes of various kinds.) The type of access we ordinarily take ourselves to have here is special in at least two basic ways. First, a person can know of his belief or feeling without observing his behavior, or indeed without appealing to evidence of any kind at all. And second, rather than this nonreliance on evidence casting doubt on the reliability of such reports, judgments made in this way seem to enjoy a particular epistemic privilege not accorded corresponding third-person judgments that *do* base themselves on evidence. For now, we need not concern ourselves with just how strong this epistemic privilege is supposed to be, for example, whether such judgments are "incorrigible" or not. Suffice it to say that they are taken to have a good prima facie claim to truth which may be overruled only in special cases. The important point is that these are taken to be genuine judgments, expressive of knowledge, which are made without reliance on "external" observation. This will need explaining, even if one is inclined to dismiss the larger claims of infallibility or incorrigibility.

The claim that introspective awareness is not inferred from observational evidence is what is usually intended by the claim that it is "immediate." As a claim about the *mode* of awareness, this just means that such judgments are not inferred from anything epistemically more basic. Beyond that, immediacy does not entail anything about the epistemic authority of the judgments. Judgments with this immediacy need not in general enjoy any special kind of certainty, as compared with some other judgments that may base themselves on observation and inference. In the case of knowledge of oneself, it is particularly clear that the judgments that may be immediate in this sense concern a subject matter (i.e., a certain person's mental life) about which judgments are made in other ways as well. A person may report on his own emotional state introspectively, but at the same time he recognizes that other people come to their own conclusions about this same state of his in quite different ways. And the person himself may on occasion employ such third-person evidence in learning about his true emotional state. Thus there are both immediate judgments and evidence-mediated judgments he may make about the same question, and for all that has been said so far, it could well be that immediacy per se does not confer any greater reliability or freedom from error on a set of judgments. As with perceptual illusion, it could be that immediate awareness is available in an area where such judgments are nonetheless prone to characteristic errors for quite independent reasons. It could be that, for a range of psychological states, immediate introspective awareness is a less reliable guide, subject to characteristic errors of its own, than are the observation-based judgments of others. The claim of immediacy then, is a claim about the specific *manner* of first-person access and should therefore be kept separate from any epistemic claims of infallibility or introspective certainty.

In addition, immediacy is to be understood as a wholly negative claim about the mode of first-person access, that is, awareness that is not inferred from anything more basic. Much of our ordinary perceptual awareness is also taken to be immediate in this sense, and this particular model of immediacy, enshrined in the etymological connotations of the word 'introspection' itself, has irresistibly suggested to many philosophers that introspective awareness is immediate because it is itself a form of perception, a kind of "inward glance." However, it is important to note at the outset that identifying introspection with a kind of perception is a substantive philosophical *interpretation* of immediacy and is not simply equivalent to it. The basic concept of first-person awareness that we are trying to capture is that of awareness that is not based on evidence, behavioral or otherwise. This basic concept of immediacy is itself not wholly free of controversy, of course, but the perceptual model of "introspective" or "first-person" access is an additional substantive thesis, which, while not without its contemporary defenders, has been subject to sustained criticism in this past century.[8] What we are identifying as the full-blown Cartesian picture

---

[8] In addition to the papers by Shoemaker mentioned in note 1, arguments against construing introspection as a form of perception may be found in Wittgenstein (1956),

of introspection combines both the strong epistemic claims of infallibility and self-intimation, and the characteristic perceptual model of just
what manner of awareness introspection is.[9] Independently of this
model, we can characterize a set of basic asymmetries between knowledge of oneself and knowledge of others that survives philosophical
attempts either to dismiss it or to explain it as a consequence of the
merely spectatorial advantages of the first-person point of view.

1.2 THE POSSIBILITY OF SELF-KNOWLEDGE:
INTROSPECTION, PERCEPTION, AND DEFLATION

What remains before us, then, is a basic asymmetry between first-person and third-person relations. A person can make reliable psychological ascriptions to himself immediately, without needing to observe
what he says and does. And this capacity lies in the nature of the first-
person position itself; it is not a kind of access he may have to the mind
of another person. Compared with the traditional Cartesian doctrine of

---

Sellars (1962, p. 33, and 1956, p. 178), Davidson (1987), and Evans (1982). In recent
years, the main defender of seeing first-person awareness as a form of internal perception has been David Armstrong (1968, 1984).

[9] Was Descartes himself a Cartesian in the sense just defined? This is a somewhat
vexed question. There is certainly a preponderance of evidence that he was committed
to some versions of the doctrines of both infallibility and self-intimation. See, for example, M. Wilson (1978, in particular p. 151). However, Descartes himself is not entirely
consistent about this, and wavers about the claim of Self-Intimation in particular. In a
letter to Gibieuf (January 19, 1642), he writes: "But I do not deny that there can be in
the soul or the body many properties of which I have no ideas; I only deny that there
are any which are inconsistent with the ideas that I do have" (Kenny 1970, p. 125). And
in the *Discourse on the Method*, he even employs a version of the "distinct existences"
argument against Self-Intimation, nowadays associated with David Armstrong: "Many
are themselves ignorant of their beliefs. For since the act of thought by which we believe
a thing is different from that by which we know that we believe it, the one often exists
without the other" (Descartes, vol. 1, p. 95).

As for the other half of the Cartesian picture, the perceptual model of introspection,
it is probably correct that he assumed some version of it, but its explicit formulation is
much clearer in other Modern philosophers, for instance, Locke in Book II of the *Essay*
(1690).

introspective infallibility, this is a relatively modest characterization of the "privileged access" a person has to his own mental life, but it is hardly either psychologically or philosophically innocuous. Various aspects of introspection's claim to either completeness or reliability surely are challenged by Freud's theory of the unconscious as well as by contemporary cognitive psychology. But perhaps more pressing than the question about the epistemic completeness or reliability of introspection are philosophical questions concerning how there could even *be* such a thing as this capacity, however imperfect its deliverances. How is it possible for there to be knowledge of some contingent matter of fact (e.g., the facts about what I believe or hope for) that is not based on observation of some kind? And in what sense is this knowledge supposed to be essentially or exclusively first-personal?

To many philosophers, these worries have suggested that so-called introspective judgment cannot be construed as the genuine "detection" of some independent psychological fact, and that the logic of "avowals" must be given an analysis that explains away their appearance as expressive of first-person *judgments*. There are a number of different forms such a "deflationary" account may take, but I want first to say something about what motivates the search for an account of this type.

As suggested, sometimes doubt is cast on the very possibility of introspective self-knowledge by the lingering assumption of some kind of perceptual model for it. One may think that if what we are doing in introspection really involves the detection of some independently obtaining state of affairs, then it could only be by means of some kind of perception. At this point, we encounter various difficulties in applying this picture, and instead of challenging the picture, philosophers may be more prepared to deny the substantiality of introspection itself. The first such difficulty is the original embarrassment of the "inner eye" and the concern that it cannot be cashed out as anything other than a misleading metaphor. There is no perceptual organ of introspection, in anything like the way there are identifiable organs of sight and hearing and the like. Further, something like a person's sensation of red is not to be analyzed into an independent object accompanied by an act of perceiving it. Aside from familiar ontological problems with the reification of sense data, and regress problems with the idea of "the perception of an appearance," there simply doesn't even seem to *be* any "appearance" or perceptual presentation of one's belief or sensation that would be the experiential basis for the quasi-perceptual judgment, for example, that one has a headache, or believes that Wagner died happy. While "representationalism" is a controversial thesis about the ordinary perception of objects in the world, on nobody's view is the awareness of one's headache mediated by an appearance *of* the headache. And in the case of attitudes like belief, there is simply nothing quasi-experiential in the offing to begin with. There is nothing it is *like* to have the belief that Wagner died happy or to be introspectively aware that this is one's belief, and that difference does not sit well with the perceptual analogy, even if the problems it encounters with respect to sensory states could be solved.

Rather different problems with the analogy arise from recent considerations in the theory of mental content. Many philosophers identify what would be linguistically expressed as a simple single belief with a state of the person satisfying a complex functional role, involving a vast array of potential inference patterns, conceptual commitments, and dispositions to behave. On such a view, the simple belief that Wagner died happy is constituted by a host of inferential commitments concerning related matters (about Wagner, death, happiness, and much else) and the truth of various counterfactuals. How, then, one may ask, could all of *this* be presented to my immediate inner perception when I am aware of what I believe about Wagner? I don't even know what "all" of this *is*; in fact, I may be explicitly aware of hardly any of it, and yet the belief I am supposedly aware of is constituted by nothing less than all this (and not by any graspable mental image, for instance). If a person is indeed aware of his own belief, it is not by being somehow perceptually presented with anything of this complexity, for there is no such presentation.[10]

---

[10] The doctrine known as holism comes in many varieties, but it should be noted that the difficulty for the perceptual model given here depends only on a quite modest claim

A closely related problem with the model is posed by "externalism" about mental content, the claim that what a thought or belief is *about* may be determined by relations the person bears to various environmental factors of which he may have no knowledge at all. For both functionalism and externalism, then, the identity of a thought is constituted by various relational properties. Paul Boghossian (1989) takes this relational feature of such views to present a prima facie case for skepticism about the very possibility of introspective awareness of one's thoughts. On this view, if some form of externalism were true, then from within the first-person perspective one would be in a position analogous to that of someone inspecting the intrinsic features of a coin to determine its monetary value, but where the value of the coin is wholly determined by, say, where it was minted and is not indicated in any way on the face of the coin (p. 16). It is such relational facts that determine the value of the coin, and these are not part of its observable features. All that introspection can deliver is awareness of the intrinsic properties of a thought-token, and hence, on the assumption of externalism, such awareness is really no better than blindness. Boghossian himself is clear that he does not mean to endorse skepticism about self-knowledge, but he does nonetheless take the difficulties presented by the assumption of externalism to be quite real ones.

I have only presented a sketch of this skeptical argument here, and I will not be concerned with the various problems that may be found with this style of reasoning.[11] Here I only want to point out how in both cases (functionalism and externalism) the appearance of a skeptical threat depends on assuming the appropriateness of the perceptual

---

about the complex constitution of a given belief state. The truth of holism would, of course, only make things worse for the model.

[11] Boghossian's paper has contributed to an explosion of literature on this subject recently. A bit earlier, both Burge (1988) and Davidson (1987) developed accounts aimed at reconciling externalism and ordinary self-knowledge. Two recent collections of papers are Ludlow and Martin (1998), and Wright, Smith, and Macdonald (1998). In addition, see Falvey and Owens (1994), as well as recent work by Ebbs (1996 and 1997).

model of introspection. This is especially clear in Boghossian's original presentation, as can be seen from his comparison of the situation of introspection with the example of the coins. For the comparison to work in this argument, we would have to understand the ordinary case of awareness of our own belief (e.g., that Wagner died happy) as proceeding via some quasi-perceptual presentation, which we then need to interpret as having a certain representational content. But this is manifestly not a person's relation to his own thoughts and beliefs, however mental content is determined. That would be just as inapt as suggesting that the way that I know that I'm thinking of my mother, rather than my aunt her twin sister, is due to the fact that she wears her hair differently. The idea that intrinsic or phenomenal features of some mental experience do not tell the person what his experience is about has been a familiar idea at least since Wittgenstein and was part of his original case against the perceptual model. And when he asks, "How do I know that I am imagining King's College on fire, and not another one just like it?," his point is not to suggest any doubt about what he is imagining, but to point out that "visual" properties do not determine content or one's knowledge of it (*Blue Book*, p. 39 and passim).[12]

How could a skeptical conclusion about our knowledge of our own thoughts come to seem unavoidable? By way of setting up the case for the deflationary analysis, Boghossian describes the options for the understanding of self-knowledge as exhausted by three possibilities: such knowledge is either based on inference, or by a kind of looking, or else it is based on nothing (p. 5). With respect to knowledge of the content of one's thought, and much other self-knowledge, it seems

---

[12] In brief, I think Peacocke, for instance, is right in claiming that "it is a datum that we do know the full, ordinary, externally individuated intentional content of our own thoughts, and of other people's utterances, without reliance on inferences from, or presuppositions about, something weaker, which is all, in some alleged stricter sense, we would be aware of on the internalist introspectionist's view" (1998, p. 79). The reference to "something weaker," i.e., something with intrinsic recognizable features of its own, is crucial to the perceptual model.

that the first possibility cannot be right. If introspective awareness is anything at all—that is, anything distinct from the knowledge of the mental life of others—then it seems it must be something different from any knowledge based on inference. As to the second possibility, examples such as that of observing the coins are taken to show that, if externalism is true, we cannot know our thoughts by inward "looking" either.[13] That leaves the option of seeing self-knowledge as "based on nothing." This, then, is taken to mean that so-called self-knowledge cannot in fact be seen as a "cognitive achievement" of any kind, and cannot sustain what he calls a "substantial epistemology." To reject a substantial epistemology for self-knowledge is to reject any form of the idea that it involves the awareness of some independently obtaining state of affairs. Boghossian briefly discusses some examples of what he means by "insubstantial" knowledge, such as the indexically grounded judgment that "I am here now," all of which examples share the feature that the appearance of knowledge is grounded purely logically (or transcendentally), and hence that the denial of any such statement would involve some kind of immediate incoherence. What this means in fact is that avoiding the "insubstantial" conclusion is even more urgent than the paper suggests. For it would not just be disappointing or deflationary if self-knowledge were to turn out to be insubstantial in this sense. (Philosophers, after all, are supposed to be hardened to such disappointments.) Rather, such a conclusion would just clash with the kind of statement being made in an expression of self-knowledge, for there is generally *no* logical incoherence in the denial of a first-person statement of some attitude. So a statement such as "I believe I was born in Minnesota," which has the appearance of an expression of self-knowledge, cannot be cognitively insubstantial in the logical or transcendental sense described. The claim to knowledge of one's own belief here could be doubted or denied without the incoherence that

---

[13] Naturally, one might balk at this conclusion, too. For instance, if a person's identity is constituted by certain causal-historical facts about his birth, etc., does that mean I cannot recognize someone by looking at him?

would follow upon denying the truth of "I am here now," and hence cannot be "insubstantial" in that sense.

However, the argument combines two quite different senses of "cognitive achievement" in order to raise the skeptical possibility. If we consider what makes the above examples cases of "insubstantial" judgments, it would seem that by contrast a genuine cognitive achievement requires that its truth conditions be in some way independent of the making of the judgment (as, arguably, they are *not* in a statement like "I am here now"). This is a general form of cognitivity that any account of introspection as a source of knowledge would seek to preserve. However, the beginning of this section of the paper assumes a definition of "cognitive achievement" as knowledge of a contingent proposition that involves either observation or inference from some observation (p. 17). And that is quite a different matter. For any definition of this latter kind clearly makes it impossible to conceive of self-knowledge as both "substantial" but not conforming to the picture of "inner observation." Thus, the argument from the three options offered for understanding the status of self-knowledge assumes the appropriateness of that picture and relies on it to raise its skeptical challenge.

There's another way of looking at the "insubstantial" conclusion, of course. If a perceptual model is *not* tacitly assumed and we take self-knowledge to be "insubstantial" only in this second, stipulated sense (i.e., "contingent knowledge not based on observation or inference"), then it may well be a conclusion to be welcomed and not avoided. By itself the conclusion would pose no skeptical threat, for all it means is that introspective awareness is "immediate," in the sense of noninferential, and in addition is not to be construed as a form of perception. One may of course stipulate such a sense of "insubstantial," but then we must recognize that nothing in it is per se incompatible with the fully cognitive status of the judgments in question.

There may, of course, still be difficulty in conceiving of the possibility of apparent judgments that are "based on nothing" in the above sense, but which still represent a genuine cognitive achievement of some kind. And that difficulty, combined with the assumption of the perceptual model, presumably contributes to the conflation of the two senses of "insubstantial." But there are in fact several aspects of one's relation to oneself as an agent which have been plausibly seen as involving awareness that is not based either on behavioral inference or any perceptual presentation.[14] A person is commonly aware of his own basic movements and bodily position without having to observe anything, internally or externally. There need not be any characteristic internal sensation present, and even when there is, it is not that on which the person bases his judgment that, for example, his knee is bent. I do not mean simply to take the idea for granted, and the case of action will receive further attention in Chapter Four, but I do take it to show that the considerations discussed above do not in any way force us to some deflationary account of first-person reports. At the very least, the burden of proof would be on someone who claims that we must adopt a perceptual model if we are to see self-knowledge as involving a cognitive achievement at all. In this respect we might compare the awareness one has of one's bodily position with a case like that of judging what time it is.[15] These are judgments of contingent fact which can, of course, be made on the basis of observation and evidence of various kinds (looking at a clock, or the position of the sun), but in a central range of cases they may involve no such observation at all. You perhaps shut your eyes, consider the question, and deliver an answer. And in cases like these, such judgments share just the features that Boghossian later cites as the earmarks of genuine cognitive achievement, and which distinguish them from the earlier cases of "insubstantial" or self-verifying judgments (p. 19). That is, these judgments are subject to the direction of one's attention, and the accuracy of one's judgment is normally dependent on the exercise of such atten-

---

[14] For an initiating discussion, see Anscombe's 1957 book on intention, in particular §§8 and 28 on 'nonobservational knowledge'. For some more recent discussion of the awareness we have of our intentional bodily movements, see chapter 5 of Wilson (1989, esp. pp. 121–24), and Peacocke (1992, pp. 90–96).

[15] See Wittgenstein's extended discussion of this case in *Philosophical Investigations* (1956, §607).

tion. Some people may in general be better at such "detection" than others, and there is naturally no trouble here in conceiving of the possibility of error, or how it might be corrected. But, nonetheless, neither the judgment that one is sitting down nor the judgment that it must by now be nearly noon need be based on any quasi-perceptual presentation. One may choose to describe this situation as one in which such judgments are "based on nothing," but that would not be equivalent to denying that they are cognitive achievements.

These considerations do not dispose of the perceptual model, of course, but they should suggest that this model is an optional one and is not forced on us simply by the guiding assumption that first-person judgments are genuinely expressive of a kind of awareness. Tacit assumption of the perceptual model plays a role in encouraging some kind of deflationary account of first-person discourse, both for reasons of general hostility to the "inner eye," and, as we have just seen, for more sophisticated reasons having to do with the theory of mental content.[16] The perceptual model has problems quite independently of these concerns, however, and it is crucial that we keep the distinction clear and do not take the substantiality of self-knowledge itself to be identified with a particular intuitive model of it.

1.3 CONSTITUTIVE RELATIONS AND DETECTION

We are pursuing an understanding of self-knowledge that would make sense of both success and failure in introspection; that is, account for a person's introspective attempt to get something right, allow for the possibility of error and ignorance, and thus accommodate some independence of awareness and the object of awareness. The comparison cases just mentioned concerning judgments of time and bodily position

[16] Again, the dialectical situation of Boghossian's own paper suggests that it is Externalism about content that is his real target, rather than the reality of self-knowledge itself.

might be thought to provide models of judgments of substantial contingent matters which need not be perceptually based. Or, if not providing models of introspective access, they might at least calm fears that such a category of judgment is a conceptual impossibility. But, at the same time, such cases suggest a purely contingent connection between the obtaining of the states of affairs in question, and the fact that we are so constituted so as to be reliable detectors of them (we know not how). The situation with respect to awareness of one's mental life has usually seemed to be something quite different. It doesn't seem that we just happen to be wired up in such a way as to be reliable reporters of our pains, intentions, or feelings of anger; and it is difficult to conceive of being a proper subject of such states but only being able to become aware of them in a third-person way. Rather, it has seemed to many philosophers to be central to our very concepts of these states that the person's own reports of them should be both "immediate" in the sense defined, and enjoy a certain authority over the reports of others; whereas by contrast it is no part of our concept of time that we should be particularly good detectors there, let alone good detectors who don't need to rely on perceptual evidence (the case of bodily position raises different questions). And the claim that, say, it is essential to a class of mental states to be available to the person introspectively has been taken as a further part of the case against viewing it as a form of perception, since in the case of external perception there is only a contingent connection between the existence of the objects and any awareness of them.[17]

There is, at any rate, a strong suspicion of a *conceptual* requirement lying at the bottom of first-person authority, and the a priori nature of such a requirement has suggested to many philosophers a different set of reasons for thinking that the "authority" in question cannot be a genuine or substantial one. On many such views, the appearance of reliable discovery of one's own mental states is in fact merely the shadow cast by certain features of our linguistic practices. Since the

---

[17] A point emphasized by Shoemaker in recent papers.

following chapters will be developing an account of self-other asym-metries that takes them to be essential to the nature of persons gener-ally, I want first to investigate the prior question of whether admitting some conceptual basis to first-person authority undermines the as-sumption of first-person reports as involving genuine cognitive achievements.

Earlier we saw how the tacit assumption that introspection must be perceptual if it is substantial at all can lead one, perhaps reluctantly, to the conclusion that some kind of deflationary account is inevitable. In recent work of Crispin Wright, we encounter a symmetrical movement that *starts* from a principled rejection of any perceptual model and moves from there to the development of an account of first-person discourse explicitly designed to be deflationary. 'Deflation' in this con-text means that either first-person psychological discourse is interpre-ted as not *reportive* at all, or the 'authority' of such statements is seen as having some wholly *non*cognitive basis. This is thought to be a consequence of an account that avoids the perceptual model by stress-ing a set of a priori conceptual connections between mentality and first-person authority. For my purposes, then, it is crucial that we keep separate the questions of conceptual dependence and the question of the substantiality of self-knowledge. It is equally important to see how, even on deflationism's own terms, the particular features of the first-person position are simply left out of such an analysis.

In a series of papers, Wright has developed an account of first-per-son psychological discourse that is designed to account for the privi-lege normally accorded such statements, while avoiding the implica-tion that such privilege expresses recognition of any properly epistemic virtue of the first-person position. On this account, our con-cepts of various mental states make first-person judgments of them "extension determining," in the sense that a person's best opinion about his intention (Wright's example) does not detect or "track" that state, but rather, for a priori reasons, determines its identity. In this way, the conceptual connection between mental state and first-person judgment is very tight, for the latter determines the former. Wright begins working out this account after canvassing various Wittgensteinian objections to conceiving of one's knowledge of one's own intentions (and other mental states) as involving a kind of inner perception.

> So far as I can see, there is only one possible broad direction for such an explanation to take. The authority which our self-ascriptions of meaning, intention, and decision assume is not based on any kind of cognitive advantage, expertise or achievement. Rather it is, as it were, a *concession*, unofficially granted to anyone whom one takes seriously as a rational subject. It is, so to speak, such a subject's right to declare what he intends, what he intended, and what satisfies his intentions; and his possession of this right consists in the conferral upon such declarations, other things being equal, of a *constitutive* rather than descriptive role.
>
> (1986, p. 401)

The constitutive role of first-person judgments is made out in terms of the distinction between extension-determining and extension-reflecting concepts. The former notion is explicated by comparison with the familiar analysis of color as a secondary quality. That notion can be expressed in terms of sets of biconditionals, whose truth is knowable a priori and which fix the meaning of the concepts in question. So, for a color concept like 'red', for instance, we specify such things as a set of normal perceivers and a set of conditions favorable for the making of color judgments, and then arrive at a biconditional of the form:

> In conditions C: X is red iff X is judged to be
> red by normal perceivers.

The details of such conceptual analyses have been the subject of much contemporary work on the proper understanding of realism and related issues, and need not concern us here. I am concerned with the application Wright makes to the case of self-knowledge and the conclusions he draws from it. The application he makes is quite straightforward. We can account for the acceptance of first-person authority with respect to intentions by seeing our concept of intention as constrained by a priori biconditionals of the following form. Assuming a normal psychological subject, and given the appropriate conditions of attention, mastery of the relevant concepts, and so on,

S has the intention to Φ iff S judges that he intends to Φ.

Wright takes such biconditionals to express our genuine conceptual commitments with respect to intentions and other psychological states, and he sees the a priori status of the biconditional as incompatible with seeing first-person judgments of intention as extension-reflecting, rather than extension-determining. If such judgments of intention were extension-reflecting, that is, involved the genuine detection of some independent state of affairs, then any a priori declaration about their reliability would be unwarranted (1989, p. 253). Thus, the claim of extension-determination is offered as the best explanation for our a priori commitment to biconditionals of the form described.

   This, in abbreviated form, is Wright's case for conceiving of first-person authority in terms of social concessions rather than in terms of cognitive advantage. Once again, but now in a different way, self-knowledge is said to fail of a "substantial epistemology." The cogency of this deflationary analysis clearly depends on the avoidance of trivializing specifications of the C-conditions, so that they do not simply build in "whatever conditions are required for the accurate detection of one's intentions." This problem gets a good deal of attention in Wright and in some of the subsequent literature (cf., especially, Holton 1993). The "insubstantial" conclusion depends equally on the case for the a priori status of the biconditional, for if instead it had the status of a good empirical generalization, then obviously the case against genuine first-person *detection* of intention would not be made. In addition, there is a surprising transition from claims about judgment-dependence of the sort represented in the biconditionals to the claims from the quoted passage against the appearance of cognitive achievement and in favor of an analysis in terms of social concessions. The inference is surprising because the original idea of the extension of certain concepts being partially determined by the judgments of appropriately placed appliers of those concepts begins life in its application to the case of secondary qualities, such as colors. But it would certainly not follow from any such analysis of color concepts that particular judgments of the color of something were not expressive of a cognitive (indeed, perceptual) achievement of some sort, and were instead a matter of some kind of social concession. So, even if the relevant biconditionals for intention could be specified nontrivially and their a priori status were secured, this would not serve to show that first-person authority was not based on some kind of genuine cognitive advantage. Nor would it even serve the purpose of ruling out a perceptual model of introspection, as the color analogy shows.

For our purposes, however, the chief weakness of any analysis of this sort is how little it ends up illuminating any of the familiar *asymmetries* between first- and third-person psychological discourse. After all, response-dependence of some form or another is a feature of a great variety of concepts.[18] Nothing in the analysis itself given here explains why there should be any difference at all in the application conditions of psychological concepts in first-person and third-person contexts. In fact, as far as the analysis goes, there may not even *be* any such difference. For we could specify a similar set of biconditionals as governing the application of psychological concepts to *others*. That is, we could specify C-conditions, competent ascribers, conceptual capacities, and so forth, in such a way as to make it an a priori matter that such ascriptions have a strong prima facie claim to truth. Indeed, on a common understanding of the sort of "interpretation theory" associated with Donald Davidson and Daniel Dennett, this is precisely how things stand with respect to (commonsense) psychological attributions generally.[19] The account of extension-determining concepts was pre-

---

[18] The idea of "response-dispositionality" as a constitutive feature of certain fundamental concepts has a wide literature by now. See, for example, recent papers by Johnston (esp. 1991).

[19] One need not go all the way in the direction of Dennett's instrumentalism to see commonsense psychological concepts as part of the class of response-dependent concepts.

See Moran (1994) for further discussion of Interpretation Theory in the philosophy of mind and the question of whether psychological discourse in general is to be understood as the application of an explanatory theory (the "theory theory" of mental terms).

sented as an account of first-person authority, and yet it does not help us to understand why it is that *first*-person ascriptions should have any *special* claim to truth. Nor does it account for why such ascriptions are routinely made without reliance on evidence, unlike their third-person counterparts. For all the biconditionals tell us, it could be that first-person ascriptions were only made on the basis of examining the behavioral evidence (i.e., one's own), but our convention dictated that we always privilege the person's own reading of that evidence as being the best possible one. Finally, any adequate analysis of the first-person would have eventually to get beyond the picture of "privilege" and "concessions" and say something about how the presumption of first-person authority expresses an ordinary rational *demand* quite as much as it reflects any deference to the person's best opinion about his own state of mind. We do not only allow his statement to stand without the benefit of evidence, we also expect and sometimes insist that he take himself to be in a position to *speak for* his feelings and convictions, and not simply offer his best opinion about them. ("Do you intend to pay the money back?" "As far as I can tell, yes.") And it is part of this same demand that not only do we not expect the person to need to base his statement on evidence, but we may regard his deferring to the behavioral evidence as a form of evasion, or else as suggesting that the state of mind he's reporting on cannot be a fully rational one.

This normative expectation, and its relation to the rationality of the beliefs in question, certainly lends some support to the suggestion that the first-person accessibility of beliefs is not a *merely* empirical matter, an extra capacity for awareness of a certain class of facts we happen to have and whose absence would leave the psychological facts in question unaffected. This suggestion is developed at greater length in Chapters Three and Four. But the nonempirical or conceptual aspect of the phenomenon does not support either a conventionalist reconstruction of first-person authority, or a deflationary analysis of the claims of self-knowledge. That psychological attributions generally presume a background of rational intelligibility is an assumption well entrenched in contemporary philosophy of mind and is widely accepted by both realists as well as instrumentalists about psychological phenomena. Introspective awareness could be perfectly substantial, even if the assumption that a person's mental life is accessible to him in this special way has a basis that is partly normative and conceptual.

1.4 "CONSCIOUS BELIEF": LOCATING THE FIRST-PERSON

It ought to seem surprising that accounts of first-person authority should fail to characterize or account for a distinctively first-person relation. I want to suggest that part of the reason for this is a concentration on the parallel (as well as the disanalogy) with the situation of making judgments about the external world. This encourages a purely theoretical model of the situation of introspection, a concentration on questions of belief and judgment as applied to some static realm of mental facts. Inadequate attention is given to the person as epistemic agent, and hence to the mutual interaction between mental life and the first-person awareness of it.[20] We saw this theoretical model at work in the case of Boghossian's tacit assumption of the Perceptual Model of introspection (which may be seen as one graphic version of what I am calling the general theoretical model), and now in Wright's conceptual analysis, which describes the abstract conditions for making a set of judgments (i.e., psychological attributions) but which leaves out of account why the presumption of truth should be any different, or differently based, in the first-person case. Neither analysis connects the privileging of first-person judgments with any of the wider asymmetries, including the distinctive *manner* in which they are made. But the prob-

---

[20] A major exception here is the recent work of Tyler Burge on the first person. See especially "Our Entitlement to Self-Knowledge" (1996) and "Reason and the First Person" (1998).

lem of self-knowledge is not set by the fact that first-person reports are especially good or reliable, but primarily by the fact that they involve a distinctive mode of awareness, and that self-consciousness has specific *consequences* for the object of consciousness.

What I mean by the concentration on the theoretical has only been sketchily indicated so far and will become clearer by consideration of a final representative account of self-consciousness that most explicitly declares its allegiance to this picture. It is a commonplace in discussions of self-consciousness to conceive of the target notion in terms of second-order states, but D. H. Mellor's "Conscious Belief" seeks to build this assumption into a complete account of the phenomenon in question. Mellor begins with what he calls an "action theory of belief," a view that needn't be disputed here, since it can be understood to stand for the basic assumption that the notion of belief (and related states) is tied to its role in the explanation of behavior. What this assumption most directly opposes itself to is the idea that belief and the like are intrinsically identifiable phenomenal states, a view that has few adherents today. It will follow from an action theory of belief that at any moment a person may be described in terms of a host of dispositional states, tacit beliefs, assumptions taken for granted, as well as explicit beliefs and desires, which together contribute to his immediate thinking and behavior. Not all of this will (or even could) be conscious at any time; some of it never will be. Hence, we need a term to describe "the new state of mind I come into when a belief of mine becomes a conscious one" (p. 88), and Mellor settles on the term 'assent'. What he describes as his main thesis, then, is "that assenting to a proposition is believing that one believes it" (p. 90).[21]

Part of what drives the analysis of conscious belief in this direction is simply the fact that "being conscious of" is undeniably a cognitive relation of sorts. It is a way of knowing something, or having it available for further thought. But, nonetheless, with respect to the aware-

---

[21] His secondary thesis is that linguistic action—speech and writing—requires second-order beliefs.

ness of mental phenomena, the case of second-order beliefs is too broad to capture either the particular character of conscious awareness or the specifically first-person character of conscious belief. As to the first point, consider the ordinary phenomena of either tacit or unconscious beliefs. A tacit belief may be something the person takes for granted but has never reflected on explicitly. Contrary to what Mellor suggests (p. 93), such a state is not simply a disposition to assent to the proposition in question (a disposition which, since it doesn't require the cooperation of a desire in order to assert itself, Mellor would place outside the class of genuine beliefs). Rather, tacit beliefs may interact with relevant desires to produce action in much the same way as do explicit beliefs. Problem solving (a desire-guided action) often requires making explicit some tacit assumptions that stood in the way of a solution. The person's action in pursuing a particular misguided line of thought is explained by reference to his maintaining the faulty assumption, and explanation of his pursuit of that false trail requires ascribing this assumption to him. And, far from the tacit belief's being a mere disposition to *assent*, its coming to consciousness in such cases is accompanied by immediate *dis*sent from the proposition one had been taking for granted.[22] It was thus a belief maintained only on condition of its not being a conscious one.

Now, if it's agreed that first-order beliefs can be either unconscious or tacit beliefs, then there's no reason why the same cannot be true of second-order beliefs themselves. Thus, for instance, a person may take it for granted that his friend, like most people, believes that dead men tell no tales, even if this thought about his friend has never crossed his mind. And, of course, he may equally well take it for granted that he himself does not differ from his friend in this respect, again without the thought ever occurring to him. In both cases, then, he has a belief about someone's belief without its ever occurring to consciousness. And in the second case it's not just a belief about someone's belief, but

---

[22] See Stalnaker (1984) for a discussion of such cases and their implications for the nature of belief and belief-attribution. See especially p. 69 and passim.

it is a *first-person* second-order belief, which, for all that, is still not a conscious belief. Similar considerations apply to the case of beliefs that are not tacit but are unconscious for perhaps more psychologically interesting reasons.

It would seem, then, that the particular features of conscious awareness of belief (what Mellor calls 'assent') cannot be described merely in terms of second-order beliefs; not when my belief concerns someone else's mental state, nor even when it concerns my own. However, more important than failing to capture the idea of explicit awareness in the account of conscious belief is the absence of any sense of what sort of difference is made by the distinctively *first-person* awareness of one's belief. We may think of the problem in the following way. We saw that I can have a second-order belief whose object is someone *else's* first-order belief, without that involving an episode of explicit awareness at all. What I now want to point out is that an analysis like Mellor's is not rescued by refining it so as simply to require explicit, episodic awareness of belief. The particular first-person character of conscious belief would still be missing. For, of course, I could be explicitly, consciously reflecting on my friend's belief about life on Mars without that making it a conscious belief of anyone's. Nor need it make any essential difference if it were my own belief that I was consciously reflecting on, if I attribute it to myself under a name or description I don't recognize. Nor even if I knowingly attribute the belief to the person I recognize as myself, using the first-person pronoun, but, say, ascribe it to myself only on the basis of reading a letter I wrote last night (where I have reason to believe I still retain this belief, even though I can't now remember why).

What any of this would leave out is the fact that to call something a conscious belief says something about the *character* of the belief in question. It is not simply to say that the person stands in some relation of awareness to this belief. If someone is looking at a tree, referring to it as an "observed tree" would not express anything about its qualities as a tree, and similarly with the unspecified awareness of someone's belief. By contrast, a conscious belief enters into different relations with the rest of one's mental economy and thereby alters its character. We speak of the 'consciousness' in 'conscious belief' as something that informs and qualifies the belief in question, and not just as specifying a theoretical relation in which I stand to this mental state. If it were simply a special immediate theoretical relation I have to this belief, then there would be no reason in principle why another person could not bear this same relation to my belief. But in such a case *my* belief would not thereby acquire the attributes we have in mind when we apply the term 'conscious' as a characterization of the belief itself. (Think of an unconscious attitude of resentment. If I become aware of it only because I fully believe the interpretation given by my analyst, the attitude does not thereby become a conscious one. There is still work to be done.)

We apply the term 'conscious' to the belief itself for reasons related to why we may apply this term to certain activities of the person, where this qualifies the activity in ways that do not obtain with respect to anyone else's awareness of it. To play the piano either attentively, or unreflectively, or deliberately to annoy someone, makes a difference to the quality of the playing. In cases like these, the cognitive terms used denote adverbial modifications of the activity itself. Similarly, it is only with respect to one's *own* activities that 'consciousness' has such an adverbial function; so that, for instance, sleepwalking, walking normally and unreflectively, and walking with conscious deliberateness are all distinct kinds of activity. In this last case, the person's consciousness of his activity is not something that stands outside it observing, but infuses and informs it, making a describable difference in the kind of activity it is. In a related manner, when my assumption that the person just referred to as "Sue" is not a boy becomes a conscious belief, this change makes a difference to its relations with my other beliefs, and to my confidence in it. My whole relation to this assumption is now different, and the belief itself no longer has the secure, taken-for-granted quality it had before. And in both cases the empirical, qualitative differences made by an activity or an attitude being a conscious one are bound up with the differences in the person's autonomy and responsibility. Just as unconsciously standing on someone's foot in a crowd is different from doing so in full awareness, so for an attitude to be a conscious one makes a fundamental difference to the person's relation to it, in addition to the bare fact of awareness and whatever empirical difference that awareness may make to the character of the attitude.

The special features of first-person awareness cannot be understood by thinking of it purely in terms of epistemic access (whether quasi-perceptual or not) to a special realm to which only one person has entry. Rather, we must think of it in terms of the special responsibilities the person has in virtue of the mental life in question being *his own*. In much the same way that his actions cannot be for him just part of the passing show, so his beliefs and other attitudes must be seen by him as expressive of his various and evolving relations to his environment, and not as a mere succession of representations (to which, for some reason, he is the only witness). And in both the case of actions and attitudes, self-consciousness makes a difference to what the person's responsibilities and capacities are, with respect to his involvement in their development. It is modeling self-consciousness on the theoretical awareness of objects that obscures the specifically first-person character of the phenomenon, whether or not this theoretical perspective takes the specific form of the perceptual model of introspection.

What we have so far characterized as the specifically first-person manner of awareness that qualifies a belief or other attitude as a conscious one is an awareness that is immediate, nonobservational, and involves reference to oneself through use of the pronoun 'I', rather than by means of some mediating description under which the person might fail to recognize himself.[23] But we will need a fuller characterization than this to account for the special features of first-person awareness. For it would still be possible for a person to have immediate awareness of an attitude of his that conformed to the above conditions but was still essentially a kind of outsider's perspective on his attitude.

[23] There is a wide literature here. See especially Perry (1977 and 1979) and Shoemaker (1968).

That is, the conditions so far specified could still apply to a case where, say, I had immediate awareness of my attitude (perhaps in the way one has immediate awareness of the disposition of one's limbs), but where the attitude was one of which I could make no sense, or whose reasons were opaque to me. The attitude could be one which I couldn't link up with other attitudes of mine, and which persisted unaltered by and in isolation from both my own criticism of it and my explicit reflection on the object that the attitude is supposedly directed upon. For such reasons, it might well be an attitude that I would not allow to play any explicit role in my deliberations about the object in question. Thus, if the attitude in question is a belief, it would then be a belief I was conscious *of*, but it would not have any of the first-person character that is indicated by referring to something as a conscious belief. Even if immediate, my consciousness of it would be just as external to it as the immediate awareness someone might happen to have of some internal bodily process. A person who only had awareness of his mental states that was immediate, but alienated, in this way could not be said to "know his own mind" in the sense we take for granted in ordinary life. If such a person would lack ordinary self-knowledge, then something is missing from our original characterization of the target notion.

A more complete characterization of the first-person perspective will require bringing the agent more explicitly into the picture, and doing so will involve taking the discussion into a range of issues concerning the agent's perspective of deliberation and self-interpretation that have not been at the center of recent discussions of self-knowledge. One thing that is unsatisfying about any perceptual model of self-consciousness is that perception is a relation that, in principle, should be possible with respect to a whole range of phenomena of a certain type. On such a model, then, there would seem to be no deep reason why one couldn't bear this quasi-perceptual relation to the mental life of another person as well as oneself. From this perspective, the restriction of this mode of access to the *first*-person is unmotivated and not essential to it.[24] Not every form of self-knowledge has a claim to "inalienability," that is, can be shown to be a form of apprehension that is essentially and exclusively first-personal in its reference, but the forms we are concerned with here do raise the question of why this sort of apprehension should be restricted at all in its scope. What I mean by restriction of scope is primarily two things. First, there is the question of why the kind of apprehension we have characterized so far should be reserved for awareness of only one's own mental life. And this requires doing better justice to the "reflexive" aspect of first-person awareness than we have done so far, including the relation of self-knowledge to some of the special features of self-interpretation that have attracted attention elsewhere in philosophy. Second, there is the restriction in scope, not to a particular person, but to a particular *class* of facts about oneself, that characterizes this form of awareness. That is, whatever the "authority" of the first-person is, we will want to understand better why the person is assumed to speak with such authority (when he is) with respect to facts about his *psychological* life, and not with respect to facts about any other "inner" processes (physiological, neurological, etc.).[25] A distinguishing fact about "intentionally characterized" phe-

---

[24] For some philosophers, that is precisely the point, or one of the points, of the defense of the perceptual model. Armstrong (1984), for instance, explicitly defends the possibility of "introspective access" to the mind of another person (pp. 113–16). In a more recent paper, Crispin Wright insists, as part of his rejection of the perceptual model, on the "inalienable" character of any self-knowledge characterized by first-person authority: "The kind of authority I have over the avowable aspects of my mental life is not transferrable to others: there is no contingency—or, none of which we have any remotely satisfactory concept—whose suspension would put other ordinary people in a position to avow away on my behalf, as it were" (1998, p. 24). A footnote to this sentence denies that "we have any satisfactory concept of what it would be to be in touch with others' mental states *telepathically*." My agreement here will already be clear, but development of this aspect of first-person authority will be taken up more fully in Chapters Three and Four.

[25] Gareth Evans and others have argued that other sorts of facts, e.g., facts about one's spatial location or bodily nature, may be known "immediately," and my formulation is meant to be neutral on this question. It is less clear whether any asymmetries of authority are thought to obtain with respect to such facts.

nomena generally (not only states of mind, but actions, practices and institutions, including linguistic ones) is that they admit of a distinction between inside and outside perspectives, the conception of them from the point of view of agents or participants as contrasted with the various possible descriptions in some more purely naturalistic or extensional idiom. The phenomena of self-knowledge participate in this duality of perspective, and it is only under some descriptions and not others that the person's own description of his state is accorded any kind of privilege. If self-knowledge is indeed a form of *knowledge*, then it will be constituted by the person having thoughts about his state, and even more basically, by his *conceiving* of himself and his state in certain ways. So, prior to understanding 'first-person authority' in terms of superiority of access, we will want to understand why the person's *conception* of his state of mind has been thought, in certain contexts, to play a privileged role in making the state what it is. The following chapter takes up various senses of 'privilege' that have been thought to characterize a person's own conception of his thought and action, particularly as these are seen as having some "self-constituting" role. Exploring the bases and limitations of such a role brings the agent's perspective more squarely into the discussion of self-knowledge by way of relating the authority of the first-person to the role of the deliberator in determining his state of mind. My hope is to provide the terms for a more detailed and realistic picture of the ordinary failures as well as successes of self-knowledge, and why some of the characteristic failures should matter in any special way to the health of the person.

CHAPTER TWO

Making Up Your Mind: Self-Interpretation and Self-Constitution

It is often said that the act of reflection alters the fact of
consciousness on which it is directed.
—Sartre, *Being and Nothingness*, p. 121

We have seen how natural it is to think that if self-knowledge is something substantial at all, it must be something that corresponds at least roughly to the Perceptual Model of it. We speak of the "realm" of the mental, and one of the more innocent things suggested by this way of speaking is that if we are to speak of awareness here, it must be like any other awareness of any other realm of empirical phenomena. At this point in the argument it hardly matters whether we think of this realm as containing states, processes, objects, or whatever. We may be willing to countenance certain apparent peculiarities of the first-person access (e.g., privacy, authority, immediacy); but if the appearance of knowledge or awareness is not to be a sham, it seems we must somehow accommodate such peculiarities within a more familiar picture of observational knowledge. Hence, the recurrent attractiveness of the picture of something like a sealed room, to which only I have access (but which I am also unable to leave).

Some version of this picture may seem to be required by even the most modest sort of realism about mental life. In the case of any given person, the thoughts, the mental phenomena, are there; and while most people have only a kind of external access to them, one person has an immediate internal access to this realm. When this picture is found extravagant, it is usually by way of rejecting either the presumed substantiality of self-knowledge or the supposedly special features of the first-person position. By contrast, rather than criticizing it as a metaphysical extravagance, I hope to show how this picture radically *underdescribes* the differences between self-knowledge and the knowledge of others. What is left out of the Spectator's view is the fact that I not only have a special *access* to someone's mental life, but that it is *mine*, expressive of my relation to the world, subject to my evaluation, correction, doubts, and tensions. This will mean that it is to be expected that a person's own awareness of his mental life will make for differences in the constitution of that mental life, differences that do not obtain with respect to one's awareness of other things or other people. For this reason, introspection is not to be thought of as a kind of light cast on a realm of inner objects, leaving them unaltered. We looked briefly at one aspect of this difference with respect to the notion of 'conscious belief', but there are several aspects of it. One or another such aspect has been taken by various philosophers to be incompatible with the ordinary assumption of either an everyday realism about mental life, or the idea that the phenomena of self-knowledge do indeed involve the awareness or detection of some set of facts. The assumption is that either realism or a substantial epistemology has got to go. What I hope to show is that, if we begin with a kind of commonsense (or perhaps simple-minded) realism about mental life, then the various

ways in which self-awareness and self-understanding make a difference to the character of one's mental life are just what we should expect. Seeing more deeply into *why* we should expect this will take us
further into the question of why there should be any apparent peculiarities of first-person access in the first place; and why the language of
"special access" saddles us with a misleading, too purely epistemic,
idea of the responsibilities of the first-person position.

2.1 SELF-INTERPRETATION, OBJECTIVITY,
AND INDEPENDENCE

The difference self-consciousness makes is bound up with a related
first-person difference, which has received less attention within philosophy of mind than in certain forms of social theory (particularly
with a Hegelian provenance). In any event, there is a general idea,
found in both Continental as well as Anglo-American philosophy, that
the way in which a person conceives, for example, his own emotional
state is partially constitutive of what that state is. Similar to what I
have claimed about the altered character of a belief that becomes a
conscious one, it is claimed that, for example, for someone to interpret
his own response as, say, either righteous indignation or as mere pee-
vishness *constitutes* his state as being of a different kind. The first-
person interpretation of an emotional state is supposed to play a role
in constituting the identity of the state that is not shared by interpretations "from the outside." This claim is often part of a larger argument
against the application of ordinary notions of objectivity or realism to
certain aspects of psychological and social life. For instance, Charles
Taylor has argued in a series of papers that the ordinary notion of
representation cannot apply to various important situations of self-
understanding.

> [B]uilt into the notion of representation in this view is the idea that
> representations are of independent objects. I frame a representa-
> tion of something which is there independently of my depicting

it, and which stands as a standard for this depiction. But when we look at a certain range of formulations which are crucial to human consciousness, the articulation of our human feelings, we can see that this does not hold. Formulating how we feel, or coming to adopt a new formulation, can frequently change how we feel. When I come to see that my feeling of guilt was false, or my feeling of love self-deluded, the emotions themselves are different. . . . We could say that for these emotions, our understanding of them or the interpretations we accept are constitutive of the emotion. The understanding helps shape the emotion. And that is why the latter cannot be considered a fully independent object, and the traditional theory of consciousness as representation does not apply here.

(Taylor 1981, pp. 100–101)

We can see how a similar question might arise with respect to the claim that 'conscious' as applied to belief indicates a difference in the character of the state itself. It was said that the relation here is not like that of an object to the observation of it. And one familiar way to spell out *that* relation would be to say that, for instance, a tree is a real independent thing whose existence and qualities are not dependent on being observed. It has full, real, objective existence. So, then, what about the facts about one's mental life? Are they not real and objective facts as well, or is even ordinary objectivity a misguided aspiration when *self*-knowledge is in question? Against this suggestion we might remind ourselves of the fact that we commonly take the question of what someone *else's* belief is to be an ordinary objective matter. (Obviously we can't be thinking of 'objectivity' in terms of 'mind-independence' here. Mindless entities don't have beliefs, yes; but this doesn't make the facts of someone's mental life any less real.) Thinking doesn't make it so in the "external world"; no more does it do so in the "inner world." Hence, one might insist, *what* my particular mental life is at any moment is something independent of what I think about it, how I interpret it, or indeed whether I am aware of it in any way at all. If we are commonsense realists about wrens and writing desks (where this is intended as a vernacular commitment, with minimal philosophical baggage), then we are, or ought to be, commonsense realists about our beliefs and other attitudes as well.

In addition, apart from any issues in the metaphysics of mind, we might also be concerned to preserve some sense of objectivity here in order to make sense of various features of the ordinary phenomenology of self-knowledge. Here we may think of such qualities as the *effort* involved in self-reflection, the struggle to get something right and the characteristic risks of being wrong. Even though introspective awareness does not base itself on observation of behavior, and even after we have weaned ourselves from the picture of observation directed to an interior, there remains the sense that one's reflection is *answerable* to the facts about oneself, that one is open to the normal epistemic risks of error, blindness, and confusion. Doesn't this require the idea of a "fully independent object" and the notion of "consciousness as representation" that goes with it? I can't make sense of my own efforts at truthful self-interpretation if I take my interpretation to be constitutively self-fulfilling, making itself true.

Unlike the claim of conceptual dependence we examined in Wright, the claim here—that one's state of mind is in some way conceptually dependent on how one interprets it—does explicitly restrict itself to a *first-person* phenomenon. No one else's interpretation of my mood is granted this constitutive role, thus it is intrinsic to the claim itself that it describes some asymmetry between self and other. But it is nonetheless an idea with many strands, not commonly distinguished. For one thing, we must distinguish the kind of phenomenon described in the quotation from Charles Taylor, which concerns the role of specific self-interpretations, from another familiar claim about the role of general conceptual capacities. It is hard to deny, for example, that a shallow or impoverished vocabulary for emotional self-description makes for a shallow emotional life; and, conversely, that richer conceptual resources make for correspondingly enriched possibilities of emotional response. A person whose conceptual universe of the emotions is limited to the two possibilities of feeling good and feeling not-so-good will certainly fail to be subject to (and not just fail to *notice*) the range of responses possible for some other person with the emotional vocabulary of Henry James. This sense of conceptual dependence is not only properly first-personal, but also restricts itself to the range of phenomena we have identified as posing the philosophical problems of self-knowledge; roughly, psychological phenomena identified under our ordinary psychological concepts (and not what might be described as their "subpersonal" components). That is, there is no temptation to invoke any such conceptual dependence when it is a matter of knowing other sorts of facts about oneself. Someone who cannot distinguish shame from embarrassment (or better, someone who recognizes no such distinction in principle, seeing only various forms of discomfort) will not be our best candidate for either emotion, whereas someone who cannot distinguish a heart murmur from heartburn could nonetheless unambiguously have either the one condition or the other.[1] My being in a particular medical (including neurological) condition does not depend on my conceptual capacities for understanding my condition. Why should it be different in the case of my envy or gratitude?

One basic reason for this difference is that someone's envy and gratitude are themselves attitudes, modes of understanding the world as well as oneself. We should expect that, unlike a medical condition, a particular mode of understanding the world will only be available to someone with particular conceptual resources. We presume a background of such resources when we routinely talk about anyone's exercise of some intelligent ability. We unhesitatingly refer to the child as sorting blocks by color. But then we look closer and find that the groupings are really only into what we would call lighter and darker colors. So maybe it's not *colors* that are being sorted. Or we find that the child cannot or will not sort anything other than blocks (not sticks, for instance), or only blocks of a certain size; nothing else is treated as

---

[1] See Williams (1993): "What people's ethical emotions are depends significantly on what they take them to be" (p. 91), where he cites Gibbard (1990, esp. chapter 7).

having a "color." So maybe the child isn't really sorting anything at all. When the background of conceptual capacities is cast into doubt, so is the original attribution of the activity or attitude that is the expression of those capacities. By contrast, although someone's ulcer may well be the symptom or by-product of his resentment, we can identify the condition of his stomach lining without making any assumptions about his conceptual capacities. This is so because the ulcer itself is not an attitude or way of seeing the world. (This is but one of the complexities and ambiguities entailed by the idea of "mental illness," and the whole medical model of emotional disturbance.)

Of course, to say that the identity of one's state of mind depends on one's general conceptual and descriptive resources is not to say that one's interpretation of it makes it what it is, nor even that, for example, one must conceive of oneself as feeling precisely *shame* in order to be in a state of shame. The idea of this variety of conceptual dependence refers to conceptual *capacities* and their implications for a person's emotional life, and does not itself entail anything at all about the consequences (causal or logical) of any particular interpretation one may adopt. That is, the claim about conceptual resources does not tell us that any particular self-interpretation made by the person must count as *right*, or even that altering the conception of his state has any consequences at all for its identity. For all that has been said so far, it could be that someone's sophisticated vocabulary for self-interpretation coexists with, or even contributes to, chronic illusion on his part about his actual state of mind (a Jamesian theme of its own.) And not only may his self-interpretations fail to be constitutively self-fulfilling, we could also imagine that his shifting self-conceptions make no difference at all to the underlying mood he is presumably trying to capture.

2.2 SELF-FULFILLMENT AND ITS DISCONTENTS

To move, then, to the level of particular self-interpretations, it may be claimed that conceiving of oneself in a certain way is *necessary* for being in a certain emotional state. And there are two versions of such an idea. The stronger idea has it that if a person is to count as being in a state of, say, envy or indignation, she must see herself under the concept of that emotion. This is normally an idea entertained only about some range of the more social, sophisticated emotions, and does not suggest itself with respect to various states of fear or rage we take ourselves to share with those humans and other creatures who don't go in for self-interpretation in the first place. But even with respect to the conceptually complex responses of envy or guilt we may have our doubts about such a claim of necessity, since such an idea amounts to the claim that one could not be in a state of envy unknowingly, or while failing to understand oneself that way. Hence, a more modest claim about necessity on this level would claim that, for instance, being envious requires that the person have a certain range of thoughts about herself and her situation, which may or may not include the specific thought that she is envious. For at least a range of cases, such an idea seems undeniable, and not without its importance for the moral psychology of understanding oneself. What is less clear is its relation to the idea of 'self-constitution' and the related doubts we've encountered about the idea of '[self-] consciousness as representation'. It doesn't seem that this more modest claim of necessity should have any such epistemic or ontological consequences.

Rather, the language of 'self-constitution', in Taylor and elsewhere, suggests that the logical relation in question is one of sufficiency and not necessity. The idea is that adopting a different formulation of one's state constitutes it as different, that is, suffices for a new description to be true of it, and this is importantly unlike one's interpretations of other people and other things. This thought can also be read in more than one way: either as claiming that the self-interpretation constitutes one's state so as to *conform* to that interpretation, thus making itself true; or more modestly, as claiming that adopting a new interpretation of one's emotional state suffices to constitute the state as *somehow* different, now requiring a different characterization from anyone. These ideas are not always distinguished, and it is not obvious that either one of them by itself should threaten any ordinary ideas about truthfulness or objectivity about ourselves, or the phenomenology of self-knowledge as the effort at the "representation of something independent." Here again we're presented with an apparent tension between a common-sense realism about mental life (or a "substantial epistemology" for self-knowledge) and some special feature of the first-person point of view. Taylor and other writers who pursue the idea of 'self-constitution' have drawn attention to genuine and important asymmetries between the understanding of oneself and others, but they and their philosophical opponents seem to share the assumption that the idea of such asymmetries is incompatible with the "substantiality" of self-knowledge.

Of the two versions of 'self-constitution' involving logical sufficiency, the more radical one claims that, at least for a certain range of cases, the person's own interpretation of his state suffices for its being that very way. On such a view, interpreting myself as, say, ambivalent, mistrustful, or ill at ease makes it the case that I am correctly characterized in those very terms. In cases like these, we may feel that "thinking makes it so" because there's simply nothing to choose between, say, *taking oneself* to be ill at ease and really being so. One condition is as distressing as the other, after all, and perhaps this is because the one simply is the same thing as the other (or a sufficient condition for it). But what makes for such cases, and how special are they within the general field of the psychological? Consider a nonpsychological case with a similar self-fulfilling character. If someone sees his marriage as a failure we may well feel that in virtue of that fact alone the marriage is indeed, to that extent, some kind of failure. To say it is "to that extent" a failure expresses the sense that for one partner in a marriage to feel it is a failure is, for logical reasons, a *constituent* of its failure, and perhaps a decisive one. No marriage can be a happy or successful one if one of the partners sees it as a mistake or a trap. Thus, certain possibilities of *simply* being wrong, just mistaken in the apprehension of the case, are not available here. At the same time, of course, there will always be logical room for hysteria and overreaction, and things don't have to be as disastrous as the person takes them to be. But even someone's exaggerated reaction makes it the case that not all is well. And the fact that this conceptual dependence will be common knowledge between the two people creates its own depressing and intriguing possibilities for unhappiness. The chronically or neurotically hurt and dissatisfied person knows that here he cannot be merely or simply *wrong*, and hence he knows that retreating to this position is a permanent possibility open to him, and one that he cannot be brought back from in the ordinary ways (e.g., by someone trying to show him that he is mistaken, that in reality things are quite different from how he sees them). Hence, the logically self-fulfilling character of the belief can be exploited to produce consequences that take it from a partial truth to something closer to the whole truth (when the breaking point is reached after the long sulk, the unreachable withdrawal, and the partner capitulates with "Fine then! You're quite right!" Bargaining relations in general provide rich opportunities for the constituting self-assertion of failure).[2]

Naturally, not every self-interpretation will work this way. In thinking about what makes for the self-fulfilling character of such descriptions, both psychological and nonpsychological, it is hard not to be struck by their "negative" or undermining character. If taking oneself to be ambivalent or mistrustful is a decisive constituent of actual ambivalence or mistrust, this must be because the contrary states of wholeheartedness or trust are themselves tacitly defined by the *absence* of certain thoughts. Any condition defined in such a way can be undermined by the presence of thoughts it logically excludes (as in the familiar paradoxes of deliberate spontaneity or unselfconsciousness). Certain basic forms of trust are defined by the absence of corresponding doubts. If I come to doubt my trust, and conceive of myself "negatively" as lacking trust, or as ambivalent, then I *am* mistrustful or ambivalent,

---

[2] In his *belief*, he cannot be simply mistaken; hence, the danger is the tacit assumption that he must therefore be *right*. But the original error lay in his casting it in the form of a question for belief or disbelief in the first place. As we will see, this problematic does indeed have correspondences in the case of self-understanding.

at least to the extent of being prone to such thoughts. We may note, as a piece of metaphysical unfairness, that the converse "positive" claims do not hold. A person will not be wholehearted about his work just in virtue of his conceiving of himself that way, nor will his marriage be successful just in virtue of his interpretive say-so. The possibilities for self-deception and plain deception are all too familiar here. In some cases, some such "positive" interpretation of one's situation may well be a necessary constituent of the state in question, but it will never be sufficient. Thus, as far as the capacity for 'self-constitution' goes, it will always be easier to constitute oneself in compromising and undermining ways than to constitute oneself as unified and wholehearted.

There is an asymmetry of entailments here, whereby it is only for the "compromising" states that their self-nomination has a self-fulfilling character. But what sort of unfairness is this really, and where should we lay the blame? Conditions like wholeheartedness or confidence are normally understood absolutely, as the complete absence of any contrary attitudes, whereas a condition like ambivalence is understood to be partial, a matter of degree. (What, indeed, would it even mean to speak of total ambivalence, undiluted by anything else?) If we conceive of the two opposed conditions in this way, then it will be a matter of logic alone that the absolute one is difficult to attain and easy to undermine, whereas the partial one remains as a kind of permanent possibility, easy to fall back into and difficult to emerge from.[3] Interpreting oneself as wholehearted will not suffice to make one so, because wholeheartedness is a complete state: it is the absence of any ambivalence, whether conscious or not. By contrast, seeing oneself as ambivalent will suffice to make one ambivalent, because ambivalence is a partial state, defined by the presence of *any degree* of doubt, and not itself incompatible with the simultaneous presence of contrary thoughts. Add to this the fact that conceiving of oneself as ambivalent

[3] Recall Wilde's Lady Bracknell: "I do not approve of anything that tampers with natural ignorance. Ignorance is like a delicate exotic fruit; touch it and the bloom is gone."

is itself a kind of self-doubt, and we get the result that only with respect to the "compromised" condition can thinking make it so. On the other side, there is no similar bootstrapping oneself into the states of wholeheartedness or trust one may associate with one's better self. As far as this sort of 'self-constitution' goes, the only possible direction is downwards.

But just because conditions like ambivalence and mistrust *are* partial or "mixed" states, this unfairness may be more apparent than real (or more self-inflicted). For it remains an open question precisely *how* far we have deviated from the condition we have defined as a "complete" one, as well as just how much this matters. It may not be very far at all; indeed, in a given case it may be just far enough, perfectly appropriate. The asymmetry depends entirely on one condition being defined as the total absence of any competing thoughts. There would be no asymmetry, no metaphysical unfairness, if both states were conceived of either absolutely or partially. And it only seems depressing, or unfair, because we forget that the fragility of the one state and the virtual inescapability of the other depends on the fact that the inescapable state is conceived of as a partial one, and thus, as far as any a priori argument can show, may approach asymptotically to the fragile "positive" state, so closely as to make the difference between them negligible. Exiling oneself from wholeheartedness may well be too easily a matter of self-fulfilling interpretation, but it may also be relatively shallow. Despite the imagery of contamination here, the depth of one's ambivalence may on this or that occasion be no greater than that of a passing thought.

If there is, for such logical reasons, a self-fulfilling character to self-interpretations of this kind, we shouldn't expect it to apply to more than a special range of cases. These will be, roughly, "partial" conditions (like ambivalence), which are defined as the contrary of some "absolute" state, which is defined so as to be incompatible with any compromising doubt about itself. This is not a trivial range of cases, but at the same time we certainly do not conceive of most of psychological life in this way. For the rest of mental life, the idea of 'self-constitution' will have to have some other meaning, if it has any application at all.

2.3 THE WHOLE PERSON'S DISCRETE STATES

I mentioned a more modest version of the idea of self-constitution, and this is the idea that for a person to alter his conception of his own mental life logically suffices for *some* significant difference in the truth about his state, though perhaps not such as to make that very interpretation self-fulfilling. There are a number of ways in which a person's reconception of his state of mind will require an altered description of his state, and for reasons that are first-personal, not shared by anyone else's conception of him. There is a sense in which such an idea accords a special "privilege" to the person's self-conception, since it is only his own conception of his state, and no one else's, that is claimed to have this logical character. But the idea of "privilege" here should not prevent us from seeing that this status given to the person's own conception does not depend on his interpretation being *true*, let alone true because it is self-constituting. One reason for this is simply that even someone's false conception of his state is part of the very person we want to understand, and so, for example, is at least *relevant* to understanding the emotion in question ("what must his envy really be like if he's inclined to misdescribe it in this way?"). Even someone's fairly gross misrecognition of his desire or fear will nonetheless be an important indication of the nature of his attitude itself. But we can see a more important reason for allowing even false self-conceptions to make a difference to what they're directed upon, once we drop the pretense that an emotion or other attitude is something like an atomistic particular. For, consider two people who both feel gratitude toward some benefactor. We might think of one person as more naive, since he sees his gratitude as something simple and free of any ambiguity, whereas the more sophisticated or cynical person sees his gratitude, and perhaps all gratitude, as bound up with resentment and aggression toward the benefactor. These two people may both be grateful, but they will undoubtedly feel and think and act differently in the expression of their gratitude, and we would expect the histories of their emotions to follow different courses. Any description of them which left out of account the differences in how they conceive of (their) gratitude would not simply be incomplete, but would be seriously misleading. Admitting all this, however, need not prevent us from imagining the case as one in which the sophisticate is seriously wrong, or misguided about himself. There is still room for the idea of accuracy and truthfulness in this domain, and for the attendant risks of error and illusion. His interpretation of his gratitude as resentful does not constitute it as such, any more than the naive person's self-understanding makes it the case that his gratitude is innocent. (And if we do see a self-fulfilling aspect to the "sophisticate's" compromising understanding of his gratitude, this will be, I suspect, under the influence of the metaphor of contamination discussed in the previous section.) But in both cases we can see that while we retain the applicability of notions of error and accuracy, it is at the same time true that a proper account of the person's state, either from the "inside" or the "outside," cannot be indifferent to his own conception of it, cannot just dismiss it as one more flawed opinion.

Retaining the possibility of being wrong does not mean that we abandon the appearance of a self-other asymmetry here. A false conception of one's state can constitute a difference in its total character, and still be false for all that. Someone may see his pride as sinful, but if there is no such thing as sin (really), then surely his conceiving of his pride this way cannot constitute it as such. Nonetheless, it will remain true that the presence of this self-interpretation suffices for his pride to be of an essentially different nature from someone else's pride, or from his own pride before he came to see it that way. And this will be true for reasons specific to its being *his* interpretation of his pride, and not someone else's. One reason for this anticipates a point to be developed shortly, concerning the "outward" as well as "inward" direction of the self-interpreter's gaze. For the person to see his own pride in these terms means for him to see the things he is proud of in certain corresponding terms. For him to interpret his pride as sinful is for him to see his wealth, his power, his beauty as essentially *unworthy*, and to see their allure as so much temptation, appealing to spiritual weakness. The more settled and unambiguous his disparaging estimation of these things is, the closer we as interpreters would come to incoherence in our own description of him, if we blithely persist in speaking of his "pride" when by our own lights this attitude has lost any connection with the ordinary requirements of seeing the object of one's pride as valuable, admirable, distinguishing. Self-interpretations are bound up with the rational-conceptual grounds of the particular attitudes; hence, past a certain point of apparent irrationality in the state we may ascribe to the person (e.g., "perverse pride"), it will be the retention of the *ascription* of pride that becomes incoherent. But well before this point is reached, it remains true that the specific terms in which the person understands his own state play a role in making it the kind of state it is. Hence, contrary to what is usually assumed, the hermeneutic privileging of self-interpretations (whether individual or social) does not require the assumption of their truth. Any outsider who wishes to understand or even to describe this person's pride at all accurately must include the fact that he interprets it in these terms, that he experiences and lives out his pride under these particular concepts.

The outsider must include these facts not only in anticipation of their likely influence on the person's pride or gratitude, but also for the logical reason that the condition he seeks to describe is a condition of the whole person. That is, the very object of the outsider's interpretation includes the person's second-order as well as first-order attitudes. The interest taken in someone's gratitude, whether by himself or by another person, is not an interest in some discrete state. Rather, it is an interest in the total orientation of the person toward his benefactor. We would have no use for a notion of a state of gratitude about which it could sensibly be asked whether 'it' remained the same when it was regarded by the person himself as dominated by feelings of resentment, unaccompanied by any desire to acknowledge the benefit received, or as the expression of a kind of shameful neurotic dependence. The original ascription of a state such as gratitude is already intended to take into account such aspects of the person's total outlook. This shows that there is a purely logical dimension to the idea that a difference in the person's own interpretation of his attitude makes a difference to what his attitude actually is, that the self-interpretation is "partially constitutive" of its object. This is due to the fact that, in the ordinary case, the total state of the person we want to characterize includes the reconception itself.

2.4 BELIEF AND THE ACTIVITY OF INTERPRETING

However, in speaking of 'self-constitution' Taylor and others clearly have something other than this logical claim in mind as well. The general idea is often illustrated by reference to the situation of a person articulating his emotional state, and a kind of causal language is invoked to describe the phenomenon. Adopting a new description of one's state is said to *alter* it: "The understanding helps shape the emotion," changing how we feel.[4] And indeed, the failure to get clear about the difference between causal and logical aspects of 'self-constitution' contributes to the appearance of mystery about the whole phenomenon, a matter of word magic or "the power of naming." Presentations of the idea of the special status of self-interpretations will sometimes make it appear as if the mere act of redescribing something (e.g., some aspect of one's own state) were being credited with the power to transform it. Not only would it remain mysterious just what sort of process

[4] "Formulating how we feel, or coming to adopt a new formulation, can frequently change how we feel" (Taylor 1981, p. 100). The reference to what "frequently" happens is itself enough to suggest that it is not a logical matter at issue here.

this is, but such a picture has voluntaristic implications from which Taylor himself is concerned to distance himself.[5]

These unwelcome implications are a consequence not only of unclarity about the combination of causal and logical considerations, but also of a peculiarity in the description of the particular cognitive act involved. Taylor and others use a host of terms for the self-interpretive activity that is said to be constitutive of our emotional responses: we adopt new formulations, vocabularies, or languages for our emotions; we interpret or articulate them differently; we "see" them this way or that. What is striking about this list is that, while these are all cognitive activities, the basic idiom of "belief" is consistently avoided throughout the discussion. And its avoidance highlights the fact that the remaining favored terms ("interpreting," "describing," etc.) all refer to what are plainly *actions* of one sort or another, and hence which *can* be performed for more than one kind of reason. The reason an activity like "describing" can be undertaken "arbitrarily" is that one can describe or interpret something this way or that, without assuming any commitment to the way things actually are. I can *describe* the Vermeer before me as a Rembrandt, perhaps as an exercise I am given to do, and perhaps even learn something thereby, without any change of mind as to who did the painting. Or I can *see* the figures in some diagram as either receding or advancing, and switch back and forth at will, without altering my judgment about anything. In this way, "describing" and so on is like "saying," which need not even involve the pretense of expressing one's actual thought. By contrast, "believing" does not describe an action that can be arbitrarily undertaken, precisely because it does involve such a commitment. A belief as such is answerable to one set of reasons, reasons connected with its truth, and is not an action performable in response to a request or as an exercise. This is why insofar as the idea of self-constitution is cast in terms of

---

[5] "(Of course, this is not to say that we can change our emotions arbitrarily by applying different names to them. We are not talking about a process that could be arbitrarily undertaken)" (Taylor 1977a, p. 70; see also pp. 64–65).

genuine activities like interpreting or describing, it will persistently raise the question of voluntarism and arbitrariness. For as far as mere description goes, a person can *describe* his own state any way he may choose, for a host of different kinds of reasons. And if *this* sort of activity is said to have the power to alter the state itself, then it is hard to see this as other than a special ability each person is credited with, to be exercised at will.

It will serve not only to demystify this last version of the idea of self-constitution, but also situate it within some of the ordinary problems of self-understanding, to show how any genuinely transforming role for the interpretation of one's state depends precisely on an understanding of 'interpretation' and the like which does *not* denote a voluntary capacity. (And conversely, to the extent that we *are* talking about an active or arbitrary capacity, it will be one without any special power to alter anything.) Verbs such as 'describe', 'interpret', and the like are fated to equivocate between a use that expresses one's genuine sense of how things are, with the same kind of commitment as belief, and a different, noncommittal use denoting an ordinary activity. Favoring verbs in this latter sense serves both to dramatize the idea of self-transforming redescription, and to obscure its genuine basis. Yet, at the same time, the presentation of the idea also requires the other, fully cognitive or "committed" sense of these verbs to play a tacit role. When Taylor speaks in the first passage quoted of "com[ing] to see that my feeling of guilt was false," he is surely talking about changing his beliefs about it, coming to believe that it was false or baseless. Yet, to believe this about one's feeling of guilt would require the same sort of reasons one would require for believing anything else and is not something to be performed at will.

In one way, it is just what we should expect that when someone comes to believe that his feeling of guilt was false, the emotion itself changes. Not only does his understanding of it change (he may now think of it as compulsive or neurotic), but what he feels changes, too. He may now admonish himself for the guilt itself and feel a mixture of relief and embarrassment. But in such a case the identity of what he *did* feel before he changed his mind about its nature is not constituted or even affected by the understanding of it that he later comes to accept. This change does not challenge the status of the original emotion as a "fully independent object"; only it has now been replaced by a different one. And insofar as we want to talk about "objects" here, it remains true that no object is so independent that it remains unaffected regardless of whatever else goes on in the world (including the "inner world").

The fact that mere beliefs about my emotions can alter what I feel *would* be surprising if the emotions themselves were not attitudes directed toward something. Coming to believe that some fear of mine is unfounded will normally change my emotional state, replacing fear with something else, perhaps relief. My fear was *about* something and dependent on my beliefs about that thing. This cognitivity is also the reason why *non*cognitive states, such as physical pain, are (regrettably) considerably less sensitive to our beliefs or to our understanding of them. One needn't claim that emotions simply *are* a species of belief in order to view them cognitively and as falling under rational criticism. A familiar fact about some emotional states is that they do *not* alter when the beliefs on which they are based are sincerely denied by the person in question—for instance, phobias that the person is aware of as such and which survive the person's recognition of them as baseless fears. (It is, of course, equally familiar that we often criticize such a state as irrational.)

So, if we can think of altering the interpretation or articulation of an emotion as involving a commitment akin to changing one's *belief* about it, and we view the emotion itself under its aspect as an attitude, we have something belief-like on both sides of the relation. In this way we may hope to shed some light on the "self-altering" character of certain self-interpretations by consideration of what are called 'second-order' attitudes, for example, beliefs about one's own beliefs. Now there are certain familiar situations of self-reflection in which determining the character of one's state of mind exhibits a peculiar shiftiness. In such cases, the more one tries to focus directly on one's current thought and feeling (e.g., about last night's quarrel, movie, phone call), the less definite or constant one's state of mind seems to become. If we picture what one is doing here as tracking down an inner state, then it can seem like a search whose object mysteriously changes just as one's introspective gaze is directed upon it. But even if this is a misleading picture, something like this general phenomenon with regard to beliefs is what we should expect. If a person is at all rational, his first-order beliefs will indeed be sensitive to his second-order beliefs about them, and they will change accordingly. He may, for instance, discover that some set of his beliefs is inconsistent, or suspect that a particular belief of his is the product of prejudice or carelessness, or, at the limit case, that it is just plain false. His first-order beliefs will then normally change in response to his interpretation of them. Here the misunderstanding involved in putting such facts of change simply in terms of offering new *descriptions* of one's emotion becomes clear. For a new description of my emotion or belief is powerless to alter it unless I *believe* the description. Clearly, it is the actual believing that is crucial to this change, and not the activity of naming or describing.

2.5 THE PROCESS OF SELF-CREATION: THEORETICAL AND DELIBERATIVE QUESTIONS

Such redescriptions of one's state of mind may be arrived at in more than one way, and only for some of them will descriptions of psychological life function differently in the first-person and the third-person cases. There is more than one spirit in which a person may reflect on his psychological state, and these involve corresponding differences in how such understanding may contribute to an altered state of mind. For example, with respect to knowledge of one's own intentions, philosophers sometimes invoke a distinction between certainty that is based on evidence or discovery, and certainty that is based on a decision made by the person. According to this distinction, uncertainty about what one intends to do is normally a matter of one's having not

yet fully *formed* an intention, and this uncertainty is ended by a decision about what to do rather than by a discovery of an antecedently
formed intention.[6] The question expressing this uncertainty will *not*
indicate a situation in which there is something I intend to do but I
don't yet know what it is. Rather, the question expresses the fact that
my intention itself is uncertain. This is practical and not theoretical
uncertainty, and the resolution of it is a decision, rather than a prediction of what I will do. Ending my uncertainty about, for example, what
I will wear is indeed coming to know something; and, like other things
I know, I can tell it to someone else so that they know it, too. But in
other ways, although we rightly speak of knowledge here, it is not
purely a theoretical or epistemic matter. My knowing what I will do
next is not based on evidence or other reasons to *believe* something,
so much as it is based on what I see as reasons to *do* something. Hence,
a person's statement of intention is not to be challenged by asking for
his evidence. When I make up my mind about what to do, and tell
someone else, I do indeed provide him with a reason to expect something, a very good reason if I'm not too vacillating, or a liar; but what
I possess myself is not an expectation, based on evidence, but an intention, based on a decision.[7]

The question, "What am I going to do?" may seem to have *only* a
practical and not a theoretical application, that is, never to express
inquiry into some antecedently formed intention. If this is so, it will be
due only to the difficulty in imagining a situation in which a person
would both need to seek to learn what his intention is, *and* have good

---

[6] For this distinction, see Hampshire and Hart, (1958), and a later discussion by Grice
(1971) and Anscombe (1957). See Velleman (1989) for a very different picture, according to which intentions are theoretical predictions to which we have a standing
motive to conform our actions.

[7] Here I have drawn on Hampshire (1975), invaluable for thinking about these issues.
It is sometimes argued that knowledge of one's future actions is indeed a matter of
prediction, since it must rest on ordinary inductive evidence, relating to one's abilities,
the empirical features of the world one relies on in planning, etc. But the claim made
here is not that inductive knowledge is irrelevant in making up one's mind, but that
after all such evidence is in, it remains for the person to decide how he will go.

enough reason to believe that he *has* some settled intention in the matter. The difficulty here is a function of the fact that even when we can imagine a situation of theoretical blindness to one's own intention, it will be hard to see this as something like mere ignorance, a gap in awareness which reflects no (practical) conflict in the intention itself. The problems with the idea of blindness to oneself of this sort do not depend on Cartesian assumptions about the mind's self-transparence. Even within a psychoanalytic explanation it will normally be the case that the contrary thoughts and attitudes which explain the subject's blocked *awareness* of the intention will themselves be reasons for ambivalence *in* his overall intention; that is, the intention itself will not be a wholehearted one. Ignorance in such a case will not be mere ignorance, not only because it will be irresistible to look for a *motivation* of sorts to explain it, but because the motivation we then impute to the person must qualify the original ascription of the intention (as conflicted or partial).

With respect to states other than intention, in any case, it's clear that the same words may express either the aim to identify a certain state of mind, or the desire to make up one's mind about some matter. Thus, for instance, saying "I don't know what I want" may either express a divided consciousness containing certain definite though repressed desires, or it may express someone deliberating about what's desirable, choosing between certain options. In the latter sort of case, the uncertainty about one's desires is an uncertainty or indefiniteness in the desires themselves, and resolving the uncertainty is a matter of forming one's desire.[8] And with respect to one's emotional life, a person may want to know what his true feelings about something are, or he may be engaged in making up his mind, coming to some settled response he can respect, or at least make sense of; that is, his inquiry may be either a purely theoretical one about his psychological state as it is, or part of the process of forming his feelings.

---

[8] Hampshire describes the situation of such a person, in which "the conclusion of his considerations will be a decision from which a definite desire emerges. He now

What we're calling a theoretical question about oneself, then, is one that is answered by discovery of the fact of which one was ignorant, whereas a practical or deliberative question is answered by a decision or commitment of some sort, and it is not a response to ignorance of some antecedent fact about oneself. When self-reflection concerning one's emotional response is of this latter sort, the declaration "I don't know *how* I feel about that" is equivalent to "I don't know what *to* feel about it"; that is, how to settle and sort out the various conflicting elements of one's immediate reaction. The corresponding theoretical question would be of the form, "I don't know what it is that I do feel," where this is equivalent to the kind of question that is a frequent occurrence in the literature of romantic love, "What is this that I feel?" The person asking this might think to himself, for instance, that previously he never thought he had any particular feelings for a certain other person, though sometimes he felt self-conscious in her presence; but now both these feelings to which he is attending and his past behavior make him believe that he *has* some definite emotional response, but he isn't sure what to call it. Perhaps when he sees her with other people, or just with certain others, he finds himself feeling something that could only be jealousy, but at first he can see no reason why he should feel anything like *that*. Naturally, if this inquiry remains a *purely* theoretical one for him, separate from the question of what he *is* to feel, his emotion is likely to be inapt or fixated, whatever it turns out to be. This would be to reduce the emotion to an interior occurrence to which he is passively subject. This, too, is familiar in the literature of romantic love. Goethe's Young Werther is a subtle and discerning observer of the movements of his own mental states. His interest in them, however, is primarily a theoretical, contemplative one, separate from questions about the world that those states of his are presumably directed upon.

When the articulation or interpretation of one's emotional state plays a role in the actual *formation* of that state, this will be because the

---

knows what he wants to do, because he has now formed his desire, and not because he now knows how a pre-existing desire is to be characterised" (1975, p. 52).

interpretation is part of a deliberative inquiry about how to feel, how to respond. And there one's attention will be directed at least equally outward, toward the object of one's response, as it is directed toward oneself. The idea of "deliberative" reflection about one's response is meant to denote something more than simply the normative appraisal of it, the sort of reflection that would terminate in some settled assessment of it. For the mere appraisal of one's attitudes, however normative, would apply equally well to past as well as to current attitudes, and indeed may have just the same application to another person as to oneself. In itself, such assessment is not an essentially first-person affair. Rather, "deliberative" reflection as intended here is of the same family of thought as practical reflection, which does not conclude with a normative judgment *about* what would be best to do, but with the formation of an actual intention *to do* something. Similarly, in the sorts of cases mentioned where seeing one's feelings of guilt as false, or one's anger as childish, "helps shape the emotion," this will be because the "seeing" in question is not purely theoretical or descriptive (even where such description includes evaluative assessment), but is rather an expression of the ordinary deliberative reflection about how *to* feel.

This distinction between theoretical questions and deliberative ones introduces a new dimension to the issues we've considered concerning the objectivity of the mental and the substantiality of self-knowledge. We are now in a position to see how there is indeed a dynamic or self-transforming aspect to a person's reflections on his own state, and this is a function of the fact that the person himself plays a role in formulating how he thinks and feels. Much remains to be said to clarify just what this role is, and the implications it has for such problems as "being objective toward oneself," in the sense pertaining to moral psychology rather than metaphysics and epistemology. But we should not confuse the introduction of the agent in self-reflection with either abandoning ordinary realism about the mental or denying a substantial epistemology for self-knowledge. It is indeed essential to our nature as persons that we are "self-interpreting animals" (in Taylor's phrase), and that the exercise of this capacity plays a crucial role in making us who we are.

And the 'self-constitution' in question here is genuinely substantial and productive and not merely a matter of something like 'logical construction'. But rather than seeing this as undermining our ordinary ideas about the reality of mental life, we should notice at this point that for *any* concept of the mental rich enough to include attitudes toward one's attitudes, this sort of mutual responsiveness is just what psychological health would involve. Hence, the question of the "independence" of the person's state of mind from his interpretation of it now takes on a very different character. For when a person's emotional state is independent in *this* sense from his other attitudes toward it, what this means is that the two sets of attitudes are cognitively isolated from each other, and thus that, for example, one's deliberative reflection on what's desirable leaves one's actual desires unaltered. Although it is a familiar enough condition in itself, this is a form of impairment that is not demanded by either the epistemological or the moral virtues of objectivity.

2.6 RELATIONS OF TRANSPARENCY

We will gain a clearer view of the interplay between these two types of inquiry by considering a related claim about how a question about one's own belief must present itself, from the first-person point of view. In the end this will also help put in proper perspective the issue of the role of the person as agent in the formation of his attitudes. Ordinarily, if a person asks himself the question "Do I believe that P?," he will treat this much as he would a corresponding question that does not refer to him at all, namely, the question "Is P true?" And this is not how he will normally relate himself to the question of what someone else believes.[9] Roy Edgley has called this feature the "transparency" of one's own thinking:

[9] The question, "Do I believe P?" might be better phrased as "What do I think about X?," where X is some issue or possibility rather than a particular proposition represented

[M]y own present thinking, in contrast to the thinking of others, is transparent in the sense that I cannot distinguish the question "Do I think that P?" from a question in which there is no essential reference to myself or my belief, namely "Is it the case that P?" This does not of course mean that the correct answers to these two questions must be the same; only I cannot distinguish them, for in giving my answer to the question "Do I think that P?" I also give my answer, more or less tentative, to the question "Is it the case that P?"

(1969, p. 90)

And more recently, Gareth Evans made a similar observation in connection with a remark of Wittgenstein's directed against the idea of self-knowledge as involving an "inward glance":

[I]n making a self-ascription of belief, one's eyes are, so to speak, or occasionally literally, directed outward—upon the world. If someone asks me "Do you think there is going to be a third world war?," I must attend, in answering him, to precisely the same outward phenomena as I would attend to if I were answering the question "Will there be a third world war?"

(1982, p. 225)

To claim that one question is "transparent" to another is not to claim that one question reduces to the other. The fact that answers the question about the war is different from the fact about a particular person's belief. As Edgley points out, the correct answers to the two questions need not be the same. But nor is it right to say, as he does, that the two questions are indistinguishable from within the first-person point of view. After all, it isn't as if, although the answers to the two questions are in fact distinct, I must remain somehow in the dark about this, or that I cannot see them pointing in different directions. It will be common knowledge, among anyone with the concept of belief, that al-

---

by P. This is both somewhat more natural and more clearly at home in a context of deliberation about some matter.

though one believes something *as* true, the fact believed and the fact *of* one's belief are two different matters. From within the first-person perspective I acknowledge the two questions as distinct in virtue of acknowledging that what my beliefs are directed upon is an independent world, and they may therefore fail to conform to it. So, rather than reducibility or indistinguishability, the relation of transparency these writers are pointing toward concerns a claim about *how* a set of questions is to be answered, what sorts of reasons are to be taken as relevant. The claim, then, is that a first-person present-tense question about one's belief is answered by reference to (or consideration of) the same reasons that would justify an answer to the corresponding question about the world.

If this serves as a clarification of the content of the idea of transparency, it raises the question of the *kind* of claim Edgley and Evans are making, and what reason there may be for believing it. Is it true as a matter of empirical fact that, as we may put it, the self-directed question and the world-directed question are always answered in the same way? Or is the claim rather that, for conceptual reasons, we cannot make sense of the idea of answering a question about one's present belief without "attending to precisely the same outward phenomena" as one would in answering the world-directed question? With respect to attitudes other than belief, it seemed earlier that we could well imagine situations where the two questions were not treated equivalently. Someone may want to know whether it is resentment that he feels, or whether any resentment is called for in this case, whether it is what he is to feel. Or he may learn of his own desire in a way that approaches the purely theoretical or behavioral, and is quite different from any reflection on what in the world is good or worth desiring. Such a division between the two sorts of consideration may well represent a failure of sorts (of rationality, willpower, or something else), but nonetheless any equivalence between them is not something guaranteed by the logic of the first-person, but looks more like a kind of normative ideal. With respect to belief, the claim of transparency is that from within the first-person perspective, I treat the question of my belief about P as equivalent to the question of the truth of P. What I think we can see now is that the basis for this equivalence hinges on the role of deliberative considerations about one's attitudes. For what the "logical" claim of transparency requires is the deferral of the theoretical question "What do I believe?" to the deliberative question "What am I to believe?" And in the case of the attitude of belief, answering a deliberative question is a matter of determining what is true.

When we unpack the idea in this way, we see that the vehicle of transparency in each case lies in the requirement that I address myself to the question of my state of mind in a *deliberative* spirit, deciding and declaring myself on the matter, and not confront the question as a purely psychological one about the beliefs of someone who happens also to be me. This is not to say that one normally arrives at one's beliefs (let alone one's fears or regrets) through some explicit process of deliberation. Rather, what is essential in all these cases is that there is logical room for such a question, about regret as much as about belief, and that the actual fear or regret one feels is *answerable* to such considerations. I may confess that my fear is beyond my control, and that I can't help being afraid of something where, by my own lights, there is nothing to be feared. But so long as I am to understand my condition as *fear* of any kind, even irrational fear, I cannot fail to accept the relevance, the force of the deliberative question "Is there anything to be feared here?" That may not be the only question for me in my situation, but if I cannot make sense of the point of *that* question directed at my state, then I cannot make sense of my state as fear of any kind, however irrational.

In characterizing two sorts of questions one may direct toward one's state of mind, the term 'deliberative' is best seen at this point in contrast to 'theoretical,' the primary point being to mark the difference between that inquiry which terminates in a true description of my state, and one which terminates in the formation or endorsement of an attitude. And so to speak of the person's role in forming his attitudes is not to invoke a kind of willful or wishful capacity for self-creation. A person adopts this role insofar as he can answer questions of the sort "What am I to believe here?" and thereby come to believe something, or answer a question of the form "Is this what I really want?" in terms of considerations of what is worth wanting, and thereby come to clarify the structure of his actual desires. The fact that we do have this capacity should not be controversial, for it amounts to the idea that part of what it is to be a rational agent is to be able to subject one's attitudes to review in a way that makes a difference to what one's attitude is. One is an agent with respect to one's attitudes insofar as one orients oneself toward the question of one's beliefs by reflecting on what's true, or orients oneself toward the question of one's desires by reflecting on what's worthwhile or diverting or satisfying. This is not the only possible stance one may take toward one's beliefs or other attitudes, but it is an essential one, and it is hardly the same thing as the free or arbitrary adoption of beliefs for reasons of convenience, fear, or fashion. There is a role for the agent here insofar as we may speak of a person's responsibility for his attitudes, and we shouldn't expect this sort of responsibility to be any simpler or immune to damage or evasion than the other kinds.

Both the shiftiness and ambiguity of self-interpretation noted by Taylor and the "outward-looking" character of first-person belief reports noted by Edgley and Evans have their source in the primacy of a deliberative rather than a theoretical stance toward one's own state of mind. This suggests that the way forward on these and other issues concerning the special features of the first-person may be as much in the area of moral psychology, broadly construed, as in epistemology or metaphysics. The phenomena of self-knowledge, not to mention the wider spectrum of asymmetries between the first- and third-persons, are themselves based as much in asymmetries of responsibility and commitment as they are in differences in capacities, or in cognitive access.

Conforming to the idea of transparency between self-directed and world-directed inquiry thus appears to be less a matter of the logic of self-reference and more a matter of assuming a certain stance toward oneself and one's attitudes. As such, then, we should expect it to be something that will apply differently to different kinds of states of mind, with different degrees of stringency, with different possibilities for and consequences of its failure or deliberate violation.

The succeeding chapters attempt to flesh out the idea that the familiar asymmetries between the first- and third-persons, whether interpreted in terms of self-constitution, or the inapplicability of ordinary notions of objectivity, realism or substantiality to self-knowledge, have both a broader application and a different basis than their confinement to more epistemological contexts would suggest. Showing this will enable us to put some of the more familiar problems of self-knowledge within a wider perspective of differences between possible relations to oneself and to others, and the temptations, philosophical and personal, to try to model one such relation on the possibilities that properly belong to the other. In particular, what we've been calling the Spectator's picture of self-knowledge shows itself to be an intellectual expression of the ordinary, nonphilosophical pressures to adopt a purely theoretical stance toward oneself in particular situations of life, pressures stemming not only from motives of evasion or "bad faith," but also from the motives of moral objectivity toward oneself. The following chapter takes up the idea of the contrast between deliberative and theoretical stances toward oneself, and the ineliminability of the demands of either one of them, beginning with the relatively straightforward case of belief.

CHAPTER THREE

Self-Knowledge as Discovery
and as Resolution

It was argued in the previous chapter that the "transparency" of the first-person, as described by Edgley and Evans, is not a logical feature of first-person discourse that applies across the board, but rather a matter of a particular (although natural) stance taken toward oneself. With respect to the attitude of belief, the claim of transparency tells us that the first-person question "Do I believe P?" is "transparent" to, answered in the same way as, the outward-directed question as to the truth of P itself. But only if I can see my own belief as somehow "up to me" will it make sense for me to answer a question as to what I believe about something by reflecting exclusively on that very thing, the object of my belief. This is indeed what one does in the ordinary case in answering the question of one's belief in a deliberative spirit. There are, however, other possible situations calling for a different perspective on oneself, and from the stance of an empirical spectator one may answer the question of what one believes in a way that makes no essential reference to the truth of the belief, but is treated as a more or less purely psychological question about a certain person, as one may inquire into the beliefs of someone else. If I have reason to believe that some attitude of mine is *not* "up to me" in this sense, that is, for example, some anger or fear persisting independently of my sense of any reasons supporting it, then I cannot take the question regarding my attitude to be transparent to a corresponding question regarding what it is directed upon. Transparency in such situations is more of an achievement than something with a logical guarantee.

The clash between these two perspectives on oneself is most clearly exemplified in such phenomena as *akrasia*, self-deception, and other conditions where there is a split between an attitude I have reason to attribute to myself, and what attitude my reflection on my situation brings me to endorse or identify with. In such a situation, someone may have good theoretical reason to ascribe an attitude to himself that he cannot become aware of in a way that reflects the Transparency Condition. It may require his best resources of theory and experience to learn what he thinks or feels about something, and one set of issues that will occupy us in this chapter is how this sort of awareness of oneself differs from ordinary self-knowledge, and why this difference matters. This difference is of both theoretical and practical significance, that is, something of importance both for the philosophical understanding of self-knowledge, and in the life of the person. For the person himself, the importance lies in the fact that he will not take himself to have attained the ordinary self-knowledge that provides reasons for action (hence, to "know his mind" in the idiomatic sense) if he can only learn of his belief through assessment of the evidence about himself, however spontaneously or reliably he may be able to do this. Success in the attribution of attitudes to oneself cannot substitute for knowing one's mind as the exercise of a deliberative, nonobservational capacity.

Part of the philosophical importance of seeing the indispensability of both the deliberative and theoretical or empirical perspectives will be in showing what's wrong with seeing the peculiar features of the first-person as reasons for doubting the "substantiality" of self-knowledge. Instead, we can see it as a rational requirement on belief, on being a believer, that one should have access to what one believes in a way that is radically nonevidential, a way that does not rely on inferences from anything inner or anything outer. What is meant by calling this a rational requirement will be made clearer later, but one impression to be dispelled is the sense of this independence of evidence as involving a kind of license or courtesy, which encourages the sort of analysis in terms of social permissions that we found in Wright and elsewhere.[1] One thing wrong with the idea of first-person authority as a matter of social concessions is that it gives a misleadingly permissive picture even of the social context. For it is not, after all, simply that we *allow* what people say about their current state of mind to go by without the benefit of evidence, and are reluctant to challenge what they say. Rather, the special first-person accessibility of mental states seems not just something we *grant* to people, but something that is a normal rational *expectation* we make of them. An examination of the first-person should account for why someone's *need* to rely on behavioral evidence to report on his mental states would suggest something wrong with him, some state of dissociation, and would raise doubts about the rationality of those attitudes of his which are not accessible to him in the normal "immediate" way.

In its most radical form, the sort of alienation we're considering would place the person in a situation he could only describe in an utterance that was a version of Moore's Paradox: I know this must be

---

[1] Wright (1986, p. 401). Rorty (1979) analyzes first-person authority as a matter of "what society lets us say" (p. 174). This is often seen by its endorsers as a roughly Wittgensteinian line, although it's unclear that there is any textual support for this assumption.

envy that I feel toward him (I believe it's raining out), although there is nothing about him to be envied (but it's not raining out). An utterance of this sort does not express a contradiction, for it appears to represent a possible (composite) state of affairs, and yet whatever thought may be seeking expression here could only be entertained under great tension. This chapter begins by looking at some of Wittgenstein's remarks on Moore's Paradox as a way of understanding what is at stake in the tension between these two perspectives, and how it is possible for them to clash at all. Some of Sartre's early thought will prove helpful here, specifically his view of the person as divided between the "self-as-facticity" and the "self-as-transcendence," and will help sharpen the criticism, shared by both philosophers, of seeing theoretical certainty as our model for the achievement of self-knowledge.

3.1 WITTGENSTEIN AND MOORE'S PARADOX

Moore's paradox itself concerns statements of either of two forms: (1) "P, and I don't believe it," and (2) "I believe that P, but P is not true." The initial problem, of course, is to say just *what* is supposed to be wrong with such statements, for the first thing pointed out about them is that they do not express formal contradictions. It is perfectly possible for both parts of such a statement to be simultaneously true, for they have different subject matters; one of them psychological, the other not. The two versions given above describe possible situations a person might very well be in: the first describes the case in which there is some fact P of which the person is unaware, and the second represents the person as believing something which is false—nothing impossible in either scenario. And noting only this much about the statements already makes it clear that to say that they describe possible situations one might actually be in is to speak much too guardedly. For it is obvious from these paraphrases that both versions describe situations that one is certainly *always* in for as long as there are any facts of which one is ignorant or any beliefs one has that are mistaken. Regrettable or not, these are not general conditions one can reasonably expect to outgrow.

So the question is, if these sentences describe either possible or actually obtaining situations, what could be wrong, then, with going ahead and asserting them? Or, indeed, what would be wrong even with the unspoken *thought* that I believe it's raining out and it isn't? Something surely *would* be wrong, both with this thought about falsity and the corresponding one concerning one's own ignorance. If so, then this suggests that the prevalent diagnosis of Moore's Paradox as the paradigm of a "pragmatic paradox" is inadequate at best, for the puzzling quality persists outside the context of utterance and speech act.[2] Were someone to think to himself, as he looks out the window, that it's raining out, and conjoin this with the thought that he doesn't *believe* that it's raining, his thought would court incoherence in just the same way as it would if he were to assert the whole thing to someone else. Since "pragmatic" analyses like these are often associated with Wittgenstein, it is worth pointing out that nowhere in his various remarks on Moore's Paradox does he offer an analysis of it in terms of what we would call the pragmatics of assertion.[3]

A different view of the paradox, which Wittgenstein certainly does consider, but which I believe he rejects as inadequate, in effect claims that such sentences are covert contradictions after all (and thus their "wrongness" reduces to a familiar kind). The basis for this idea is the denial that first-person statements of the form "I believe that P" are in fact statements about the speaker as a believer at all, but are instead to be understood simply as the speaker's way of presenting the embed-

---

[2] By 'pragmatic analysis' I mean any account which explains the paradox in terms of the self-defeat of the purposes of assertion (by representing oneself as disbelieving what one is asserting as true). Searle (1969) was perhaps the first to give an explicit development of this view.

[3] In addition to the sustained discussion of Moore's Paradox in section 10, part 2, of *Philosophical Investigations* (Wittgenstein, 1956), there are frequent remarks on the paradox in both volumes of the *Remarks on the Philosophy of Psychology* (1980a, b) and in both volumes of *Last Writings on the Philosophy of Psychology* (1982 and 1992).

ded proposition P. That is, when someone says, "I think it's raining out," his statement does not refer to his (or anyone else's) state of mind, but is instead simply a more guarded way of making the assertion about the rain. So in this context the word 'believe' is not operating as a psychological verb at all. On this view, then, the two parts of the Moore-type statement do *not* in fact have different subject matters (one part about the rain, the other about someone's belief); instead, they're both about the rain, and hence their conjunction really does form a contradiction. And so what was puzzling about the original statement reduces to the fact that it is a contradiction after all, but in a disguised form. We may call this the Presentational View, since its central idea is that in the first-person present-tense use, the verb-phrase "I believe" does not in fact have any psychological reference, but is instead a mode of presenting the relevant proposition.

There are indeed first-person utterances in the indicative mood that employ apparently psychological verbs like 'believe' but are nonetheless *not* reports or self-ascriptions. Expressions such as "I'm afraid I'll have to ask you to leave now" or "I thought I told you to wait in the car" are not presented or received in the spirit of informative reports about one's fear or earlier thought. They have a different function. But it is not plausible that after we have catalogued these various other functions, it will turn out that *no* such first-person psychological statements actually have a reporting function, that none of them count as something said with the intention of telling another person my thoughts, beliefs, and feelings. All that is meant by a "psychological" reference here is the idea that, for instance, in its third-person or past-tense versions, a statement such as "My wife thinks I'm in Oslo" says something about someone's state of mind, a claim that would be made true or false not by the *speaker's* actual whereabouts, but by facts about his wife and her beliefs. Describing someone's state of mind in this sense, whether accurately or not, is a perfectly ordinary accomplishment. So, a full accounting of the Presentational View about 'believe' in its first-person, present-tense version would have to explain how verbs like 'believe' that serve to describe a person's state of mind in their third-person and past-tense uses lose that function and take on a wholly different one in the case of the first-person present-tense use.

It is this type of view Wittgenstein is alluding to when, for instance, he concludes one line of thought about Moore's Paradox with the advice, "Don't regard a hesitant assertion as an assertion of hesitancy" (*Philosophical Investigations*, p. 192). That is, we are to see the hesitancy expressed by the apparent reference to one's belief (as in "I *believe* it's still raining out") as qualifying the assertion about the rain, and not as describing anyone's state of mind. However, to ascribe the Presentational View to Wittgenstein one would have to understand this passage and related ones as not just warning against a confusion to which we may be prone, but as claiming that, for instance, hesitancy can *only* apply to assertions and not to persons and their states of mind. This is not what he says; and had it been what he meant, it would have made less sense to warn against confusing one thing with another than simply to declare that the very idea of an assertion of one's own hesitancy (or doubt, or conviction) can only be an illusion. But there certainly are situations in which one does intend to make an assertion about one's own hesitancy, or one's conviction, or one's belief *as* a fact about oneself. To insist on this much does not depend on any metaphysics of "inner states," or any ideas about what, if anything, *constitutes* a person's belief.

And to deny this minimal idea would be to claim that while you can talk and think about the psychological life of other people, you are peculiarly barred from doing so in your own case. There's no need to downplay the profound differences of such thought and talk in the two cases, but the task of understanding these differences can only be short-circuited by an analysis that implies that you cannot think or talk about the very same matters that another person does when he talks about what you believe or intend. Were this the case, you would not simply lack first-person authority; rather, you would be unable so much as to entertain the thought that there is something you believe or something you want, nor would it be possible for you even to have *mistaken* beliefs about such matters. There would be one person in the world whose psychological life would not be so much as darkness to you, for you could not even turn your attention to it.

However, we *can* take it as part of Wittgenstein's view that what we call first-person authority is systematically connected with blindness of a certain sort, but this blindness does not consist in being unable to think of oneself as a psychological subject. There are instead special conditions on conceiving of oneself as a psychological subject, conditions that do not apply to one's understanding of other people. Wittgenstein expresses one such condition, which will occupy us shortly, in one of his more well known remarks on Moore's Paradox, when he says, "If there were a verb meaning 'to believe falsely,' it would not have any significant first-person present indicative." (*PI*, p. 190). And, as before, whatever problem there would be for the significance of such a first-person statement of false belief would apply equally to the corresponding first-person *thought*. If so, then, *certain* attitudes toward the person as a psychological subject will have their home in our relations with others, and will have at best only some problematic application to oneself. One of Wittgenstein's themes, I take it, is that the first-person indeed has a special status in our thinking, but that this status is not exclusively one of privilege. Not every way of conceiving of others is a possibility (or the same possibility) in thinking of ourselves, but this restriction does not mean that the very idea of conceiving oneself psychologically (e.g., as a subject of belief) is ruled out for grammatical or other reasons. Some have been tempted to such a view as a convenient way to dissolve the philosophical problems of self-knowledge, but this is an overreaction, and Wittgenstein himself explicitly repudiates the conclusion that there is no properly psychological use of verbs like 'believe' in the first-person present tense.[4]

---

[4] For example: "The language game of reporting can be given such a turn that a report is not meant to inform the hearer about its subject matter but about the person making the report" (*Philosophical Investigations*, p. 190). The psychological use of 'believe' is more explicit in §502 of *Remarks on the Philosophy of Psychology*, vol. 1: "But now, we do nevertheless take the assertion 'He believes p' as a statement about his *state* [*Zustand*]; from this indeed there results his way of going on in given circum-

For all that, we can agree that the normal function of the first-person present tense of 'believe' is to declare one's view of how things are out there, and this follows from the fact that to believe some proposition *just is* to believe that it is true. What is believed is believed as true, and hence the possibility of answering the question about one's belief in the "outward-looking" way described in terms of "transparency."[5] However, Wittgenstein does not deny that the two questions may relate to what are different matters of fact. Nor does it even mean that a person cannot admit the difference between the two from within the first-person point of view. It is, after all, one thing for it to be raining out, and quite another for me (or anyone else) to believe that it is. There are in this way two quite different types of commitment involved in my avowing a belief of mine. On the one hand, in saying "I believe it's raining out" I commit myself to the state of the weather being a certain way. My avowal of this belief expresses the fact that it is not an open question for me whether it is raining or not. At the same time, however, I must acknowledge myself as a finite empirical being, one fallible person in the world among others, and hence acknowledge that my believing something is hardly *equivalent* to its being true. And even when a person's fallibility is not the issue, anyone must recognize that his believing P is nonetheless an additional fact, distinct from the fact of P itself.

Neither commitment is avoidable, although it is clear that each can pull one in a different direction. Insofar as I recognize myself as a finite human being, I must acknowledge that the question of what my belief is concerns an empirical matter of fact distinct and independent from the question about the object of belief. For me to deny this, either

---

stances. Then is there no *first-person present* corresponding to such an ascription? But then, may I not ascribe a state to myself now in which such-and-such linguistic and other reactions are probable? It is like this, at any rate, when I say 'I'm very irritable at present'. Similarly I might also say 'I believe any bad news very readily at present.'"

[5] On a related point, see Wittgenstein (1980), §815: "Asked: 'Are you going to do such and such?' I consider *grounds for* and *against*." See also Velleman (2000) for a discussion of the sense in which beliefs "aim at truth."

implicitly or explicitly, would be for me to deny that what my beliefs are about, what my attitudes are directed upon, is an independently existing world. And yet here I am, assuming transparency, answering the question about my belief as if these were *not* distinct matters, *without* directing my attention either to the behavioral evidence or the inner state of the person whose beliefs I'm reporting. It may thus seem like there is some evasion, or at least some questionable indirection involved here, if I answer a question about one subject matter by means of reflection on another logically independent one. Or, it may seem that my stance toward the question of what my beliefs are does implicitly deny the fact that, on one level at least, this concerns a matter of empirical psychological fact about some person.

Whether or not there is any implicit denial here of one's status as an empirical human being, it does seem appropriate to distinguish between different levels at which one conceives oneself as a psychological subject. Believing involves taking something to be true; and of course, one also takes other people to have true beliefs sometimes. But the beliefs of other people represent facts (psychological facts, to be sure) on the basis of which one may make up one's mind about some matter, whereas one's own beliefs just are the extent to which one's mind *is* (already) made up. That is, the beliefs of another person may represent indicators of the truth, evidence from which I may infer some conclusion about the matter. I may trust them or mistrust them. With respect to my own beliefs, on the other hand, there is no distance between them and how the facts present themselves to me, and hence no going from one to the other.

It is for reasons of this kind that Wittgenstein says (in the same discussion), "One can mistrust one's own senses, but not one's own belief" (*Philosophical Investigations*, p. 190). And this must mean not that I take my beliefs to be so much more trustworthy than my senses, but that neither trust nor mistrust has any application here.[6] One way to

[6] The ancient contrast between the seductive, misleading Senses and the trustworthy dictates of Reason can be seen, in part, as resting on a failure to recognize a related

express this might be to say that, in any particular case, it is a fully empirical question for me whether my own senses or another person's beliefs reveal the facts as they are. And even when my confidence in either one of them is complete, this confidence itself will be an empirical matter, based on various things I may know about either my own senses or about the other person, and including considerations of trust, evidence, and reliability. Whereas, from the first-person point of view, the relation between one's own belief and the fact believed is not evidential or empirical, but is instead categorical. That is, to speak of one's belief is just to speak of one's conviction about the facts, and not some additional thing one might be convinced by. Hence, it is quite a different matter to take one's own belief about something to be true and to take someone else's belief to be true, even when these beliefs concern the very same proposition.

Some such distinction is necessary if we are to understand Wittgenstein's remark about mistrust as something other than a declaration of our greater complacency in the relation to our beliefs than in the relation to the deliverances of our senses; or, say, as describing the matchless confidence one has in one's own judgment that cannot be approximated by the confidence one has in anyone else's.[7] Instead, what is being described here is the distinction in kind or category between the sort of thing one may treat as evidence on which to base one's judgment, and the judgment itself that one arrives at. As an empirical matter, the fact of anyone's believing P leaves open the question of the truth of P itself, although another person may close this opening by inferring from a psychological fact to a nonpsychological one. But

---

difference in kind between the two. The Senses can be compared to an unruly mob, in conflict with itself, because they belong to the category of deliverances *on the basis of which* one forms a judgment. But, insofar as Reason represents the unifying judgment one forms *from* this basis, it is not a faculty superior to or in competition with the Senses.

[7] Similarly, for several of the *Maximes* of La Rochefoucauld (1959) (e.g., "Everyone complains of his memory, but none of his judgement," #89), it would be a mistake to see them as purely psychological, and not also categorical, remarks.

for the person herself, if her belief that it is raining does not constitute the question's being settled for her, then nothing does. To have beliefs at all is for various questions to be settled in this way. Referring to a *categorical* rather than an empirical relation here is a way of saying that to be a believer at all is to be committed to the truth of various propositions. "Taking my beliefs to be true" is not an empirical assumption of the sort that I might make with respect to another person. Rather, it is the categorical idea that whatever is believed is believed as true. Skepticism itself does not avoid this conceptual relation between belief and truth, for the skeptic renounces belief itself and the commitment it entails. (Doubting, then, will bring with it *different* categorical commitments.) Nor is this relation absent from those situations where I have reason to think that my judgment in some matter is skewed, and I therefore have less than total confidence in my own opinion. For in that case the relation between belief and truth expresses itself in the fact that insofar as I lack confidence in my judgment about X, I have no settled belief about it. For conceptual reasons, the degree of doubt or mistrust will entail a corresponding qualification in the original attribution of the belief to me. This is not an empirical matter, and it doesn't apply to one's relation to the beliefs of others. What is unavoidable from the first-person perspective, then, is the connection between the question about some psychological matter of fact and a commitment to something that goes beyond the psychological facts.

3.2 SARTRE, SELF-CONSCIOUSNESS, AND
THE LIMITS OF THE EMPIRICAL

This distinction of levels, and the possibilities of tension between them in one's relations with oneself, are thematic in the early work of Sartre. In Sartre's language, consciousness of anything at all involves a kind of negation, a distancing or distinguishing of the subject of consciousness from its object. Indeed, he will sometimes say that consciousness just *is* this "negating" of the in-itself (the world of facticity) by the for-itself (the conscious subject which "transcends" that world). Consciousness of *oneself*, then, will involve this same distancing and separation of the "transcendental" subject from that aspect of the person which such self-consciousness is directed upon. Hence, he normally identifies the object of self-consciousness with the aspect of the person as a "facticity" rather than as "transcendence," that is, with one's status as an empirical psychological subject, a particular human being. And so, for him, self-consciousness of one's own belief involves a distancing of oneself from the perspective of the declaration or endorsement of one's belief.

> If I *believe* that my friend Pierre likes me, this means that his friendship appears to me as the meaning of all his acts. . . . But if I know that I believe, the belief appears to me as pure subjective determination without external correlative. This is what makes the very word 'to believe' a term utilized indifferently to indicate the unwavering firmness of belief ("My God, I believe in you") and its character as disarmed and strictly subjective ("Is Pierre my friend? I do not know; I believe so").
>
> (1956, p. 114)

Considered as an empirical phenomenon, the fact of one's belief is just a fact about one's psychological life, like anyone else's, a "pure subjective determination." As such, it bears no special relation to the truth, or only one of aspiration, and fallibility is built into the attribution of any such attitude. It is this perspective on belief that naturally finds expression in the familiar metaphors of interiority (one state occurring inside me, which may or may not correspond to what is going on outside of me), but the contrast between the two perspectives, and the possibility of their conflict, does not require the imagery of an inside and an outside. What is crucial is the distinction between what is true of the person as such (a state of belief), and what truth independent of the person that state commits her to.

Sartre's case of the akratic gambler who resolves to stop gambling is in some ways a more helpful example for considering the two

stances and the contrasting roles of commitment (*of* oneself) and theoretical knowledge about oneself. For the gambler to have made such
a decision is to be committed to avoiding the gaming tables. He is
committed to this truth categorically, as the content of his decision;
that is, insofar as he actually has made such a decision, *this* is what it
commits him to. For him his decision is not just (empirical) *evidence*
about what he will do, but a resolution of which he is the author and
which he is responsible for carrying through. But now, at the same
time, he does know himself empirically too; he knows his history, and
from this point of view his "resolution" is a psychological fact about
him with a certain degree of strength. And it is the psychological
strength of this resolution that justifies any theoretical expectation that
he actually will avoid the gaming tables. From this theoretical point of
view on his (past) resolution (as facticity rather than as transcendence)
it appears to him then as an ungrounded, inconstant thing on which
to base any confidence about what he will in fact do. In Sartre's view,
his relation to his decision is transformed when it becomes for him an
empirical object of consciousness, and he sees it as one of his facticities
rather than identifies with it as a transcendence.

> The resolution is still *me* to the extent that I realize constantly my
> identity with myself across the temporal flux, but it is no longer
> *me*—due to the fact that it has become an object *for* my conscious-
> ness. . . .
>
> It seemed to me that I had established a *real barrier* between
> gambling and myself, and now I suddenly perceive that my former
> understanding of the situation is no more than a memory of an
> idea, a memory of a feeling. In order for it to come to my aid once
> more, I must remake it *ex nihilo* and freely.
>
> (*Being and Nothingness*, 1956, p. 70)

Contrary to what the wording of this passage may suggest, it is not
simply the fact that his resolution has become an object for his consciousness that makes it suddenly appear as something ephemeral.

After all, the awareness of another person's resolution (as empirical fact about him) need not diminish its substantiality or reality in my eyes.[8] Indeed, as empirical realities, the acts and intentions of other people may present themselves with the status of something more substantial and lawlike than one's own perpetually modifiable resolutions could ever hope to achieve. So it should not be assumed that it is apprehension of the empirical aspect alone that makes the gambler's resolution appear to him as less than reliable. Rather, his anxiety is provoked by a disengagement from his resolution, a hedging of his endorsement of it, combined with the simultaneous desire to rely on it like a natural fact. He relates to his resolution as something independent of him, like a machine he has set in motion and which now should carry him along without any further contribution from him. He seeks confidence about his own future behavior at the empirical level, but then realizes that any such theoretical confidence is utterly inadequate on its own to settle his mind, because it can only be totally parasitic on his practical-transcendental resolution. His problem lies in the fact that if he *needs* empirical support, that can only be because he feels that his resolution is not strong enough on its own. And he now realizes that the empirical perspective cannot provide any additional strength of its own, for all of it is borrowed from the strength of the resolution itself. Hence, the resolution itself appears as inadequate ("no more than the memory of an idea, a memory of a feeling"), and at the same time he feels helpless to provide it with any additional strength, because he is seeking it in the wrong place. With his attention diverted

[8] In his discussion of freedom of the will, Hume provides a beautiful illustration of the apprehension of the will of another person in all its facticity as constituting a "real barrier" in the most literal sense. "A prisoner, who has neither money nor interest, discovers the impossibility of his escape, as well when he considers the obstinacy of the gaoler, as the walls and bars, with which he is surrounded; and, in all attempts for his freedom, chooses rather to work upon the stone and iron of the one, than upon the inflexible nature of the other" (Hume 1977, §8, "Of Liberty and Necessity," p. 60).

See also Sartre's own remarks on the sense of the primacy of the suffering of others, achieving *being* in a way denied to one's own experience (1956, pp. 141–42).

from the practical reasons that issued in the resolution in the first place, and considering it now purely as a psychological phenomenon discovered in himself, there seems nothing especially compelling in it.

What, then, does being both responsible and psychologically realistic about oneself mean in such a situation? One of Sartre's themes is the thought that the person cannot simply *accept* such a theoretical conclusion, however empirically well grounded, without that opening him to the charge of indulging in *acquiescence* in his weakness under cover of being hardheaded and without any illusions about himself. What I am aware of concerning myself empirically, as a facticity, cannot substitute for what I am committed to categorically—commitments I have simply in virtue of having any beliefs about the world or any decisions about my action. Being "without illusions" about oneself is precisely such a theoretical relation, and someone for whom this is the supreme virtue, the one unchallengeable imperative, will be to that extent in a relation of bad faith and evasion with respect to his beliefs and his actions. (This has not prevented the interpretation of the early Sartre as a champion of just such a "heroism of disillusion.") There is one kind of evasion in the empty denial of one's facticity (e.g., one's history of weakness and fallibility), as if to say "Don't worry about my actual history of letting you down, for I hereby renounce and transcend all that." But there is also evasion in submerging oneself in facticity, as if to say, "Of course, whether I will in fact disappoint you again is a fully empirical question. You know as much as I do as to what the probabilities are, and so you can plan accordingly."

These considerations may also provide us with the beginnings of an explanation for why *akrasia* can be such a peculiarly corrosive condition. For it often begins with the tactical substitution of the theoretical point of view for the practical one. Hence, I may tell myself that I know I'm bound to backslide at some point, so it's better that I do so on *this* occasion in a controlled and self-aware manner. Here I would be presenting this thought as an attempt to bring the theoretical perspective to the aid of my practical ends. But soon my accumulated history of backsliding provides more and more good theoretical evidence for predictions of my future conduct that conflict with what I decide to do, and it is these predictions that get vindicated, rather than my decisions. What gets obscured in this process is the provisional status of the original "tactical substitution" that was, after all, presented in the guise of a practical concern, to minimize the harm of anticipated backsliding. My so-called decisions are now shown to be poor things both epistemically, as indicators of the future, and practically, as effective contributors to my well-being. But, at the same time, the theoretical perspective demonstrates its success on its own terms (that is, predictively), while also presenting itself as looking out for the efficacy of my decisions. Hence, my theoretical understanding of myself is shown to be much more reliable than my practical self-understanding, and my akratic behavior itself provides more and more evidence of the superiority of the theoretical over the practical point of view on my decisions and my future.

But even when I am confident about myself and not worried about backsliding, this does not mean that I can be complacent about my resolution as constituting a real empirical barrier between gambling and myself, for I must recognize that the resolution is mine to keep or to break at any time. For me, the fact of my resolution cannot be something on which I may base a confident prediction, because I must recognize that the resolution only exists as a fact on which anyone can base a prediction insofar as I continue to endorse it. And my endorsement is in principle answerable to how I relate myself to the reasons in favor of some course of action. They are what brought me to the decision in question in the first place, and the decision is only as strong as my hold on those practical reasons. If they seem insufficient to me such that I seek to avail myself of empirical, predictive reasons for my confidence that I will avoid the gaming tables, then to that same degree I lose the empirical basis in fact for making that prediction, for I thereby reveal myself as *un*resolved about the question.

And naturally these limitations in the empirical relation to oneself do not apply to another person's relation to one's resolution. In thinking about another person, there is no demand that predictive reasons defer to practical ones. I may believe that someone's resolution to do something is based on (what I take to be) rather poor reasons, perhaps because some of them are founded on his believing my lies or responding to my bullying. But this need not interfere with my relying on his decision as part of his total psychological state, a fact about him upon which I base my expectation of what he will do. As an object for *my* consciousness, his decision retains full psychological reality and can be apprehended as a phenomenon in the world like any other, with its own evidential import.

With respect to beliefs, the parallel asymmetry would be the instability in the idea of trust or mistrust being applied to one's own belief, in the sense of treating the empirical fact of one's *having* the belief as evidence for its truth. If a generally reliable person believes that it's raining out, that fact *can* certainly be taken as evidence for rain. But in my own case, as with the resolution not to gamble, I must recognize that the belief is mine to retain or to abandon. (In Sartre's language, "I posit my freedom with respect to it" [*Being and Nothingness*, p. 109].) That is, my belief only exists as an empirical psychological fact insofar as I *am* persuaded by the evidence for rain, evidence which (prior to my belief) does not include the fact of my being persuaded. If I am unpersuaded enough to need additional evidence, then by virtue of that psychological fact itself I lose the empirical basis for any inference from a person's belief to the truth about the rain. For someone's *un*confident belief about the rain provides much less reason for anyone to take it to be good evidence for rain itself.

3.3 AVOWAL AND ATTRIBUTION

Moore's Paradox provides us with a kind of paradigm formula for difficulties arising from the introduction of an empirical or theoretical point of view whose deliverances may clash with what we want to say from the point of view of a rational deliberator, a point of view "transcendent" with respect to the psychological facts as currently constituted. For empirically, I can well imagine the accumulated evidence suggesting both that I believe that it's raining, and that it is not in fact raining. Theoretically, these are perfectly independent matters of fact, and I can in principle recognize the possibility of their co-occurrence, just as I can imagine my future conduct clashing with what I now decide to do. But, as I conceive of myself as a rational agent, my awareness of my belief is awareness of my commitment to its truth, a commitment to something that transcends any description of my psychological state. And the expression of this commitment lies in the fact that my reports on my belief are obliged to conform to the condition of transparency: that I can report on my *belief* about X by considering (nothing but) X itself. Hence, a situation that one can conceive of as a theoretical, empirical possibility clashes with the conception of oneself as a rational agent. And, of course, were one *not* a rational agent, there would be no psychological life to have empirical views about in the first place. Hence there is no philosophical resolution to be found in some exclusive adherence to the empirical perspective, for that would fail even to describe the conditions of such a clash.

When a person's relation to her belief conforms to the Transparency Condition, then the belief is expressed by reflection on its subject matter and not by consideration of the psychological evidence for a particular belief attribution. That is to say, one is not treating the belief-attribution to oneself as a purely empirical or theoretical matter. We have seen that, were it to make sense for one to take such a purely theoretical view of oneself, then the thought expressed in a Moore-type sentence would describe a perfectly coherent empirical possibility on which one could sensibly report. Hence, we will gain a better understanding of the limitations of the theoretical or empirical point of view on the self by examining situations in which transparency fails, and hence one's relation to oneself approaches a fully empirical one. The limits of the empirical point of view on oneself will in turn shed light on how it can be, among other things, a *rational* requirement that one have a kind of access to one's beliefs that is not based on evidence of any kind.

In various familiar therapeutic contexts, for instance, the manner in which the analysand becomes aware of various of her beliefs and other attitudes does not necessarily conform to the Transparency Condition. The person who feels anger at the dead parent for having abandoned her, or who feels betrayed or deprived of something by another child, may only know of this attitude through the eliciting and interpreting of evidence of various kinds. She might become thoroughly convinced, both from the constructions of the analyst, as well as from her own appreciation of the evidence, that this attitude must indeed be attributed to her. And yet, at the same time, when she reflects on the world-directed question itself, whether she has indeed been betrayed by this person, she may find that the answer is no or can't be settled one way or the other.[9] So, transparency fails because she cannot learn of this attitude of hers by reflection on the object of that attitude. She can only learn of it in a fully theoretical manner, taking an empirical stance toward herself as a particular psychological subject. We might say that the analysand can *report* on such a belief, but that she does not *express* it, since although she will describe herself as feeling betrayed she will not in her present state affirm the judgment that this person has in fact betrayed her. When the belief is described, it is kept within the brackets of the psychological operator, 'believe'; that is, she will affirm the psychological judgment "I believe that P," but will not avow the embedded proposition P itself.

The distinction between reporting and expressing a state of mind has figured in various philosophical discussions since Wittgenstein. In recent work on *akrasia* and self-deception, Georges Rey has developed similar terms for describing the difference between beliefs and other attitudes of which I become aware by virtue of their *explanatory* role, and those which I am aware of because I *avow* them, that is,

---

[9] At this point one might ask whether this means that we must give up the original attribution of the belief in question. To do that, however, we would need a reason to give decisive weight to the avowal, which is but one piece of evidence, over all the other evidence accumulated in and out of therapy.

explicitly endorse them.[10] On this view, a *report* on an attitude of mine has an explanatory basis, grounded in evidence, and need not imply a commitment to the attitude's truth or justification, any more than its third-person equivalent would. Instead, the attribution is made in order to identify the states, forces, or whatever else that is driving the actual psychological machinery. An *avowal* of one's belief, by contrast, is not made on any psychologically explanatory basis, and is rather the expression of one's own present commitment to the truth of the proposition in question. Rey describes both self-deception and *akrasia* not as involving conflict between first- and second-order attitudes, but as constituted by conflict between attitudes one avows and those he calls one's "central" explanatory attitudes.

Part of his case against seeing self-deception as purely a matter of second-order attitudes is given by his description of what he calls an "educated neurotic" who knows enough psychological theory and has sufficient experience of his own "case," to confidently ascribe some repressed attitude to himself. As with our previous analysand, we can see here that the person's first-order and second-order attitudes are not in conflict: he has a first-order attitude of resentment, and he has the correct second-order belief that this is his attitude. And yet clearly something is wrong if he cannot consciously avow the first attitude and can only ascribe it to himself on the evidence. So what is wrong with this person's access to himself? One might resist Rey's suggestion that he remains self-*deceived* even with his perfectly accurate second-order awareness (the idea of "deception" seems to require some element of falsity), but it would still make sense to say that the original attitude of resentment remains *under repression*, even with the person's own ability to report on it. And at the very least we can say that such a person does not have ordinary first-person knowledge, and hence that *this* notion is not capturable by an account restricted to higher-order attitudes. What's missing, on this view, is the person's *endorsement* of the attitude he ascribes to himself, the ordinary ability to declare oneself.

[10] See Rey (1989).

Much as I think one can learn from Rey's general account in that paper, a central problem with it is that he understands the distinction drawn here to be a distinction between two different *kinds* of attitude, the "central" and the "avowed" ones. He illustrates this idea with the comparison between our psychological terms such as 'belief' and a natural kind term such as 'jade' that has a divided reference between two distinct kinds of stone. Just as we can greet this discovery by simply saying that there are two kinds of jade, so we may say that each psychological attitude may come in either a central or an avowed variety. But if the beliefs I express when I avow them (by saying either "P" or "I believe that P") are simply of a different *kind* from the beliefs and other attitudes that are the central explanatory ones, then it is completely unclear how we may see the two as *clashing* at all. And yet without the clash we lose the phenomenon the distinction is supposed to help us understand. For if they are anything at all, conditions like *akrasia* and self-deception are some kind of *conflict* within the person, expressive of conflicted relations to the same thing, and this sense is lost if we see the avowed belief that P and the central explanatory belief that not-P as distinct attitude types, and each all right in its own way. This picture would return us to an unanalyzed instance of Moore's Paradox, with no way to say what's wrong. That is, I would be able to *report* on the "central" explanatory attitude that I feel betrayed by this person while I *avow* the belief that I have *not* been betrayed (I look inside and see one thing, and I look outside and see another.) But avowing and reporting cannot be thus isolated from each other, if for no other reason than that any avowal is itself behavior, and thus at the very least a central part of the evidence for the *explanatory* attitude of belief. Hence, in principle the "two attitudes" could never be of utterly distinct types.

Preserving the sense of conflict within the self, whether in a therapeutic or other context, requires that we see the meaning of a psychological term like 'belief' as univocal across the two contexts. Only thus can the idea remain available to us that, although when I avow my belief I do not avail myself of psychological evidence of any kind, I nonetheless take what I say in that context to be *answerable* to the whatever psychological evidence there may be. If I am known to vacillate on some question, where the interests of other people are dependent on what I really do believe, my avowal of my belief may well be met not by denial of its truth, but by the demand that I take in the full empirical background of my own inconstancy before I announce my belief so confidently. This same answerability to the empirical, even for a statement that doesn't base itself on evidence, emerges in Anscombe's discussion of two possible stances toward an expression of intention. A well-known remark of hers says that "if a person says 'I am going to bed at midnight' the contradiction of this is not: 'You won't, for you never keep such resolutions' but 'You won't, for I am going to stop you'" (1957, p. 55). Since an expression of intention is not a prediction, it is not contradicted by a contrary prediction (but by the expression of an opposed intention). To say this is not, however, to deny that in declaring the intention the person is committed *both* to the practical endorsement of the action and to the expectation of a future event. In the case where it is the person's constancy that is doubted, it is not open to him to respond to the other person's doubt by saying, "True enough, I never do keep such resolutions. But nonetheless: I'm going to bed at midnight" (that would be the "empty transcendental" form of bad faith from the discussion in 3.2). Rather, his statement of intention expresses his responsibility for both perspectives on one and the same action. And, in declaring his intention, the speaker tells his audience something about the future that he may doubt or count on like an ordinary prediction. This requirement of univocality is recognized by Anscombe later, although not explicitly related to the earlier remark, when she says: "If I say I am going for a walk, someone else may know that this is not going to happen. It would be absurd to say that *what* he knew was not going to happen was not the very same thing that I was saying *was* going to happen" (p. 92). The person who announces that she is going for a walk does not base her statement on evidence; and yet her statement is something that may be true or false, something whose truth or falsity *may* be a matter of evidence for another person.

Despite the difference in basis between attitude-statements made through attribution and those made through avowal, the same psychological terms refer to the same phenomena whether spoken in the first-person or third-person voice.[11] We should, then, see the stance of avowal and the stance of explanation as two ways of becoming aware of the same thing, and the Sartrean and Kantian language employed earlier is meant to convey this idea of different stances toward what is in some sense the same state of affairs, the same person. When I *avow* a belief, I am not treating it as just an empirical psychological fact about me; and to speak of a *transcendental* stance toward it is meant to register the fact that it is explicit in the avowal that it commits me to the facts *beyond* my psychological state; and as a commitment it is not something I am assailed by, but rather is mine to maintain or revoke.

If, then, we are looking at two routes to knowledge of the same facts, we must ask: What would be missing from a restoration of self-knowledge that remained theoretical or descriptive in this sense? Why should one route, the ordinary nonevidential way of avowal, be privileged in any way in our daily lives? A form of privilege for avowal is maintained even in contexts where this is detached from assumptions of accuracy or completeness. It is virtually definitive of psychoanalytic treatment, for instance, that it does not begin by taking first-person declarations as necessarily describing the truth about the analysand's actual attitudes. And this might be taken to mean that the knowledge of oneself it seeks to culminate in would ideally dispense with avowal as something unsophisticated and unreliable, substituting for it something more interpretive and theoretically grounded. But any such suggestion would neglect, at the very least, the crucial therapeutic difference between the merely "intellectual" acceptance of an interpretation, which will itself normally be seen as a form of resistance, and the process of working-through that leads to a fully internalized acknowledg-

---

[11] Again, the claim is not that there are *no* contexts in which, e.g., 'believe' has such a different function in speech that it is wrong to see it as reporting on one's state of mind. The claim of univocality says only that this is not always so, and that a person's belief *can* be reported on by the person herself as well as by others.

ment of some attitude which makes a felt difference to the rest of the analysand's mental life.[12] This goal of treatment, however, requires that the attitude in question be knowable by the person, not through a process of theoretical self-interpretation but by avowal of how one thinks and feels. That is, what is to be restored to the person is not just knowledge of the facts about oneself, but self-knowledge that obeys the condition of transparency. But why should it matter, aside from convenience or reliability, that the knowledge is arrived at in a certain way, so long as *what* is known is the same?

In focusing this question, we should consider what an idealized but still purely theoretical relation of expertise toward oneself would be missing. This will put us in a position to understand how it is not just permissible but essential that ordinary first-person knowledge proceed independently of evidence, and hence why a nonempirical or transcendental relation to the self is ineliminable. Obviously, not everything we know about our own attitudes is known through avowal, nor need it be. But even so, something is amiss if some attitude *cannot* be known through avowing it. The deliverances of an "ideal symptomatic stance," as we are imagining it, could be as spontaneous as the most basic judgments we make about the world. Nor need there be any loss of special reliability: what is learned about one's attitudes in this way might well be so certain and so complete as to be unchallengeable by anyone else. Further, we need not think of the evidential basis here as restricted to anything like overt behavior, but could also include one's dreams, passing thoughts, associations, and feelings. That is, theoretical expertise as we are imagining it here could extend to the private "inner" realm as well, such that only the person himself could report on it and his reports were invariably accurate. Thus, we would be providing everything possible in the way of "privileged access," but without the person's awareness of his attitudes being expressible through his avowal of them. And yet, for all of this immediacy, accuracy, and

[12] In Freud, see especially "Remembering, Repeating, and Working-Through" in Freud (1953–74), vol. 12, p. 147.

reliability, there still is a sense in which such a person would remain opaque to himself.

What such a case provides us with is a full-blown realization of the theoretical, or perceptual, picture of self-consciousness that both Wittgenstein and Sartre want to combat. The criticism of this picture of privacy is usually thought to lodge in its metaphysical extravagance: an inner eye focused upon essentially inner events that no one else, in principle, could witness and which I am unable to reveal or describe to another person. But I think what the realization of this picture enables us to see is that the deeper criticism to which both philosophers are pointing is that under the *guise* of metaphysical extravagance this picture of privacy presents an essentially superficial view of the differences between my relation to myself and my possible relations to others. For in essence what we have here is a picture of self-knowledge as a kind of mind-reading as applied to oneself, a faculty that happens to be aimed in one direction rather than another. Hence, in filling out the picture of such a person's self-knowledge we may even dispense with any work of interpretation on her part altogether. That is, she may know these psychological facts with immediacy, in a way that does not depend on any external "medium," and which involves no inference from anything else, and yet the idea is that she would still not enjoy ordinary first-person knowledge.

How is our ordinary self-knowledge different from this sort of self-telepathy? In Chapter One I argued that any philosophical account of self-knowledge must be an account of knowledge *from the first-person position*, and that this target is strangely easy to lose sight of. We are now in a position to see something about why this is so. For the first-person perspective, and the authority of the first-person, has two distinct aspects that normally run together but can in principle come apart, and only one of them fits the traditional understanding of a purely epistemic capacity. One aspect is the familiar feature of epistemic immediacy; the idea that, whereas other people must rely on what I say and do to tell what I think, *I* can say what I think without observation, evidence, or inference of any kind. Immediacy by itself doesn't entail that the awareness that is gained in this way is more accurate or reliable than any other, let alone that it is as such epistemically privileged over the evidence-based reports of others. But we can stipulate the inclusion of such privilege for current purposes, as in the previous example, and still not have described another aspect of the first-person position: that in ordinary circumstances a claim concerning one's attitudes counts as a claim about their *objects*, about the world one's attitudes are directed upon. It is part of the ordinary first-person point of view on one's psychological life both that evidence is not consulted, *and* that, for example, the expression of one's belief carries with it a commitment to its truth. What we've been calling the Transparency Condition is equally a feature of ordinary first-person discourse. But as we've seen, it is no more than ordinary, and when endorsement fails, then so does transparency, for without endorsement the person cannot declare his belief through avowal of it. He might still, however, retain a kind of immediate epistemic access to it. The dimension of endorsement is what expresses itself in one aspect of first-person authority, where it concerns the authority of the person to make up his mind, change his mind, endorse some attitude or disavow it. This is a form of authority tied to the presuppositions of rational agency and is different in kind from the more purely epistemic authority that may attach to the special immediacy of the person's access to his mental life.

These two aspects to first-person authority are not unrelated, of course, and the kind of unity they form will be taken up in the following chapter. But it is important to stress their distinctness to see why it should be a matter of any consequence, either philosophically or in the life of the person concerned, that what is known in self-knowledge should be knowable in the special manner we associate with the first-person position. For insofar as it is possible for one to adopt an empirical or explanatory stance on one's beliefs, and thus to bracket the issue of what their possession commits one to, it will be possible for one to adopt this stance to anything theoretically knowable, including private events or attitudes that one may be somehow aware of immediately, without inference. The kind of alienation we have been picturing here would remain possible on even the most generous epistemology for self-knowledge, so long as it was construed purely theoretically. We may allow any manner of inner events of consciousness, any exclusivity and privacy, any degree of privilege and special reliability, and their combination would not add up to the ordinary capacity for self-knowledge. For the connection with the *avowal* of one's attitudes would not be established by the addition of any degree of such epistemic ingredients.

Any treatment that took upon itself the task of restoring self-knowledge would have to restore a capacity that conformed to what we've been calling the condition of transparency. The person might be *told* of her feeling of betrayal, and she may not doubt this. But without her capacity to endorse or withhold endorsement from that attitude, and without the exercise of that capacity making a difference to what she feels, this information may as well be about some other person, or about the voices in her head. From within a purely attributional awareness of herself, she is no more in a position to *speak for* her feelings than she was before, for she admits no authority over them. It is because her awareness of her sense of betrayal is detached from her sense of the reasons, if any, supporting it that she cannot become aware of it by reflecting on that very person, the one by whom she feels betrayed. The rationality of her response requires that she be in a position to *avow* her attitude toward him, and not just describe or report on it, however accurately, for it is only from the position of avowal that she is necessarily acknowledging facts about *him* as internally relevant to that attitude (say, as justifying or undermining it), and thereby (also) as relevant to the fully empirical question of whether it remains true that she indeed has this sense of being betrayed by him. Otherwise, her own sense of the truth about that person floats free of her sense of what sustains her attitude toward him. From the purely theoretical or explanatory point of view she might respond to the information that her sense of betrayal is in fact groundless by saying, "Quite so, but how is that relevant to the psychological question of what my attitude actually *is* [that is, Rey's 'central attitude']? Surely I *do* feel betrayed by him. We both agree that this is the unavoidable conclusion to draw from the rest of my thoughts, feelings, and behavior. And I'm as certain of that as ever."

3.4 BINDING AND UNBINDING

The point of referring to such things as "commitment" and "endorsement" here has been to show the limitations for self-knowledge of such a form of "certainty." We may compare the case of belief with the case of decision and the two different possible ways of knowing what one will do. We may imagine Sartre's akratic gambler as in a state such that he can only learn of the strength of his resolution to avoid the gaming tables by empirical psychological reflection on himself, and *not* by practical reflection on his *reasons* for quitting gambling. To the extent that he cannot become sure of what he will do by reflection on normative, practical considerations rather than predictive considerations, he does not take the commitment or direction of his will to be a function of what his best practical reasons are. His actual will, such as it may be, is not understood by him as a response to those reasons, and what determines its strength or weakness is something quite independent of them.

What is wrong with the "direction of gaze" here, the shift to the theoretical or empirical perspective, is that it suggests that his reflection on his best reasons for belief or action still leave it an open question what he will actually end up believing or doing. This is not a stable position one can occupy and still conceive of oneself as a practical and theoretical deliberator. One must see one's deliberation as the *expression and development* of one's belief and will, not as an activity one pursues in the *hope* that it will have some influence on one's eventual belief and will. Were it generally the case (for Sartre's gambler, say) that the conclusion of his deliberation about what to think about something left it still open for him what he *does* in fact think about it, it would be quite unclear what he takes himself to be *doing* in deliberating. It would be unclear what reason was left to *call* it deliberation if its conclusion did not count as his making up his mind; or as we sometimes say, if it didn't count as his coming to *know* his mind about the matter.

Nothing further in the way of *evidence* about himself could establish the connection between his reflection on the world and his knowledge of what he will in fact do or what he does in fact believe. Considering himself empirically (or theoretically), he must see these as quite separate questions. Nothing but some commitment on his part could make it the case that his world-directed reflection on his reasons for belief or action does indeed settle the question of what he does believe or what he will (in fact) do.

Demanding that evidence about oneself provide the link between one's present thinking and one's future action would be precisely to undo the status of one's thinking as deliberation, as making up one's mind about what to do. Undoubtedly, such epistemic disengagement is sometimes called for (e.g., as when I repeatedly fail in following through on some "decision" of mine), but emerging from this condition cannot be through my accumulation of evidence of the correlation between what I think now and what I do later. Similarly, for our analysand, if she is unable to learn of her attitude toward the person by whom she feels betrayed by thinking about *him*, if here she can only attribute beliefs to herself but cannot avow them, then she will not come to avow them by engaging in more and better attributions to herself. (The theoretical stance toward oneself constitutes itself as a self-sufficient realm.) When I deliberate about something, the conclusion of my deliberation settles the question for me only in virtue of my attitude toward this activity, not in virtue of what I may believe about its effect on me. The aim and conclusion is the binding of oneself to a certain course of action (or proposition), not the production of a state of mind that I might then treat as (further) empirical evidence about how I should proceed.

The interplay between these two stances toward one's own thought takes an external form in certain familiar situations of decision making. To break a deadlock over, say, whether to take some job, I might decide to settle the question by flipping a coin. I tell myself if it comes up heads, I'll take the job, otherwise not. So it comes up heads; and then my first thought on confronting the result is: Should I really be bound by this? Do I really want to take this job? I'll flip it again to make sure; if it comes up heads *again*, then I'll know.

This is a recognizable quandary of binding and unbinding oneself. Insofar as I recognize myself as someone who can bind himself, I must recognize that I can also always unbind myself. There's nothing irrational in settling a question by a coin toss, but if it is up to me what the position of the coin shall mean, then it is up to me whether it means anything at all. I can opt out at any time. It is one and the same capacity that makes it possible for me to assign this meaning to the coin toss and to revoke that meaning when the result appears to be not what I wanted or expected.

When I detach myself from the result in this way, I may tell myself that tossing the coin was really a way for me to *find out* what I really wanted to do all along (hence reasserting the theoretical stance). It may be the only way I have of putting myself in the position where I can vividly imagine living with a particular decision. And when I do so, I find that I don't like it. So with this device I learn something about myself and what I'm prepared to live with. But of course what I am attending to when I make this discovery is not the behavior of the coin, but the scenario presented by a certain option, and all the reasons that make me uncomfortable with it. The coin toss can only have the desired psychological effect (vivid imagining) if I at least *sort of* believe that the way the coin lands commits me in a certain direction. Therefore, in the position I am in now, I have no reason to toss the coin a second time. *It* couldn't tell me anything I don't already know now. Indeed how could I invest it with this meaning (e.g., as telling me what I will do) if I know ahead of time that I am not committed to abiding by the outcome? The coin cannot *make* me do anything, and I cannot think of it as *revelatory* of the future (here the sense of my activity would drift into a form of divining).[13]

---

[13] One might ask here: If there is a problem with investing the coin toss with this meaning when I know beforehand that I am not committed to abiding by it, why isn't

If I am committed to the first result of the coin toss, then I know what I shall do and I have no further questions. If I am *not* committed to it, then there are several problems with tossing the coin again. First, assuming I have some *reasons* for revoking my commitment to the first result, they will presumably be practical reasons concerning the desirability of taking a certain option. In that case, I should be concentrating on *them* to decide what to do (if, indeed, the vividness of my earlier encounter with them doesn't already settle the question for me). Second, in revoking my commitment to the previous result, I have now produced good empirical evidence for believing that I may well opt out of the result of the coin toss I'm currently considering. I cannot pretend I don't know this now. And at the very least this diminishes my confidence that I *can* commit myself to the result of this coin toss. (Whether I can commit in a certain way has now become an empirical question for me.) And without the commitment, the whole procedure really is an empty ritual, even when considered as a psychological device for clarifying my preferences. The upshot then is: if I'm committed to the previous result there's no point in tossing the coin again, and if I'm *not* committed to it there is either no need to do it again (because the real practical reasons are now present to me) or I must acknowledge myself as *unable* to do it again and commit myself to its result.

Only in virtue of a commitment of mine does the coin toss mean anything; just as only in virtue of a conviction of mine is there a belief of mine with some evidential value (a commitment to abide by the coin toss, a conviction about the facts). There's no point to anyone considering my mental state (e.g., as evidence about some matter) if it is not understood to (already) bind me to some view of the facts. Without it representing such a commitment of mine, it cannot serve as evi-

---

there the same problem when, as in the normal situation, I know that, although I am now committing myself in this way, I am always free to *un*commit myself? Why doesn't *that* knowledge make it impossible for me to go through the whole charade?

For now, the brief answer is: believing that I am always free to uncommit myself is not the same as having reason to think that I will do so. (The first is a transcendental claim to agency, the second is some empirical reason I may or may not have.)

dence, for myself or anyone else. However, it is not the pointlessness of a second coin toss that is of most concern here, but rather how in both cases something in the guise of an empirical *strengthening* of one's position is in fact an undermining of one's position as deliberator. I can describe tossing the coin a second time as an expression of epistemic caution (as if I were confirming the previous result), just as I can view my retreat to the theoretical stance of attribution as taking in a more complete body of evidence (including now the fact of my own belief). But, in fact, to toss the coin again just *is* to undo its status as deciding the question for me; just as to decide to treat my own belief as evidence *is to* suspend my conviction about the matter.[14]

It is not essential to whatever is missing from such a theoretical perspective that there be any lack of certainty about the contents of one's mind. At one point Wittgenstein remarks that "We say 'I hope you'll come', but not 'I believe I hope you'll come.'"[15] But what is wrong with the position of belief here? Whatever would be bizarre and less than welcoming in being told "I believe I hope you'll come," the problem is not that you are here being offered mere belief instead of something expressing greater certainty. The sense of something wrong in this encounter would not be mitigated by the amendment, "No, you misunderstand me. I'm quite *sure*, in fact *I have no doubt* that I hope you'll come." The essential thing would still be lacking—that which is provided by the ordinary expression of oneself in "I hope you'll come." But if something would be missing, it seems fair to ask what more could reasonably be demanded of the person speaking here. After all,

---

[14] This process of discovery, commitment, and then detachment that reopens the original question can be reiterated, of course. Someone may detach from the decision or desire at which he arrives through this process, and now consider *it* as new evidence for his overall attitude. The dialectic is limited only by sanity or exhaustion. For further elaborations, see Freud's "Notes upon a Case of Obsessional Neurosis" (the "Rat Man," 1909), in Freud (1953–74), vol. 10, pp. 153–249.

[15] Wittgenstein (1967), §79.

one may think, she is speaking her mind, to the very best of her knowledge of it, not holding anything back. So what is it that is wanted by the person unsatisfied by all this, the person who feels let down by this scrupulous self-description? That she should somehow speak *more* than sincerely, that is, speak somehow *beyond* her own present knowledge of herself? In one sense this is precisely the demand, insofar as it means that what is wanted from the expression of hope is something that is not settled by evidence about herself or other theoretical considerations. And this will indeed involve speaking beyond one's present knowledge of oneself to the extent that even the most searching theoretical self-description will still leave room, in principle, for disavowal, for a failure to identify with what one discovers.

CHAPTER FOUR

The Authority of Self-Consciousness

The expression *gnothi seauton* has been repeated often enough and
in it has been seen the goal of all human endeavor. That is quite
right, too, but it is equally certain that it cannot be the goal if it is not
at the same time the beginning. The ethical individual knows himself,
but this knowledge is not a mere contemplation (for with that the
individual is determined by his necessity), it is a reflection upon himself
which itself is an action, and therefore I have deliberately preferred
to use the expression "choose oneself " instead of know oneself.
—Kierkegaard, *Either/Or,* vol. 2

4.1 EXPRESSING, REPORTING, AND AVOWING

In the previous chapter I sketched out a picture of self-knowledge as
involving the ability to *avow* one's state of mind and not merely to
attribute it to oneself; and I argued that it is this feature of the first-

person position that accounts in part both for the way in which first-person reports are made without appeal to evidence, and why the ability to make reports of just this sort should be bound up with the rationality of the person. All of these claims require further development, both to clarify this line of thought and to relate these basic ideas to other, perhaps more familiar ones in the literature on the first-person.

The notion of avowal has been developed here in relation to the earlier idea of transparency. A statement of one's belief about X is said to obey the Transparency Condition when the statement is made by consideration of the facts about X itself, and not by either an "inward glance" or by observation of one's own behavior. An avowal is a statement of one's belief which obeys the Transparency Condition. This may seem to reopen the question of whether "first-person statements" that obey this condition are to be seen as genuinely first-personal at all. If a statement like "I believe that's a goldfinch" is made in this "outward-directed" manner, how can it retain any reference to the speaker and his state of mind; and without that reference, how can it be seen as a statement of self-knowledge? And how is such a view different in the end from the Presentational View, according to which statements of the form "I believe P" have only the *surface* form of statements about the speaker and his belief, and are really only more or less guarded ways of presenting a claim about P itself?

One way of understanding the Presentational View is as claiming that a certain class of utterances do not assert or *report* the speaker's state of mind, although they do *express* it. Undeniably, a plain statement such as "That's a goldfinch," while it expresses the speaker's belief, does not describe it or report on it. Hence, if it is shown that the putative belief-statement "I believe that's a goldfinch" is only a way of saying the same thing, then statements of that form too may be seen as expressions rather than reports of the speaker's belief. This brings the Presentational View into relation with expressivism more generally, as a claim about some class of utterances (e.g., moral, aesthetic, first-personal). If avowal is to play the ineliminable role in self-knowledge claimed here for it, we must bring out what is distinctive about it, both in relation to the "mere" reporting on one's state, and in the sense of expressing it as implied by the Presentational View.

In post-Wittgensteinian philosophy of mind, expressivism is a broad claim about first-person utterances generally and not just about statements of belief or other attitudes. Hence, statements like "I'm in pain" have been the primary examples for expressivism. In such a case the claim is that the apparent reference to oneself here is illusory because such statements are not descriptions or *reports* in the first place. They are instead to be understood as behavioral expressions of pain, akin to crying or wincing. And like crying or wincing, such expressions cannot in themselves be manifestations of *self-knowledge* since they are not reports in the first place. Only a report of one's state, or some other fact-stating utterance, can be something that is true or false, justified or unjustified. Hence, expressivism about a class of utterances (e.g., moral discourse, first-person discourse) prevents the question of knowledge from even arising. If the statement "I have a headache" is not a report about some person's condition in the first place, then it raises no question for us as to how the person can be in a position to make such a report, or with what authority such claims are made. Expressivism should thus be seen not an *account* of self-knowledge or first-person authority, but a rejection of those very ideas.[1]

The central idea for expressivism is to finesse the questions concerning how claims of a certain sort can be made (moral claims, first-personal claims), and what the authority or basis for such claims may be, by denying that the discourse in question is in the business of making claims or reports in the first place. In claiming a logical equivalence between "I believe that P" and the plain statement "P," the Presenta-

[1] Expressivism with respect to sensations has been suggested to people by Wittgenstein's comparison of the utterance "I'm in pain" with the expressive behavior of moaning in pain. See *Philosophical Investigations*, §244, and *Blue Book*, p. 68. I find myself in agreement with McDowell (1996) both in his denial that Expressivism represents Wittgenstein's considered view of the matter, and in finding such a strategy to be a "cop-out" (p. 22, note 21).

tional View leads to a form of expressivism. For the assertion of "P" by itself is certainly something different from a report on one's state of mind and raises no philosophical questions concerning the basis for a psychological report. And at the same time, the simple assertion "P" *is* certainly an *expression* of one's belief in P, in the broad sense of 'express' meaning simply to manifest or reveal. (Speaking *is* a form of expressive behavior, after all.) So the Presentational View functions as an additional argument in favor of the view that statements of the form "I believe that P" both *are* expressions of one's belief, and are *not* reports of one's belief.

Laying it out like this highlights the fact that it is only as a *negative* claim that expressivism has any distinctive philosophical role to play. For to call some range of utterances "expressions" is not by itself to cast any doubt on their also being reports, statements of fact, or anything else. And conversely, when we classify an utterance as a statement or report, we are not thereby *denying* that it is also an expression. The sudden exclamation "The brakes don't work" both states a fact and expresses the speaker's belief; and, depending on the context, it may well also express his panic or frustration. Any statement a person makes is an utterance, and every utterance is an action, and every action of the person may be said to *express* various things about him (including his states of mind). Expressing and reporting are not in themselves mutually exclusive categories. The presentation of the neo-Wittgensteinian argument obscures this because it makes it seem as if the point at issue is whether or not first-person utterances are expressions, and hence that the denier of the Presentational View must deny that such utterances are expressions. But this is not so. The crucial claim in the expressivist argument is not the positive claim but rather the *denial* that members of this class of utterances ever function as statements or reports. It is for this reason that when understood as a claim about first-person utterances generally, expressivism comes to the incredible idea discussed in the previous chapter (3.1) to the effect that a person cannot talk about his own state of mind, or make judgments concerning it, even while his various interlocutors can.

As I am understanding the terms, then, 'expression' is our most general category, encompassing both verbal and nonverbal behavior, as well as both the overt, deliberate declaration of one's state and the involuntary manifestation of it. Understood this way, reporting or describing one's state is a particular *way* of expressing it, manifesting it. It is a special way, of course, involving a judgment about one's state of mind and the special responsibilities of *asserting* that judgment. The denial of this general possibility, as put forth in expressivism, is therefore more properly put forward as the claim that first-person expressions of pain or belief are *mere* expressions; that is, not to be included among the verbal expressions that are also assertions or reports of one's state. This general denial loses all plausibility (and is explicitly rejected by Wittgenstein) when we recall that the category of reports is quite broad, broad enough to include ascriptions made on any basis whatsoever, as well as those made on no basis. Thus, whatever may be true in more typical "immediate" first-person discourse, what we've called the "merely attributional" report on one's belief *must* count as a genuine report and not a mere expression. The difference here is that it is a report that does base itself on evidence of one sort or another, or on the authority of another person, and need not carry with it the endorsement of the belief attributed. In this way, what our analysand says about her own resentment is clearly a report or ascription in the same straightforward sense that what the analyst tells her involves ascribing beliefs or other attitudes to her. So a general thesis of expressivism has little to recommend it.

Once we see that any report is also an expression, it should be clearer why we need a third category, 'avowal', to frame the philosophical questions about first-person authority. And if we agree that it cannot be impossible in general for a person to think and speak about his own state of mind (especially since he succeeds in talking about the mental life of others), then the more substantial point that remains at issue can be put as the claim that *avowals* still count as reports; that is, that conforming to the Transparency Condition does not entail the collapse of a report into a "mere expression." This remains at issue, for it might still be thought, after the rejection of expressivism generally, that when a first-person assertion of belief conforms to the transparency requirement, *those* at least must be cases in which the apparent reference to one's state of mind is illusory, and hence where the assertion is not expressive of *self*-knowledge.

But in fact, if we don't beg the question in favor of something like the Presentational View, it's hard to see how conforming to transparency should be incompatible with a statement retaining its apparent reference to oneself. What conforming to transparency comes to is the commitment that beliefs I call my own are beliefs I can endorse as true. But that commitment is internal to the very concept of belief and cannot itself annul the prima facie reference to oneself in a statement like "I believe it's stopped raining." Any understanding of belief that provides for the minimal idea that believing involves "holding true" will entail that it is at least possible to announce one's belief by reporting on the truth as one sees it. If my intention is to report on my belief as such, and I know (how could I fail to know?) that my belief about X is what I hold to be true of X, then my intention will not be thwarted if I make this report by considering what is true of X. Here we might again compare the case of belief with that of knowledge of one's own future behavior: a person *may* have a purely predictive basis for knowing what he will do, but in the normal situation of free action it is on the basis of his decision that he knows what he is about to do. In deciding what to do, his gaze is directed "outward," on the considerations in favor of some course of action, on what he has most reason to do. Thus his stance toward the question, "What am I going to do now?" is transparent to a question about what he *is to* do, answered by the "outward-looking" consideration of what is good, desirable, or feasible to do. When he answers this question for himself and announces what he is going to do, his answer does not somehow lose its first-person reference because his process of answering it conforms to the transparency requirement. What he has gained, and what his statement expresses, is straightforward knowledge about a particular person, knowledge that can be told and thus transferred to another person who needs to know what he will do.

Further, consider some of the implications of even this modified version of the Presentational View (restricted to avowals, in our sense). It would mean that, far from avowability being a condition of genuinely first-personal awareness, avowing one's belief is strictly incompatible with maintaining reference to *oneself*. And so as a consequence, when our client in analysis moves out of the position where she is only able to attribute a belief to herself and now avows it consciously, this cannot be seen as a development of her self-knowledge, for with this transformation in her relation to her belief her utterance loses its reference to herself. On such a picture, then, the *only* knowledge she could have that was properly about herself was the alienated, opaque attribution of attitudes to herself, attribution that falls short of full endorsement since that would annul its status as a properly psychological judgment. But of course it is *attributional* self-knowledge that is the expression of an essentially *third-personal* stance toward oneself, so the consequence of adopting even this weakened version of the Presentational View would be the perverse idea that only an essentially third-person perspective on oneself could count as a vehicle of genuine self-knowledge.

The case of the analysand has been described in such a way that she has every kind of access to her belief, short of avowability. And the result is a kind of idealized attributional knowledge that nonetheless seems both impaired and something different from the target notion of ordinary self-consciousness. The case was described so as to highlight the natural conclusion that it is avowal that makes for the difference between merely attributional knowledge and genuinely first-personal awareness of one's belief. This is a natural conclusion, but of course avowal could not count as *any* form of self-knowledge if conforming to transparency ipso facto annulled the reference to oneself in statements putatively expressive of self-knowledge. Thus it was necessary just now to bring the Presentational View back into the discussion, rehearse the earlier reasons for rejecting it, and add to those some additional reasons specific to the issue of avowal. The conclusion to be secured by these considerations is that avowal is indeed a vehicle of self-knowledge, and that it is what makes the difference between genuine first-person awareness and a purely theoretical or attributional knowledge of one's states, however idealized.

4.2 RATIONALITY, AWARENESS, AND CONTROL: A LOOK INSIDE

The remainder of this chapter concerns why avowability should have any special place in our thinking about first-person knowledge, and why the capacity for this particular form of awareness has traditionally been thought to have a special importance to the overall psychic health of the person. In particular, I hope to show that the picture developed so far of what is distinctive about this form of awareness best accounts for the relations (suggested or assumed throughout the history of writing on the subject) between self-knowledge and the freedom and rationality of the person, and why the "immediacy" of first-person awareness should have any importance beyond that of easy accessibility.

We can begin by returning to the question of just what is supposed to be wrong or incomplete in the analysand's purely theoretical knowledge of herself (see the end of the previous chapter). We may agree for now that what she has doesn't count as ordinary first-person awareness of her sense of betrayal, but isn't it just as good? Or if it's not quite as good, aren't the advantages of genuine self-consciousness purely on the order of greater convenience, immediacy, or reliability?

An answer along the following lines has already been suggested. When there is an attitude of mine that I cannot become aware of through reflection on its *object*, it suggests that the attitude is impervious to ordinary rational considerations relevant to the maintaining or revising of the attitude. As in the case of the analysand's sense of betrayal, if she cannot become aware of it by reflection on the very person she feels betrayed by, that suggests that the persistence of the sense of betrayal has nothing to do with her sense of the facts about *him* that would either justify or undermine the attitude. And if the persistence of the attitude is impervious in this way to considerations of its justification, the attitude itself cannot be a fully rational one and must instead be seen as a kind of fixation. A belief that cannot be avowed is thus cognitively isolated, unavailable to the normal processes of review and revision that constitute the rational health of belief and other attitudes. Thus, we could explain why it is that the capacity not just for awareness of one's beliefs, but specifically awareness through avowal, is both the normal condition and part of the rational well-being of the person.

Something along these lines is indeed the account I wish to defend. I mentioned in Chapter One (1.3), and it has been guiding my discussion since then, that the self-knowledge that is of special interest to philosophers (as distinct from all the various things a person may know concerning himself) appears to be not just a capacity we happen to have, whose absence would leave the rest of one's mental life unaltered. Rather, it seems that the capacity for specifically first-person awareness of one's state of mind is necessarily tied up with *being* a subject of mental states in the first place. This conceptual connection could be secured by arguing from the systematic rationality that defines attitudes like belief, to the requirement that such attitudes be accessible to the person as part of ensuring their rational adjustment to each other and to new experience. But the connection of the capacity for self-knowledge with rationality requires a great deal of care to avoid both overestimating the ordinary need for awareness of one's own beliefs, and underestimating what is special about the "immediate" character of first-person awareness. We can see this by briefly considering a general argument, shared by a number of philosophers, for seeing the very possession of beliefs and other attitudes as bound up with a capacity for awareness of them.[2]

---

[2] The denial of the contingency of the relation between mental states and the capacity for first-person awareness of them is an important part of the case against construing self-knowledge as a kind of perception, for perception is characterized as a contingent, causal relation between an object and a perceiver. Hence, Sydney Shoemaker, for in-

Early in *The Character of Mind*, Colin McGinn offers the following intuitive considerations in favor of seeing the rationality of attitudes as requiring self-conscious awareness of them.

> Since a person is not simultaneously aware of all of his beliefs, it is perfectly possible—indeed commonplace—that conflicts among beliefs go unnoticed; it is thus possible to believe something as well as believing its opposite, precisely through lack of omniscience about what you believe. But once such a conflict comes to awareness one or the other belief must go—normative considerations then operate to determine your beliefs. . . . If a person were not aware of his beliefs, then he could not be aware of their inconsistency; but awareness of inconsistency is (primarily) what allows normative considerations to get a purchase on beliefs; so the rational adjustment of beliefs one to another seems to involve self-consciousness, that is, knowledge of what you believe. Without such self-consciousness the control of logic over thought would be deprived of its compelling force; rationality as we know it requires knowledge of the contents of one's own mind. (1982, p. 20)

On the following page of the book, the connection is drawn with the "further thesis, namely that the very possession of propositional attitudes requires self-consciousness." It is certainly natural to think that the capacity we have for awareness of our own beliefs and other attitudes ('self-consciousness' in that sense) is bound up with our rationality in some way, and with the rationality of the attitudes to which we have this access. One immediate reason for this would be the manifest *ir*rationality that often characterizes attitudes that are under repression of some kind, and to which we do not have immediate introspective access.[3] And on a natural picture of the function of self-consciousness,

---

stance, has explored this general type of argument in several papers as part of his general case against the Perceptual Model. In particular, see Shoemaker (1988), (1990), and (1991), which cites the argument from McGinn that follows.

[3] This is noted by McGinn later in this same passage.

this connection between repression and *impaired* rationality makes perfect sense. If some attitude of mine is out of reach of the light shone by consciousness, then I cannot "see" it in order to check it out and adjust it to the rest of my beliefs and desires. As with the intelligent, directed control of other things, the rational adjustment of one's beliefs and other attitudes requires, at the very least, *awareness* of what is being subjected to control.

But at the same time, we might wonder about the naturalness of the picture of this requirement. For there is more than one thing we might understand under the heading of "adjustment" and "sensitivity to reasons." There is no need to challenge the idea that the concept of belief (and that of other propositional attitudes) is of something systematic and normatively controlled, so that having a belief involves having a network of other beliefs, which are mutually rationally supportive. But if what McGinn means by "the rational adjustment of beliefs" is simply whatever it is that keeps one's belief-system in good working order, avoiding gross inconsistency, updating and revising beliefs in the light of the constant flow of experience, and so on, then there is no reason this regulation could not take place below the threshold of consciousness, perhaps at a wholly "subpersonal" level. Think of the constant flow of perceptual experience and the updating and revising of the beliefs about one's immediate environment. The purposes of belief-regulation do not require that the *person* get involved here at all, and hence there is no need for the person to have awareness of the contents being regulated. Looked at this way, there is no more reason to think that the rational regulation of belief requires awareness of the beliefs in question than there is to think that the regulation of heartbeat, respiration, or metabolism requires conscious monitoring, or even a creature with the capacity for consciousness at all. And as this comparison suggests, not only do such activities not seem to *require* the conscious control of the person, but it seems that they *could not* require this, for it is difficult to imagine how life could proceed at all if such monitoring *were* needed for proper functioning. In our biological as well as our cognitive lives, it must be the case that the majority of these processes take care of themselves, however "rationalizable" they may be in their functioning. Otherwise, we couldn't get going with the more reflective activities of the whole person like deliberate action or self-criticism. It may be true, even trivially true, that *I* myself cannot revise my beliefs unless I am aware of them. But my beliefs, like the flow of perceptions, interact and undergo revisions all the time without any intervention on my part. Their general rationality does not need my constant supervision. Indeed, it is not clear that it would even be coherent to require such global supervision as a general condition of rationality.[4]

In addition, it's worth noting an ambiguity in McGinn's reference to the "control of logic over thought," which makes it harder to see that there is a real question here as to *why* an inconsistency should be any harder to maintain once the person as such is made aware of it. Near the beginning of the passage he says, "Once such a conflict comes to awareness one or the other belief must go—normative considerations then operate to determine your beliefs"; and toward the end, "Without such self-consciousness, the control of logic over thought would be deprived of its compelling force" (20). Both sentences employ a language of necessitation here ("must go," "compelling force"), and so we might understand these claims normatively, as statements of what reason or logic requires. Logic requires the abandoning of one of two conflicting beliefs, for what is meant by "conflict" here is precisely that they cannot both be true. This, however, is a requirement of the logic of belief regardless of whether the beliefs in question are conscious, unconscious, or whatever. The normative force of the laws of logic is not dependent on the belief as an object of awareness at all. On the other hand, if we interpret the language of necessitation in this passage more purely psychologically, as a description of what must actually happen in the life of a believer, then the claim is hardly true without

---

[4] Apart from the difficulties in imagining such a psychological condition, such a requirement of explicit awareness and intervention would appear to involve an infinite iteration of levels related to those the Tortoise imposed on Achilles.

exception. More than one interlocutor has cheerfully maintained two conflicting beliefs after some Socrates has pointed out their inconsistency. And to the extent that it *is* true, it remains something of a mystery why, in such a case, consciousness should make such a difference, especially since in plenty of other situations of life beliefs are revised and updated, and inconsistency is avoided, without any awareness of the beliefs in question. The psychological "necessitation" or control of logic over belief is often strongest when no explicit reflection is involved.

(The ringer on the telephone is turned off. I know this because I turned it off earlier. But now the phone rings, and I pick it up and say hello. I might have remained stuck in self-contradiction, but mercifully my beliefs have revised themselves and I can assume—if I bother to— that I misremembered turning off the ringer. Meanwhile, life goes on.)

Further, if what we understand by the "rational adjustment of beliefs" is not just whatever processes, personal or subpersonal, manage to maintain order, but the actual deliberative activity of the agent, then the idea that this requires the awareness of one's own beliefs raises a different set of questions, which will occupy us in the remainder of this chapter. Briefly, I will be arguing that, whereas awareness of one's beliefs is too strong a requirement on "rational adjustment" when this is interpreted in the first way (roughly, the sense consistent with "functional regulation"), it is too weak a requirement when "rational adjustment" is understood in this second way, as a description of the person's deliberative relation to his own beliefs. For, as we have seen, the awareness of a person's beliefs, even one's own, can be arrived at in various ways, and nothing in the argument as given takes us to an account of, or an explanation of the need for, specifically *first-person awareness* of one's beliefs. The picture of the need for self-awareness here does not distinguish specifically first-person awareness from the sort of awareness of an attitude that any other person would require if he wanted somehow to alter one's state of mind, a need much the same as the sense in which I need to *see* the furniture in my room if I am going to rearrange it. But this is a badly "external" picture of the sort of "control" or authority a person exercises over his attitudes. To see how ordinary rationality is indeed bound up with specifically first-personal awareness, we need a broader understanding of the notion of "first-person authority." This will help in understanding why the "immediacy" of first-person awareness should matter at all, either to the philosophical account of self-knowledge or to the rationality of the person.

4.3 FROM SUPERVISION TO AUTHORITY: AGENCY AND THE ATTITUDES

> In many people it is already an impertinence to say "I."
> —Theodor Adorno, *Minima Moralia*

When we speak of "authority" in connection with first-person statements of belief and other attitudes, this idea has various dimensions. There is, of course, the epistemic authority of the report, indicating that the person making the report is in a superior position to know; and hence we can see the idea of "authority"' as describing the relation of the person to the facts reported, facts about a particular person's state of mind. But there is also a sense of "authority" as applied to the relationship of the person to the report itself, indicating the person as responsible for the report, as its author. And it is not just the *report* that the person is author of, but also, in a central range of cases, the person can be seen as the author of the state of mind itself, in the sense of being the person who originates it and is responsible for it. This is how Stuart Hampshire, for instance, describes things in passages like the following from his *Freedom of the Individual*, distinguishing a person's beliefs from those thoughts which seem to just "come" to him passively.

> I make up my mind, and decide, when I formulate my beliefs. I do not observe them. But there are countless thoughts that occur to me, and that pass through, or that linger, in my mind, and of

these only a small minority constitute beliefs. The beliefs are those thoughts which I endorse as true. I do not merely find them occurring or lingering: I decide in their favour. . . . A belief is a thought from which a man cannot dissociate himself.

(1975, pp. 97–98)

Elsewhere, the rational person is said to be "the responsible author of his beliefs" (p. 80), and the question he asks himself about his belief or desire is normally answered by a decision rather than a discovery (p. 76). One idea to be explored, then, is the connection between the ideas of knowledge of oneself (including the authority attaching to one's declarations) and responsibility for oneself (including one's thoughts).

Hampshire is not endorsing a voluntarism about belief here, as if one's beliefs were normally picked out and adopted at will. The agency a person exercises with respect to his beliefs and other attitudes is obviously not like that of overt basic actions like reaching for a glass. But to see the point in speaking nonetheless of "agency" here, compare the case of sensations with that of attitudes, with respect to the person's active or passive relations to them. A sensation of pain or vertigo really is something one may be passively subject to, something that just happens (even though one may then bear another kind of responsibility in anticipating or dealing with it). Beliefs and other attitudes, on the other hand, are stances of the person to which the demand for justification is internal. And the demand for justification internal to the attitudes involves a sense of agency and authority that is fundamentally different from the various forms of direction or control one may be able to exercise over some mind or another. We can begin to see what characterizes this sort of activity and responsibility by distinguishing different kinds of desire. Some desires, such as those associated with hunger or sheer fatigue, may be experienced by the person as feelings that simply come over him. They simply happen. On some occasions their occurrence may be inexplicable to him, and their inexplicability in such cases need not diminish their force. Like an alien intruder, they must simply be responded to, even if one doesn't understand what they're doing there or what the sense of their demands is. The person's stance toward such desires, and how he deals with them, may be little different from his stance toward any other empirical phenomenon he confronts. From this angle, a brute desire is a bit of reality for the agent to accommodate, like a sensation, or a broken leg, or an obstacle in one's path.

Other desires, however, may be states of great conceptual complexity, attitudes that we articulate, revise, argue about, and only arrive at after long thought. Thomas Nagel, for instance, distinguishes between "motivated" and "unmotivated" desires, and by now the general distinction is familiar from various contexts.[5] When someone wants to change jobs, or learn French, or avoid being seen, these are "motivated" or "judgment-sensitive" desires in that they depend on certain beliefs about what makes these various things desirable. This dependence is twofold. First, the desire to change jobs depends for its justification on various beliefs (about oneself, about one's present job and prospects elsewhere). Were the person to lose these beliefs, he would lose justification for the desire. And second, losing *justification* for this desire is supposed to make some difference to whether he continues to *have* this desire. The actual existence of the desire may well not survive the discovery that the new job prospect involves even more heavy lifting and a more toxic environment than one's present situation. This connection can fail, of course, and when it does the person may be open to familiar forms of criticism, and may be baffling to himself. It is the normal expectation of the person, as well as a rational demand made upon him, that the question of what he actually does desire should be dependent in this way on his assessment of the desire and the grounds he has for it. For the person himself, then, his motivated desire is not a brute empirical phenomenon he must simply ac-

[5] Nagel (1970). In the chapter from which I just quoted, Hampshire (1975) distinguishes between "thought dependent" and "thought independent" desires, and, more recently, T. M. Scanlon (1998, chapter 1) employs a concept of "judgment-sensitive" attitudes, with specific reference to desires.

commodate, like some other facet of reality he confronts. For this sort of desire, as a "judgment-sensitive" attitude, owes its existence (as an empirical psychological fact) to his own deliberations and overall assessment of his situation.

In fact, by far most of the desires we act upon are of this sort, and not of the sort that simply assail us with their force (despite the traditional concentration by philosophers since Plato on the "brute" desires of hunger and lust). For a desire to belong to the "judgment-sensitive" category it is, of course, not necessary that it be *formed* as the result of deliberation. For very few of our desires come into existence as the conclusion of an explicit exercise of practical reasoning. Equally, however, very few of our beliefs about the world arrive as the conclusion of any explicit *theoretical* reasoning that we undertake. It is nonetheless essential to the category of belief that a belief is a *possible* conclusion of some theoretical reasoning. Unlike a toothache, or a tooth for that matter, a belief is of the right grammatical kind to be the conclusion of one's reasoning. Similarly, what is essential for a desire to count as "motivated" in the relevant sense is for it to be the possible conclusion of some practical reasoning. This already indicates a categorical difference between such desires and mere feelings, including such things as the sensation of thirst, and brings us a bit closer to the particular sense of 'activity' that should be characteristic of our relation to our judgment-sensitive attitudes.

For there's more than one way of being active with respect to an attitude or other mental state of one's own. Consider again one's relation to one's feelings and sensations. In what sense do we understand sensations or "brute" desires as mere happenings to which the person is passively subject? After all, a person *can*, of course, inflict various sensations on himself, and can do this quite actively and freely. He pinches himself and produces the very sensation he intended to. But this is not what is meant by the passivity of sensation. True, as the person doing the pinching, he is active, but the sensation itself is the passive effect of his action. It has no *telos* of its own; it is *merely* an effect, much as if he had produced a scratch on himself. By contrast, a person thinking that it's getting late or his hoping for rain are not *effects* he produces, even when they result from a process of thinking on his part. Instead, such attitudes are constituents of his thinking and are thus more analogous to the act of pinching than to the sensation produced by that act.

A desire that is not judgment sensitive may in principle, of course, be produced through various external means, too, just as some sensation may be the effect aimed at by one's intervention. It may be treated as the passive object of one's manipulation, and the sense in which a person can be "active" with respect to it is the expression of a kind of external control. While this external sense of activity will make most sense as applied to the realm of sensations and the judgment-*in*sensitive desires and appetites, a person may also, in certain circumstances, adopt a similar manipulative stance toward some properly judgment-sensitive attitude of his as well. In various cases a person may produce in himself various desires, beliefs, or emotional responses, either by training, mental discipline, drugs, the cooperation of friends, or simply by hurling himself into a situation that will force a certain response from him. But exercising this sort of control over one's attitudes is not the expression of "activity" relevant to autonomy or rational authority. In such cases of producing a desire in oneself, the resulting attitude is still one I am essentially passive with respect to. It is inflicted on me, even if I am the one inflicting it.

There is, of course, another way in which a person may assume responsibility for some aspect of his psychological life, one that does not apply to sensations but *only* to his relation to his judgment-sensitive attitudes of one sort or another. Consider the distinctive kind of responsibility a person assumes for his desire when it is the conclusion of his practical reasoning; say, someone's coming to the conclusion that what he really wants to do is cancel his trip to Isfahan until he can stay longer than a week. In such a case, he is not only prepared to justify this desire if asked, but the presence or absence of justification makes a difference to the presence or absence of the desire itself, and the direction of his desire is in fact guided by the direction of his thought about what is desirable. Here he is active with respect to his desire not because he has *produced* it in himself, but because he takes the general question of what he wants here to be the expression of his sense of what he has best reason to pursue in this context. Were those considerations to be undermined, the desire itself would be undermined. And that means there is a kind of control he does *not* take himself to have here, in that he won't take himself to be in a position to *retain* the desire, or to reproduce it at will, if he were to lose or abandon the considerations that supported it, and the object in question now seemed worthless to him. Or rather, perhaps he could find some way to retain it, if we think of this now as a purely causal question, a choice of effective means to somehow maintain the presence of this desire. But if his "activity" with respect to this desire were confined to this sort of external control, this would be the very expression of his alienation from it, even though he managed to produce it in himself.

This "external" sort of activity and responsibility is not essentially first-personal at all. It is no different from the ways one may make oneself partly responsible either for the actions or for the thoughts and attitudes of another person. I can take responsibility for the beliefs of another person when I believe I can exert some influence over them, redirecting them in one way or another. But I do not thereby see the other person's beliefs as the expression of *my* sense of the balance of reasons. In seeking to redirect them, I need not myself share the reasons I offer to the person to change his mind. My concern is with what may appeal to *him*, and this may be a matter of reasons I can respect, or instead simply a matter of either my flattery or intimidation (relations which only the very most sophisticated may attempt toward themselves). This stance toward changing his mind need not be crudely instrumental, but it is internal to any such relation of two that it can develop in that direction. By contrast, the specifically first-personal responsibility that a person has for his own desire is essentially not instrumental. The person's responsibility here is to make his desire answerable to and adjustable in the light of his sense of some good to pursue.

It is not a responsibility that reduces to the ability to exert influence over one's desires, and that is why the idiom of "control" is misleading in this context.[6] When the desire is (already) the expression of the person's reasons, there is no *need* for exerting any control over it. As in the case of ordinary theoretical reasoning, which issues in a belief, there is no further thing the person *does* in order to acquire the relevant belief once his reasoning has led him to it. At the beginning of his practical reasoning he was not aiming to produce a particular desire in himself (as he might with respect to another person), but rather holding open his desire to how the balance of reasons falls out.

This is the same sense of activity and responsibility we rely on in ordinary reasoning with others where the operating assumption must be that the person is in a position to respond to the considerations offered, to see the point of some criticism, and thereby determine whether such considerations shall count here and now as a reason for changing his mind. Otherwise, the whole activity of offering certain reasons and countering other ones would be quite senseless. Without the understanding that the person you're speaking to is in a position to exercise some effective agency here, there would be no point in criticizing his reasoning on some point since otherwise what would *he*, the person you're talking to, have to do with either the process or the outcome? He might be in a superior position to view the results of

---

[6] For these reasons, I think Dennett is mistaken in claiming that "one changes one's own mind the way one changes somebody else's" (1977, p. 308). This claim is elaborated in another paper with regard to altering one's desires: "Acting on a second-order desire, doing something to bring it about that one acquires a first-order desire, is acting upon oneself just as one would act upon another person: one *schools* oneself, one offers oneself persuasions, arguments, threats, bribes, in the hopes of inducing in oneself the first-order desire. One's stance toward oneself *and access to oneself* in these cases is essentially the same as one's stand toward and access to another" (1976, pp. 284–85). In a sense, there would be nothing to argue with here once it was understood that these scenarios do not describe the ordinary situation of the formation of desires (or other attitudes) through deliberation, explicit or otherwise. We *can*, but we typically do not, arrive at a new desire by first identifying it as something to acquire and then acting on the second-order desire to adopt it. Changes in our beliefs, desires, and other attitudes are only occasionally the result of such techniques of self-management.

your intervention ("from the inside," as it were), but both of you would have to simply await the outcome.[7] Instead, it seems clear that the very possibility of ordinary argument (and other discourse) presumes that the reasons he accepts and the conclusions he draws are "up to him" in the relevant sense.

Acknowledging this sort of agency and responsibility does not involve us in any sort of voluntarism about the formation of beliefs or desires, any more than we need to see ordinary argument with others as aiming at getting one's interlocutor somehow to adopt a new belief by sheer act of arbitrary will. Sometimes, as in various conditions of psychic impairment, the first-person claim to this kind of responsibility is hollow, unfit to be taken seriously. And in such situations, rather than taking my declaration to settle the question (of what I really believe), I may be *obliged* to treat it for the moment as just so much data, something that may be a more or less good *indication* of my actual belief or desire. How one emerges from such a condition is a question unlikely to have helpful general answers, but there would be nothing that counted as agency or deliberation at all if a person could not generally claim the conclusion of his reasoning as making it the case that, as a matter of psychological fact, *this* is his belief about the matter.

4.4 THE RETREAT TO EVIDENCE

This suggests a further dimension to the relevant idea of "authority," and the limitations on replacing it with a more purely epistemic notion to describe the position from which a person may be said to speak his mind. If the authority in question were just a matter of the person's normally having the best-informed view of the facts in question, and

---

[7] See Philippa Foot's remark that reasons are not like medicine you take in the hope that it will work: "When given good evidence it is one's business to act on it, not to hang around waiting for the right state of mind" (1958, pp. 104–5).

if we have agreed that this assumption may lapse in various circumstances, then it might be asked what would stand in the way of a more complete supersession of this assumption, perhaps made possible by some future science of the mind. A fairly modest version of the idea of "first-person authority" will understand it not as entailing either infallibility or perfect access, but as a feature of discourse, as the authority a speaker is ordinarily granted to declare his thought and feeling, and have that declaration count (normally decisively) as telling us what the person's attitude is. This is not the assumption of all discourse, naturally, nor is its abrogation restricted to institutional settings such as the psychotherapeutic. But the fact that on a given occasion, or with respect to a given subject matter, we *can* suspend the assumption that the speaker's genuine attitude is given by his statement of it may easily produce the impression that the idea of such authority was a dispensable assumption to begin with. It has certainly seemed to various contemporary philosophers as if this assumption reflected a prescientific prejudice which we would do well to abandon. And yet, imagining a suspension of first-person authority across the board would be a very different matter from imagining such a suspension with respect to this or that particular site of psychic conflict. Within a familiar kind of therapeutic context we may imagine, for example, that what the person *says* about his reaction to his grandmother's death is treated not as authoritative for what his attitude is, but as simply more data, more (verbal) behavior for interpretation, from which, together with other information, his actual attitude may perhaps be inferred. The therapist takes the person's report of his state into account, but only as a piece of evidence not itself any more authoritative than various other aspects of behavior and history.

And, of course, the client himself may be well aware that his words are being taken this way. But now, if the person, being aware of this aspect of the situation, can only say what he *seems* to believe or feel here, his limitation in this condition is not only that he cannot see clearly into the contents of his mind and report what's there. Getting into the spirit of this kind of discourse, let's imagine he now expresses uncertainty as to his true thoughts about this event. But then, to be fair, even his expression of uncertainty itself can't be taken as authoritative, but only of symptomatic value—indicative, but perhaps misleadingly so, of his actual state of mind, which perhaps isn't uncertain at all. At this point he may well feel the need to express his frustration or despair, but any words he produces now can only amount to verbally gesturing at his own state of mind, not speaking his mind. He may attend to his own words, to what he is saying now, to see what they may reveal about his thought. But then, in distancing himself from them, they lose even the symptomatic value they had when he naively spoke them with conviction. For their value as evidence depended on his giving them his backing; but now, without any conviction in them, as mere words, issuing from somewhere within, who or what are they supposed to be indicative of?[8]

If we try to imagine the abrogation of first-person authority as quite generalized, covering all questions about a person's current beliefs, desires and other attitudes, there is difficulty in imagining the simplest forms of explicit reasoning and concluding. If a person can only de-

---

[8] Even the pressure to split the person into more than one Self testifies to the unavoidability of this authority at some level of description. In his remarks on Moore's Paradox, Wittgenstein presents this situation:

> "Judging from what I say, *this* is what I believe." Now, it is possible to think out circumstances in which these words would make sense.
>
> And then it would also be possible for someone to say "It is raining out and I don't believe it," or "It seems to me that my ego believes this, but it isn't true." One would have to fill out the picture with behavior indicating that two people were speaking through my mouth. (*Philosophical Investigations*, p. 192)

We split the person into two, one of them describing the other, because to understand the speech as an assertion at all, we have to treat *some* Self as giving itself authoritative utterance here. So in this case, one Self can talk *about* the apparent beliefs of another only by abandoning the symptomatic stance and arrogating to itself the authority to speak its *own* mind, to declare how things actually seem to it ("It seems to me that my ego believes this . . ."). With those words, the speaking Self moves from attribution to avowal.

scribe what he seems to believe about any matter, then if he is, for instance, asked some factual question that requires some figuring out, he cannot even take the answer he delivers to necessarily report the actual belief he has arrived at. On this view, what he announces confidently as the conclusion of his thinking is one thing (e.g., "Yes, I do think you save time if you avoid the tunnel, but it's easier to get lost"), but his actual belief, as an empirical psychological matter, is another. The radical abrogation of first-person authority means that he cannot take for granted that the conclusion he arrives at just is, now, what he genuinely believes about the matter. Thus, his problem is not only that the current of his true beliefs and feelings runs somewhere out of *sight* of his consciousness, but also that this current seems to run its own course and have nothing to do with his explicit thinking about the people and things his feelings are supposedly directed upon.

In this way, the authority that would be lacking here is not simply the epistemic authority of the truthful observer, but also the person's authority to make up his mind and have that actually count for something, count as determining his belief. The loss of *this* authority is not made good by supplementing it with expert knowledge from the outside of what his real attitudes are, knowledge that might be offered to him by a doctor or some other well-meaning informant. Just being provided with the *information* about his belief is not enough. For if he cannot see the empirical question of what he believes as answerable to his current explicit thinking about the matter, then just being informed what his belief is leaves open the question whether this information shall count as a *reason* for him or not. As it is, he is no better off than if he had been told that some other person has this belief, or that he himself once did at some other time. This suggests that the primary thought gaining expression in the idea of "first-person authority" may not be that the person himself must always "know best" what he thinks about something, but rather that it is *his business* what he thinks about something, that it is up to him. In declaring his belief he does not express himself as an expert witness to a realm of psychological fact, so much as he expresses his rational authority over that realm.

4.5 FIRST-PERSON IMMEDIACY AND AUTHORITY

While we have seen that we do have reason to relate the capacity for self-consciousness to the rationality of the person, we need better charactcrizations of both the notion of "self-consciousness" and of "rational control." Otherwise, we haven't yet distinguished first-person awareness and *its* kind of authority from the kind of awareness one would need of another person's beliefs and other attitudes in order to exert some rational influence upon them. One could, of course, simply build in "immediacy" or independence of observation to the account of the kind of awareness we're trying to capture, but how would that help? In particular, it's hard to see how it would help in understanding why an awareness stipulated as "immediate" should matter to rationality in the case of one's own attitudes once it is acknowledged that this particular manner of awareness is not relevant to the *general* possibility of such rational control. So long as we are thinking of the relation in terms of the requirements of "rational control," the requirement of immediacy seems unmotivated, since the rational direction of other items (including another person's attitudes) may require awareness of them, but it doesn't require that this awareness be arrived at in any particular way. We need a less "external" picture both of the person's awareness and his rational stance toward his attitudes if we are to see how these capacities relate to the specifically first-person authority from which, in normal circumstances, a person claims to speak his mind.

A related context where we confront the issue of knowledge that is peculiarly "immediate" is in the agent's knowledge of his own intentional action. A familiar point since Anscombe's *Intention* is that an indefinite range of true descriptions will apply to the behavior that constitutes a person's action, and it is only under some of these descriptions and not others that the action will count as intentional.[9] In one of her examples, someone is pumping water from a cistern, and in the course of doing so he is also clicking out a particular rhythm on the pump handle. The first description gives part of his aim; the second, we may assume, does not. Anscombe focuses her discussion of intentional action with the claim (which is more of a working hypothesis than a definition) that "intentional actions are ones to which a certain sense of the question 'why?' has application" (*Intention*, p. 11). In the course of distinguishing the kinds of cases where this question is *denied* application, she mentions two that are of particular interest for the present discussion. One is the familiar situation where the person simply didn't *know* that the description in question (e.g., clicking that rhythm) applied to what he was doing. Perhaps this exclusion is clear enough; if someone doesn't know he took my umbrella instead of his own, it won't make sense to ask him *why* he did this or to count it as intentional (he grabbed an umbrella intentionally, but he didn't intentionally grab *mine*).

But Anscombe adds a further restriction, relevant to our question about immediacy. After introducing the idea of "nonobservational knowledge" (i.e., "immediate awareness" in our sense) and illustrating it with the example of a person's ordinary awareness of the position of his limbs, she says that the relevant question "why" would *also* be refused application were the person to say, "I knew I was doing that, but only because I observed it" (p. 14). Here we get closer to our question about "merely attributional" awareness of one's state of mind. For while I take Anscombe's point to be an intuitive one, we can ask the same sorts of questions about it. That is, we will all agree that a person will need to *know* that he is doing a particular thing if we are to ask him for his reasons in doing it, but why should the particular *manner* in which he acquires this knowledge matter to its status as intentional? Why isn't the knowledge itself enough, however it may be arrived at? And why should the action's status as intentional (under this descrip-

[9] Anscombe (1957).

tion) depend on the agent's awareness of it having this very special basis in particular, viz., a basis that is independent of observation, evidence, or inference?

What we might call Anscombe's Condition on intentional action tells us that the relevant question "why" is refused application if the agent's awareness of what he is doing (under the relevant description) is not "immediate" in our sense. Anscombe herself does not offer explicit argument for this claim, or in any case her argument is not any shorter than the entire's book's case for a distinctively "practical knowledge" as something ignored in modern philosophy's "incorrigibly contemplative conception of knowledge" (p. 57). But we might reconstruct the following sorts of considerations in favor of the condition in such a way as to relate it to our question about avowal and rationality. An action is intentional under a certain description when that description (e.g., "pumping water") can be seen as answering to some aim the person is pursuing. If the person is doing that action intentionally, then he is doing it for reasons that he takes to justify it as contributing to his aim. These reasons would be what is specified in the special sense of the question "why?" whose applicability Anscombe takes to mark off the intentional actions. For him to be pumping the water for justifying reasons is for him to see that action as contributing to his aim; if he doesn't see it as contributing to his aim then we may conclude that he is not doing that thing for the sort of reasons (i.e., justifying reasons) that make an action intentional. The description under which an action is intentional gives the agent's primary reason in so acting, and the agent knows this description in knowing his primary reason. This description is known by him because it is the description under which he conceives of it in his practical reasoning. It is the description under which the action is seen as choiceworthy by him, as aiming at some good to be achieved. The agent takes the question of what he is doing to be answered by his decision as to what is worth pursuing, and that question is not a predictive or explanatory one to be answered by observation of himself. Hence, we arrive at Anscombe's Condition: If he can only know what he is doing by observing himself, that would be because, described in *these* terms (e.g., clicking out the rhythm) his action is *not* determined by his primary reason, is not undertaken by him as the pursuit of some aim. Otherwise, he would know what he is doing in knowing his practical reasons for adopting this aim. For him to say, "I knew I was doing that, but only because I observed it," would be to imply that under that description the event does not form part of his aim. For an agent to conceive of himself as capable of forming an intention and implementing it (which, I take it, is necessary to conceiving of himself as an agent at all) he must take his intentional action to be determined by his reasons, and thus he is in a position to know a true description of his action in knowing his reasons.

The basic point can be expressed in a loosely Kantian style, although the idea is hardly unique to Kant. The stance from which a person speaks with any special authority about his belief or his action is not a stance of causal explanation but the stance of rational agency. In belief as in intentional action, the stance of the rational agent is the stance where reasons that justify are at issue, and hence the stance from which one declares the authority of reason over one's belief and action. Anscombe's question "why" is asking not for what might best explain the movement that constitutes the agent's action, but instead is asking for the reasons he takes to justify his action, what he is aiming at. It is as an expression of the authority of reason here that he can and must answer the question of his belief or action by reflection on the reasons in favor of this belief or action. To do otherwise would be for him to take the course of his belief or his intentional action to be up to something other than his sense of the best reasons, and if he thinks *that*, then there's no point in his deliberating about what to do. Indeed, there is no point in calling it "deliberation" any more, if he takes it to be an open question whether this activity will determine what he actually does or believes. To engage in deliberation in the first place is to hand over the question of one's belief or intentional action to the authority of reason.

Of course, this authority can be partial or hedged in various ways. When I know this to be the case, for instance when I know that I am akratic with respect to the question before me, that compromises the extent to which I can think of my behavior as intentional action, or think of my state of mind as involving a belief rather than an obsessional thought or a compulsion. Nor does a person speak with first-person authority about such conditions.

The authority the agent does speak from (when he does) as well as the fact that his declaration is made without observation of himself both stem from the fact that the person's own relation to his attitudes and his intentional actions must express the priority of justifying reasons over purely explanatory ones. In this, his position is fundamentally different from that of another person, such as a rationalizing interpreter, who is seeking to explain either his actions or attitudes. The reasons that *explain* an action are states of mind of the agent, which may themselves be either veridical or mistaken. When a belief that is an explanatory reason is a false belief, this need not affect its explanatory validity in the slightest. But naturally this is not the agent's own relation to his reasons, which must be *guiding* or justifying reasons, and which are facts distinct from and independent of his beliefs.[10] What provides a reason for betting on a certain horse is the *fact* that it will win, or evidence for that fact, not one's *belief*, however strong, that it will win. And that fact would constitute a reason for the bet, even in the absence of the corresponding belief. (The relevance of the horse's own confident belief in winning is, of course, another matter, being part of the evidence itself.) A person's own attitude toward how his beliefs and desires relate to his action is not "subjectivist," or simply a matter of good fit among the states themselves. His belief is not *for him* a psychological datum that could even in principle justify his behavior purely

---

[10] See Raz (1978), p. 3. Raz's distinction between guiding and explanatory reasons is similar to Francis Hutcheson's distinction between "justifying" and "exciting" reasons. See Hutcheson (1728), pp. 308–9.

in its role as a psychological state. Otherwise, he would take himself to have as much reason to make the bet whether his belief is true or false, so long as he's got it. On the other hand, a rationalizing interpreter *will* take that behavior to be rationalized by the belief, whether it is true or false. The interpreter can afford to treat the belief as a psychological datum and go on from there to use it in a rationalizing explanation. The agent himself does not have this option, and, as we have seen, he would not be rational if he did. And rationalizing interpretation, of all things, must seek to preserve the assumption of the subject's rationality. So the interpreter's stance and its success presuppose the stance of the reasoning agent; and further, they presuppose that belief is treated *differently* from within the two stances.

As before, in the discussion of Rey (Chapter Three, 3.3), such considerations can suggest that we are dealing with two different attitude types or two different concepts of belief. But in fact I think that these very considerations, including the differences between beliefs considered as explanatory reasons and as justifying reasons, are inevitable features of the kind of unity displayed by the concept of belief or any other "judgment-sensitive" attitude. Throughout this discussion, I have sought to accommodate the assumption that the meanings of psychological terms do not alter across first- and third-person contexts, while at the same time insisting on certain fundamental asymmetries in these two contexts. There has been no attempt to show that concepts such as belief do not play more than one role, for it is hard to see how anything remotely like our concept of belief could fail to play a sort of dual role: as explanatory of behavior and as bearer of truth values. As long as there are believers, and as long as beliefs purport to represent the world, it will be possible to ask of any belief both whether it is true or false, and how it disposes the believer to act. The two aspects of belief depend on each other, since the explanatory aspect requires an assumption of rationality, and *that* requires that the believer himself not treat his belief as an opaque psychological fact. In his awareness of his beliefs, he either acts upon them as he acts upon recognition of some aspect of the independent world, or he subjects them to revision.

Instead of positing two different attitude types or two different concepts of belief, we may speak of different interests in the same concept. From the agent's perspective, the question of the truth of his beliefs is prior to the question of how they will dispose him to act. Beliefs "aim at truth" and do not enter into his practical reasoning in a way that brackets the question of their truth. The interpreter, on the other hand, will be interested in how beliefs explain behavior, and this is a role played by false beliefs quite as often as by true ones. Any representational state will have such a dual aspect, one under which it is treated as transparent to the world in a certain way, another under which it makes a contribution to the behavior of the agent. Naturally, these different interests in belief are not *restricted* to the first- and third-person uses, respectively. In communicating and reasoning with others, for instance, we are concerned with the truth, and not just the explanatory adequacy, of the beliefs we take them to have; while, on the other hand, in understanding oneself, one will sometimes need to bracket the question of the truth of one's beliefs and concentrate on their explanatory role. And the fact that in the *past*-tense case the person's own relation to his belief may approximate to that of an outside interpreter provides additional reason against thinking of the two roles as involving different concepts. For it is not credible that any shift in meaning occurs when one says (or thinks) something of the form "I believed it then and I believe it now."

Anscombe's Condition does not tell us that observation plays no role in the agent's awareness and execution of intentional action. The empirical world (e.g., in the form of a pump-handle and what it is or is not connected to) must cooperate, and Anscombe's agent, like any other, will need to pay attention to what he's doing. The point is not that an action counts as intentional only if the agent has complete knowledge of what he is effecting without the benefit of observation at all, for no action will satisfy that condition. Rather, this condition says that the special "why question" is being rejected if the *only* way the person has any awareness of that action (under that description) is by empirical observation of himself. The rejection of the question means that, under this description, the person does not have justifying reasons for what he is doing.

It is because the agent's perspective is characterized by the dominance of justifying reasons over explanatory ones that the immediacy of avowal is not only a possibility for the agent but also something of a requirement, in the sense that it is an expression of the person assuming responsibility for his thought and action. But the responsibility in question and the relevant sense of control are not restricted to the production of effects. For there are really two aspects to immediacy here, what we might call "epistemic" and "practical" immediacy. With respect to the latter, it is because the deliberator declares the authority of reason over his thought and action that at the conclusion of his thinking there is no further thing he *does* to make that conclusion his actual belief or his intention. The goal of deliberation, whether practical or theoretical, is conviction, about what to do or what to think. In the case of practical deliberation, reaching a conclusion means making a decision, hence forming an intention; reaching a conclusion in theoretical deliberation means achieving conviction in the form of a belief about what is the case. In both forms of reasoning, it would be an expression of the failure of reasoning were it to terminate not in conviction itself but rather in my apprehending a particular thought, or even appraising it as best, which I then need to find some *way* to make my own, my actual state of mind. (As in other straits, having lost authority, I could only fall back on *control*.)

Again, the point is never that various forms of alienation are not possible, or perfectly common, but rather to describe the unalienated conditions of the first-person perspective so that we may see in what sense these states *are* states of alienation, even what they are alienation *from*. In a certain case, I may see how all the evidence points to a conclusion I cannot bring myself to believe, or I may reason my way to a conclusion about what to do that leaves me with a further task of somehow managing to commit myself to it. But to find myself in such a condition is to confess that here in this situation, with respect to this issue, I am unable to reach conviction. In what must be the standard situation of deliberation, however, the person's conclusion *is* his belief or intention, not something he now needs to find a way to impose upon himself. Here he is not "working on" his states of mind, the way he might with respect to another person, nor is he trying to produce results in himself.[11] If he were, then he would indeed need to "see" what the states of mind are that he is trying to manipulate, the way the akratic person relates to his desire. Rather, in conceiving of the questions he's asking as part of the specific activity of deliberating, he has asserted the determination of the answer by justifying reasons rather than explanatory ones.

So, this is part of what I meant earlier in saying that the relation between rationality and self-knowledge suggested by McGinn provides a kind of "outsider's" picture of the sort of "control" or authority a person exercises over his attitudes. This would be to picture the role of self-knowledge as like the periodic need to get under the hood and see what's going on before making any adjustments (and from such an explanatory perspective the states or entities discovered would have to be something like Rey's Central Attitudes, the psychological machinery driving the system, leaving out the question of the person's own endorsement or disavowal of what is discovered). We could compare this with the two ways a person might "move his arm." In the ordinary case, he does not do any further thing in order to accomplish the moving of his arm. He simply does it, and he can do it with his eyes closed, without needing to observe anything (not on the "inside" either). In an abnormal case, on the other hand, the arm might be paralyzed and he manages to move it by picking it up with his other hand. That's "moving his arm," too. But here his relation to it is like the relation he has to the arm of another person, and in such cases he will need to observe

---

[11] See Hampshire (1975): "He who employs some method or technique to get rid of an idea acts upon himself exactly as he might bring about an effect in the mind of another. The man who changes his mind, in response to evidence of the truth of a proposition, does not act upon himself, nor does he bring about an effect" (p. 100).

what he is doing to bring it off. In the ordinary case of intentional action, I do not "move my body" as I might move a piece of equipment, nor do I relate to my attitudes as mental furniture to be arranged.[12]

Similarly, with respect to "epistemic immediacy," it is because the rational agent declares the authority of reason over his thought and action that he does not apprehend himself under a particular description when he is deciding what to think or do. Several writers on self-consciousness have stressed that the target notion requires that the awareness in question should be expressible using the first-person pronoun in its "subject-use"; that is, independently of any identifying description to secure reference.[13] This is, however, part of the same requirement of "immediacy" in first-person authority. When a person employs the "I" as subject, she is apprehending her state of mind without the *mediation* of any identifying description of herself. This is the semantic equivalent of immediacy in the sense of the sort of "nonobservational knowledge" that has come up in connection with Anscombe and elsewhere. When a person has what we've called "merely attributional" knowledge of his state of mind, the access he has to himself *is* based on observation, and his reference to himself is mediated by some identifying description. By contrast, the employment of "I" in its "subject-use" expresses an apprehension of oneself that is properly first-personal and not merely attributional. The use of the first-person pronoun in its "subject use" reflects the fact that attention is directed wholly outward, at the justifying reasons relevant to the truth of some proposition for belief. Outside of special (and obvious) cases, it is not facts about *me* or what descriptions I fall under which are relevant to the truth of a proposition for belief. In deliberating about some matter I do not even take as fixed whatever stock of beliefs and desires I may bring to the problem, for entering into the spirit of rational deliberation

[12] See the discussion of this distinction in Wilson (1989), pp. 84–86 and 122–24.

[13] The distinction between the use of 'I' "as subject" and "as object" is originally Wittgenstein's, from the *Blue Book* (1958). Sydney Shoemaker placed the "subject use" at the center of contemporary discussions of self-consciousness in "Self-Reference and Self-Awareness" (1968).

means that I acknowledge that reflection on the problem may lead me to abandon or revise any one of them.[14] The "immediacy" of self-consciousness and first-person authority, the fact that I can be aware of my belief without inference or evidence, is a function of the fact that information about myself that I would gain through inference or evidence about myself is ruled out as irrelevant to the question of what I am to believe.

4.6 INTROSPECTION AND THE DELIBERATIVE POINT OF VIEW

In seeking to explain and vindicate avowal as a privileged form of knowledge of oneself, I have been relating the capacity for "immediate" or "introspective" awareness of one's attitudes with the capacity of the person to make up his mind. And in the course of this I've tried to understand the "authority" of "first-person authority" not as an all-or-nothing feature of the logic of the first-person, but as bound up with this same capacity, and hence subject to the same failures and partiality. A person is credited with first-person authority when we take the question of what he *does* believe to be settled by his decision as to what he *is to* believe; and this assumption is not guaranteed by logic alone or the semantics of the first-person.

[14] In "Practical Reasoning," Stroud (2000) argues that "no fixed general description of a person of a certain kind can capture the full question of what a particular person should (or has most reason to) believe or do. The question of what I should believe in the situation in which I find myself is not the same as the question of what anyone who fits a certain general description should believe, even if I fit that description and know that I do. In asking the question about myself, I am in effect asking whether that description is *all* that is relevantly true of me and my situation or, if it is, whether it should continue to be true of me. Even if I grant that I now have the beliefs in question, the question is whether I should continue to believe everything I now believe. The question of what to believe is in that sense always open, whatever I believe at the moment. I do not mean that it cannot be answered, but only that the answer is never simply dictated by what I already believe. To detach the best conclusion I have to be ready to subject even my earlier beliefs to further scrutiny or criticism" (p. 33).

This chapter's discussion of the "immediacy" of self-knowledge has focused on features of the situation of deliberation that might in other contexts seem removed from the idea of Introspection as a faculty of awareness.[15] At this point, I want to discuss the continuity between the two sets of ideas by way of explicating how the discussion of avowal belongs to the philosophical account of self-knowledge. As mentioned in Chapter One, the knowledge of oneself that has been of interest to philosophers does not include any and all knowledge where the person himself is the subject. Clearly, knowledge of such things as one's own parentage, weight, or tax bracket doesn't raise the sorts of issues philosophers have traditionally been concerned with here. Nor even will all knowledge of one's own mental life be "introspective" in the sense at issue. Rather, there is broad agreement among philosophers about a set of features that would have to be shared by the sort of access in question, and which a proper philosophical account would have to explain. The two primary ones are "immediacy" and "authority." A proper philosophical account of self-knowledge should tell us how it is that a person can speak about his own mind, without appealing to evidence about himself, where that independence of evidence contributes to rather than detracts from the authority of what he says. It is also widely acknowledged that the target notion of a philosophical account of "self-knowledge" is restricted to awareness that is expressible by the use of the first-person pronoun in its "subject-use," which is the use that is not only indexical but whose reference to a particular person is not based on any identifying description.[16] We can either consider this a third element of the broad agreement about the self-knowledge of interest to philosophers, or see it as ultimately a part of the general condition of immediacy, as was just suggested.

[15] Following Shoemaker, I use the term 'introspection' neutrally to denote whatever the special access is that a person has to his own thought, and not to imply any version of a Perceptual Model of this access.

[16] There is a good bit of controversy about the nature and varieties of what Shoemaker calls "immunity to error through misidentification" and Evans calls "identification freedom," which I am not entering into. A related controversy stems from Anscombe's

The account developed here attempts to understand these features together, to show how they relate to and contribute to each other. What we are now in a position to see, I think, is that obeying the constraints on the target notion of self-knowledge that are widely agreed upon, and seeking a unified account of them, reveals that the notion itself is not simply that of a faculty of awareness, and that the immediacy in question only has importance for self-knowledge as a consequence of the person's normal capacity for the avowal of his attitudes.

A third feature is part of this broad agreement, but it has received less philosophical attention than the others, in part because it's somewhat harder to define. And this idea is that whatever "self-knowledge" of the relevant kind is, it should be something we can understand as having a special *importance* to the person, an importance beyond the usefulness of having some way of knowing, for example, one's own parentage or tax bracket. There is broad agreement, that is, that the capacity for first-person awareness does somehow matter to the overall rationality of the person, that its absence would not be just the lack of one particularly efficient avenue to knowledge of a particularly relevant and interesting person. But this defining idea of importance, though it has usually been tacitly relied on, has not usually been pursued together with the understanding of immediacy and authority. With the exception of the discussions in McGinn and Shoemaker and a few others, the idea that the capacity for first-person awareness has a special relevance to the psychic health of the person has mostly operated as a kind of background assumption in contemporary philosophy of mind, and not investigated on its own. And, as I argued earlier in this chapter, when we *are* offered an explanation of how self-knowledge should matter to rationality, the account given does not point us toward the special forms of immediacy that are agreed to characterize properly first-personal awareness. What we need, I suggest, is an understanding

---

claim that some of these very features of the first-person pronoun prevent it from being a referring expression at all (Anscombe 1975).

of how first-personal awareness matters to the well-being of the person, an understanding that relates this to the specific features of immediacy and authority that characterize the forms of first-person discourse that have attracted philosophical attention.

The idea, then, is that the attempt to frame an account of the philosophically relevant notion of "self-knowledge" that obeys the constraints of these defining features and seeks to account for them together obliges us to relate the faculty of awareness to the stance of deliberation. For the points of common agreement about self-knowledge pose the following questions for anyone seeking a philosophical account of it. Why should knowledge of oneself of this specifically first-personal form be thought to matter to the rationality or psychic health of the person? That is, why should it be thought to matter any more deeply than knowledge of oneself acquired in some other way, or any other "information" relevant to one's practical interests (as, decidedly, knowledge of *oneself* will often be)? In general, the lack of such knowledge may of course pose difficulties for the person, but such ignorance is not per se damaging to rationality. Second, why should it be this *particular* form of awareness of oneself, characterized by its independence of observation and evidence, that matters in this special way to psychic well-being? Or, the way we've been pursuing the question lately: in those cases where a person is unable to know his mind by avowing it (and is instead, perhaps, restricted to merely attributional awareness of some attitude of his), why should this suggest anything amiss with the attitude and the person's relation to it? And last, how does this particular form of awareness make for any special authority in the judgments made from it? Or, to relate this question to the feature of Immediacy, why should it be that the independence of evidence exhibited by the person's own statements of his state of mind makes for a kind of authority that is not shared by another person's statements about the same thing when these *are* based on good evidence? That is, how is it that not being based on evidence contributes to rather than detracts from the authority of such judgments?

4.7 REFLECTION AND THE DEMANDS OF AUTHORITY:
APPREHENSION, ARREST, AND CONVICTION

To help see how the answers to these questions fit together, and to round off the case for seeing avowability as basic to self-knowledge, I want briefly to consider a way of looking at self-consciousness that explicitly understands its special importance to the person in terms of his assertion of a specific form of authority with respect to his mental life. There is a tradition of thought, roughly Kantian, but with sources both in Locke and in early Stoicism, which aligns, or even identifies, reflective consciousness with rational freedom. In more or less obvious ways, the argument of the last two chapters has drawn on this tradition. But naturally these must sound like two quite different ideas. "Self-consciousness" sounds like the description of a faculty for awareness of the contents of a particular mind, one's own. As such, it is unclear why it should be thought to have any *more* relation to freedom or rationality than another other faculty of awareness might. The operation of this faculty of awareness may well involve the intelligent operations of such "activities" as selecting, noticing, and responding; but much the same could be said of the conduct of the human faculties of ordinary vision and hearing. Nothing along those lines suggests any reason to think there's any *deeper* relation between *self*-consciousness and rational freedom.

The argument we looked at from McGinn showed one way in which we could see the capacity for self-consciousness as tied more centrally to rationality, for it was argued there that awareness of the contents of one's mind is necessary for the basic maintenance of coherence and consistency in one's beliefs. However, even aside from the ambiguities and difficulties in this idea we discussed, the picture of self-consciousness provided there is still basically that of a faculty of awareness, and thus, as with vision and hearing, something that is surely an important *aid* in maintaining good rational functioning, but hardly something with a claim to be the very expression of one's rational autonomy. (The scenario is still one of looking under the hood when there's a problem; in principle things can run fine on their own.)

To make sense of the philosophical tradition of "self-consciousness as reflection," we would need to move from the requirements of rational *control* to a conception of something closer to rational *authority*. For it is one thing to be able to exercise a certain intelligent control over the contents and operations of some mind, whether one's own or that of another person, and quite another to speak or act with any authority with respect to it.

The considerations of Chapters Three and Four, and the general criticism of the "theoretical" picture of self-knowledge, have been in part an attempt to prepare the ground for a better understanding of this other tradition of thought about self-consciousness. Why might self-consciousness be thought to bear a *special* relation to the rational autonomy of the person, so much so that certain philosophers have been inclined to *identify* one with the other? This identification can't make sense if self-consciousness is understood simply as a faculty of awareness, and yet I've been trying to show how we can approach this idea even while staying close to an understanding of "self-knowledge" that is fairly mundane, almost prephilosophical, and which begins from some of the basic differences between self and other that have attracted the attention of contemporary philosophers of mind with no particular ambition to retrieve the post-Kantian tradition of reflection.

Sartre has come up in these pages, and he is of course particularly blunt and relentless in making the identification between self-consciousness (or sometimes just "consciousness") and freedom that I have in mind. In *Being and Nothingness*, he presents a picture of self-consciousness as the positing of one's freedom with respect to whatever psychic structures, drives, or traits of character are discovered in consciousness. He describes this activity as a "negating" or "nihilating" of the elements that are the objects of self-consciousness; and this implies both that I see myself as *distinct* from these forces and facticities, and that I temporarily *suspend* their psychological reality, subject to my renewed endorsement of them, my identification with them. This idea has some claim to be *the* guiding theme running throughout the book, and is expressed in passages such as the following: "Consciousness is a pure and simple negation of the given, and it exists as the disengagement from a certain existing given and as an engagement toward a certain not yet existing end" (p. 615). And even more baldly: "Choice and consciousness are one and the same thing. But if it has been well established that consciousness is a nihilation, the conclusion is that to be conscious of ourselves and to choose ourselves are one and the same" (p. 595).

Let's assume we're talking about "*psychic*" givens here, that is, some attitude of mine that I become aware of in the particular first-person manner characteristic of reflective consciousness. Why should consciousness of some "given" of my own psychic life be bound up with (even: equivalent to) the assertion of my freedom with respect to it? Sartre is often read as endorsing a kind of crude voluntarism in passages like these (either about one's attitudes or one's character), but there is no need to read him that way. When he says such things as that "there is no inertia in consciousness" (p. 61), we can understand him to be saying that no attitude or impulse apprehended by reflective consciousness has any right to continued existence apart from one's free endorsement of it. When I am reflectively aware of some attitude or impulse of mine, I am thereby made aware that its persistence in me (as a "facticity") is not a foregone conclusion stemming from the inertia of psychic life, and in particular that its counting as a reason for me in my current thought and action is my affair. This idea is not without its own unclarities, but it is quite different from saying that I am free to pick and choose among the convictions, values, and desires I would like to have. His language does suggest, however, that it is a consequence of such reflection that a situation of choice is somehow *forced* on the person, such that whatever he does now with respect to this "psychic given" must count as either his commitment to it or his acquiescence in it.

In part, Sartre is availing himself of the familiar metaphor of "stepping back" from some content of consciousness, and thereby "positing one's freedom" with respect to it. The question I want to raise here is, what is supposed to be special about *self*-consciousness, about specifically first-person awareness of some attitude or impulse, such that it places the person reflecting in a position in which any response of his to this awareness now represents a "choice" on his part, or is in some way an expression of his freedom? The interest of such a claim depends on its purporting to illuminate something about the first-person position, but this aim can easily go out of focus. For, consider a similar claim about the consequences of my awareness (however acquired) of *another* person's impulse or attitude. It seems it should make as much sense in that case, too, to say that once I am so aware, then anything I do in response to this knowledge can be said to represent a choice on my part either to engage with it, seeking to alter it, or acquiesce in it, leaving it alone. Naturally, we'll say, a person normally has greater access to and control over his *own* "psychic givens" than those of other people, but even this is not *always* true, and in many cases this will only be a matter of degree. So in principle I *can* brace myself and "posit my freedom" toward *any* "psychic given" I may encounter, either my own or those of anyone else who strays into my range of influence. If the identification of consciousness and choice in the passages above comes to no more than this idea, then its significance begins to shrink to a vanishing point, and it certainly doesn't tell us anything about the distinctive consequences for responsibility of specifically first-personal awareness of one's own impulses and attitudes. You might as well say that *any* information I encounter "raises the question" for me of what, if anything, to do about it. Any "inescapability of choice" of this sort begins to fade in interest. What is the difference supposed to be with respect to what I learn about my *own* states of mind in reflection?

And yet it is clear that Sartre is after a notion of authority here that *is* properly first-personal, and inalienable from it, not in the sense that various forms of alienation are not possibilities, but that they are possible *as* forms of alienation. That is, self-consciousness is figured here as forcing the issue of some kind of commitment that the person cannot shift on to another, with the understanding that, like commitments of other kinds, it remains in effect even when the person alienates himself from it or otherwise fails to fulfill it. Something like this idea finds expression in contemporary moral psychology, where a similar equation is sometimes made between reflective consciousness and the ideas of freedom and authority. In *The Sources of Normativity*, Christine Korsgaard relates these ideas in the following way: "For our capacity to turn our attention on to our own mental activities is also a capacity to distance ourselves from them, and to call them into question. I perceive, and I find myself with a powerful impulse to believe. But I back up and bring that impulse into view and then I have a certain distance. Now the impulse doesn't dominate me and now I have a problem. Shall I believe? Is this perception really a *reason* to believe?" (p. 93). A few pages later the connection is made more explicitly between self-consciousness and the forcing of a situation of choice, when she says, "The reflective structure of human consciousness sets us a problem. Reflective distance from our impulses makes it *both possible and necessary* to decide which ones we will act on: it *forces* us to act for reasons" (p. 113, my emphases).

Both the language of "decision" or "choice" and the idea of self-consciousness as making these unavoidable are picked up on by Thomas Nagel in his gloss on this passage from *Sources*:

> The new data provided by reflection always face us, in other words, with a new decision. . . .
>
> [T]he reflective self cannot be a mere bystander because it is not someone else; it is the very person who may have begun with a certain unreflective perception, or desire or intention, but who is now in possession of additional information of a special, self-conscious kind. Whatever the person now concludes, or chooses, or does, even if it is exactly what he was about to do anyway, will either have or lack the endorsement of the reflective view. . . .

Given that the person *can* either try to resist or not, and that he is now self-conscious, anything he does will imply endorsement, permission, or disapproval from the reflective standpoint.

(1996, pp. 200–201)

Again, what is pictured here is how the situation of reflective consciousness of some psychic given makes inescapable for the person a situation of decision, inescapable in the sense that anything the person now does will represent a choice of his, even if only by default. And we want this point to hold at a deeper level for the first-person than the sense in which I may always be said to "decide" to offer or withhold endorsement from the desires of some other person to whom I am indeed a "mere bystander" (for once I am aware of *them*, it will also be true that they will "either have or lack the endorsement" of my perspective and assessment). The metaphor of "stepping back" from our current mental activities is a richer and more complex image than it may seem on the face of it, and the language in the passage from Korsgaard brings out some of its distinguishable features. "Stepping back" from an impulse of mine is a metaphor of distancing, obviously; but also one of observation and bringing into view, and of separation and distinguishing (as in the sense that this impulse is one thing and I another), and of confrontation and facing (suggesting something unavoidably in my path). But in addition, it is not only an image of the reorienting of one's *position*, for the idea of "stepping back" also presumes a prior situation of ongoing action. Thus, "stepping back" involves the halting of one's forward movement, the interruption of an action, suspending one's motion in pursuit of some aim.

In particular, there are two senses of "suspension" at work in the passage from *Sources*. Self-consciousness is said to bring with it the capacity to "call into question" either a present belief or desire of mine, or some inclination impelling me toward belief. That is, I can suspend its legitimacy, while I subject it to rational assessment and determine for myself whether I can endorse this as a reason to believe (*mutatis mutandis* for desire or other attitudes). But it is also said that performing this stepping back from my impulse means that "now the impulse doesn't dominate me." When this happens, it is not only the legitimacy of the impulse that is suspended, but its actual psychological force in me. Insofar as it no longer dominates me, I am not simply free to *appraise* it, but also free to choose whether this shall be something I act upon or not. For, of course, I remain free to approve or disapprove of an impulse that *does* nonetheless continue to dominate me, just as I may with respect to anyone else's inclinations or attitudes. There is nothing peculiarly reflective or first-personal about the ability to make a normative assessment of some perception or impulse. But when I "suspend" the force of some impulse in this latter "effective" sense, my stance toward it makes a difference to what happens, and I can actually refrain from proceeding with it.

And this brings us to a capacity that is indeed something specifically first-personal, which we see in the interplay between these two senses of "suspension," in just how withholding endorsement can (and normally does) make a difference to the empirical role of the state in question. If we could forget for a moment the hard cases of internal conflict, common as they are, in which reflection of any sort is powerless to loosen the grip of some dominating impulse, we can see this capacity at work in the situation of ordinary deliberation and the effective authority we take for granted to determine what considerations are to play a role in answering some question before us. ("Shall I go to the sea this summer since that is what I always do? Or is that very fact a reason to go to the mountains instead?") Here we do seem to encounter an asymmetry between self and other, which throws some light on the relation between self-consciousness and rational freedom. For only in the first-person case is it true that when I "suspend" some impulse to believe in the first "appraising" sense (roughly, the sense of "call into question," or "hold subject to my endorsement") I thereby "delegitimize" it in inference and in its interactions with my other attitudes. In ordinary deliberation, when I come to question some belief I began with, that means that I am denying it a role as a premise in my reasoning or a guide to action. The "stepping back" from it means that it no longer has the ordinary inferential or functional role that belongs by nature to a belief of that sort. I may not be able at that moment to "cast it from my mind," but I can bracket its role in my explicit reasoning. This is a genuine empirical difference in my state of mind, and not simply some externally applied appraisal of it. And this alteration is the expression of a capacity that is reserved for first-personal reflection. This sort of reflection on oneself is not a matter of simply *appraising* one's state of mind; the answer to such a question is not simply the normative assessment of it, as good or bad, worthy or unworthy. For again, I can engage in the normative estimation of any attitudes that may swim into my ken, mine or someone else's. But only with respect to my own state of mind am I in a position to determine what it is by deliberative reflection on it. By contrast, if my appraisal of someone *else's* impulse or attitude is going to make any difference to its actual functioning, I'm going to have to do considerably more than simply reflect on it and come to some conclusion of my own about it (such as *tell* him about it, at least, and be found worth listening to, etc.).

The idea is not that one's attitudes are always determined, in this unmediated way, by the conclusions of reflection, and nothing in the passages from Korsgaard or Nagel suggests that they are. Rather, the claim is that first-person reflection entails special responsibilities because it is the expression of a capacity that is exclusively first-personal, albeit one subject to its own possibilities of infirmity. And that capacity is not simply one of special awareness, nor, as we've just seen, awareness plus some form of appraisal. The question asked by the agent at the end of the passage from *Sources* is "*Shall* I believe?," which is a different question from either the theoretical (predictive) question "Will I believe?" or even the normative question "What ought I to believe?" What it is shown to be is a "deliberative question," in the sense introduced in Chapter Two (2.5), a question that is answered by a decision or commitment of oneself rather than a discovery of some antecedent truth about oneself. This is a perfectly homely assertion of one's freedom. It is what is exercised in the undramatic situations of making up one's mind about some matter: I decide that my conclusion was hasty or based on a failure of imagination, and that conclusion itself is thereby pulled out of circulation, either temporarily or for good; I decide that I can't keep looking for my keys and holding everyone up, and I thereby alter my intention; I decide on reflection that my eagerness to tell an embarrassing story about my ex-wife actually reflects more badly on me than on her, and my desire changes. To take oneself to be in a position to ask and answer this sort of question about one's belief or intention is to take oneself to be in a position to *make* something true in one's answering it. This is not a position one is in with respect to another person's state of mind, whatever *influence* one may be able to exercise upon it. And it is this capacity for counting or discounting something as a reason, and the agent's awareness that the exercise of this capacity is part of understanding himself as engaged in reflection in the first place, which explains why, in Nagel's words, "the reflective self cannot be a mere bystander." The reason is that, unlike either descriptive or evaluative inquiry, reflective (deliberative) questioning takes upon itself the capacity to play a constituting role in determining the psychological facts themselves.

It is understanding the special status of this capacity, I'm suggesting, that helps to account for the relation of self-consciousness to the categories of freedom, choice, and decision, as it comes up in various traditions of thought; and, in particular, understanding the sense in which self-consciousness is said to make the applicability of such categories *unavoidable* for the person. When Nagel says that "*whatever* the person now concludes . . . will either have or lack the endorsement of the reflective view," and that "*anything* he does will imply endorsement, permission or disapproval" (my emphases), it is natural to understand the sense of unavoidability invoked here as a logical or grammatical one. But the descriptive necessity in question is of a conditional sort—conditional on the person being self-conscious and capable of trying to resist or not. It is a statement of the same type that is made when we say that, given certain general conditions, an object must have *some* temperature or other, or be of *some* color or other. Or rather, it is akin to such statements, but with more actual grip on what it applies to, since in this case it is a statement that we apply to ourselves and to which we hold ourselves. In the context of discourse about human thought and action, to claim that some predicate out of a specific range of possible descriptions *must* apply (given certain conditions) is to claim that some category of responsibilities is necessarily applicable to the person. For instance, it is sometimes said that for any person who is conscious and capable of movement, there is at any moment some answer to the question of what he or she is doing (even if nothing more momentous than waiting and worrying). And this means that there is always some set of actions and omissions for which the person is responsible, since to be an agent is to have a range of actions open to one. Here again, this is intended as a claim of categorical necessity, the claim that some set of predicates of action must apply to the person here (just as, even more basically, the physical person must be in *some* posture or other).

I take it that a parallel claim about Reflection is expressed in the passage from Nagel, which brings us closer to understanding the alignment between the ideas of freedom (or decision, choice) and reflective self-consciousness that we see in Sartre and elsewhere. For any person who is self-consciously reflecting on his state of mind, there will be some answer to the question of what stance he takes toward what he discovers there, whether of "endorsement, permission or disapproval."[17] Given his awareness, some such stance or other is unavoidable because it is unavoidably this person's business whether some "mental presentation" shall count for him as a reason or not. In this way, a situation of choice is made unavoidable for the person, since he is reflectively aware of his thought, and to be capable of thought is to recognize the possibility, in principle, of thinking otherwise. Under these conditions, even evasion or abandoning oneself to this impulse

---

[17] The very word "stance," like "posture," has a familiar categorical use to indicate not some particular thing done or not done, but rather a general category of assessment, within which some specific predicate out of the range defined by that category must have application. Both etymologically and logically, "attitudes" belong to this same type.

to determine one's future thought or action must count as "tacit consent," just as with respect to one's basic posture the recognition of the possibility of change can make doing nothing at all an expression of "choice by default."

If this line of thought is on the right track, the modal meaning of "reflection demands a reason" will not be that an act of reflection always succeeds in finding or producing a reason. Instead, the claim is that the stance of reflection, being the stance from which the status of some "psychic given" *as* a reason may be constituted or suspended, makes it the case that any response to that "given" can now be understood in terms of the person's responsibilities, and hence as implying either "endorsement, permission, or disapproval," or simply passive allowance. If I know myself to be irrational here, and I am trying to be psychologically realistic about myself, I will not say in reflection that it is up to me (ultimately, entirely) what forces in me will in fact produce actions or further thinking on my part. But it will still be my concern, and not the business of any other part of me, what counts for me as a reason (even though I may fear that I will in the end act against my reasons). And even such a "cautious" or "realistic" attitude toward my reflection does not avoid the commitments of the posture of reflection, for even resignation and acquiescence involve acceptance of a predictive reason about what I will in fact do. That is, even when engaged in that degree of "self-objectification," I nonetheless can't help assuming the authority to accept my history of backsliding as an actual reason to believe that any further resistance on my part will be pointless. What is unavoidable, then, is the stance from which the question before me functions as the deliberative question of what I *shall* believe, or want, or intend.

4.8 THE REFLECTIVE AGENT

In this way, we can begin to see a kind of convergence in the special importance ascribed to the capacity for self-knowledge both by contemporary philosophy of mind, and in what I've called the philosophical tradition of Reflection. Genuine self-consciousness, properly first-personal awareness, cannot be simply a matter of a special route of awareness to knowledge of a specific realm of psychological facts. Rather, in addition to the idea of awareness, the (target-) notion of conscious belief itself brings with it the assumption of a particular first-personal *stance* toward the belief in question, the stance of rational agency. Let me conclude this part of the discussion with a few final remarks on what sense of "agency" is relevant here.

Earlier we tried to imagine a case where first-person authority was suspended across the board. In such a situation, the person's utterances and promptings could only be treated as so much data or evidence, from which his real beliefs may be inferred. On some particular occasion this could be the person's own relation to what he says or thinks about his belief or desire. We are now in a better position to see what would be incoherent in generalizing this situation.

The picture of self-knowledge usually referred to as "Cartesian" is a thoroughly perceptual one, the familiar metaphor of the "inner eye." But in *one* way of reading Descartes on belief and introspection, he both presents us with a canonical expression of the Spectatorial picture *and* diagnoses what's wrong with it when he comes to explain how error is possible. That is, we could suppose there really is something like a "theater of ideas," and that each person has a kind of private access to it. But now, in the generalized situation just described, the passing show I witness really is just so much "data" to me, which it is now up to me to affirm or not as representing the facts. "By the mere intellect I do no more than perceive the ideas that are matter for judgement; and precisely so regarded, the intellect contains, properly speaking, no error."[18] An idea as such is something I may be passive with respect to. It may be implanted in me by God or the external world or by an Evil Demon. But for that very reason it cannot be identical with my belief about some matter, for my judgments are *my* affair, some-

[18] *Meditation* 4, ¶8, in Descartes (1911–12).

thing I am responsible for, through the exercise of my infinite liberty to affirm or deny. (God is not responsible for either the correct or incorrect use of my power of judgment.)

The problem with the idea of generalizing the theoretical stance toward mental phenomena is that a person cannot treat his mental goings-on as just so much data or evidence about his state of mind all the way down, and still be credited with a mental life (including beliefs, judgments, etc.) to treat as data in the first place. For any given mental presentation of mine, just as for any utterance, it may be true that I *can* treat it as data, something which gives me a more or less good indication of my genuine belief. But for there to be judgments or deliberation in the first place, I cannot adopt this point of view on my mental life quite generally. At some point, I must cease attempting to infer from some occurrence to my belief; and instead *stake* myself, and relate to my mental life not as something of symptomatic value, but as my current commitment to how things are out there. And so, for this reason the abrogation of first-person authority is not made up for by improved theoretical access to myself.

In this chapter I have argued the case for seeing the ability to avow one's belief as the fundamental form of self-knowledge, one that gives proper place to the immediacy of first-person awareness and the authority with which its claims are delivered. In pursuing this case, I have also tried to provide some foundation for the connection between this capacity and the freedom and rationality of the person, a connection alluded to in other traditions of thought. This argument has involved giving a more central place to the person as reflective *agent*, and criticizing both certain theoretical accounts of self-knowledge and certain ordinary stances toward oneself that presume (or enact) a more "spectatorial" relation between the person and her own thought. The agent belongs here because the difference between being in a position to attribute some belief to oneself and being able to avow it is a matter of the person's commitment of herself, rather than something settled by the evidence about herself. When our analysand learns attributively that she feels betrayed by someone in her life, or that someone has deprived her of something, it remains open to her whether to accept those feelings at face value, perhaps adding to them other things she knows, and accept this together as constituting a sufficient reason for believing that she has indeed been betrayed or deprived. It remains open to her, since when she learns this she must recognize that she might well *not* accept the proposition "This person has betrayed me" as a premise in her further reasoning about what to think or do. Nothing in the psychological attribution imposes this conclusion upon her; the issue remains hers to decide. (It is along these lines that I suggest we understand the Sartrean thesis that "there is no inertia in consciousness" ([p. 104], with any such "discovery" about oneself only sustaining its own truth for the person "up to now.") The transition from attribution to avowal is thus an expression of the person's rational freedom, an assertion of authority. It is this assertion, this commitment, that makes it possible for her declaration to conform to the Transparency Condition, the announcement of her belief without reliance on the psychological evidence about herself. At that point, the proposition itself gains admittance as a basis for her further thought, both practical and theoretical. And this expresses the dominance in her self-reflection of justifying reasons over explanatory ones, for the premises of reasoning are not propositions about someone's beliefs, but propositions about the objects of one's beliefs, the facts themselves. This expresses a relation to one's state of mind that is exclusively first-personal and not shared by the best telepaths of our philosophical imagination. The agent belongs at the center of the picture because if I am able to avow my belief, and thus speak my mind without the support of evidence about myself, it is because, within that context anyway, I am taking what I believe to be up to me.

CHAPTER FIVE

Impersonality, Expression, and the Undoing of Self-Knowledge

Dr. Richards has noted "the widespread increase in the aptitude of the average mind for self-dissolving introspection, the generally heightened awareness of the goings-on of our own minds, *merely as goings-on*." This is nothing to the generally heightened awareness of the goings-on of other people's minds, *merely as goings-on*.

—Wallace Stevens, *The Necessary Angel*

This final chapter does not so much continue the argument of the previous four as bring the foregoing account of first-person authority into contact with a few of the wider problems in moral psychology which that account should help us to consider with greater specificity—problems that lie beyond the basic question of self-knowledge of beliefs. In the epigraph above, for instance, the connection being drawn in passing by both Stevens and I. A. Richards, between a point of view on the self that is at once objectifying ("merely as goings-on") and undermining ("self-*dissolving* introspection"), is, in one way, familiar enough not to require a gloss from either writer. And yet, of course, the imagery itself suggests two movements in *opposition* to each other, the inward gaze at once "fixing" one's state while at the same time somehow undoing it, which suggests that the difference can't be seen as simply a matter of two names for the same phenomenon. So we need a better understanding of why adopting an observer's stance toward one's own mental life (what we've been calling a "theoretical perspective") should contribute, in a certain range of cases, to the undoing of the very state subjected to this objectifying gaze. Part of the answer to this should already be in place, and the discussion to follow takes it into a range of more intricate cases. What should emerge is an articulation of the relations between philosophical pictures of the nature of introspection (e.g., the "observational model" in its various guises) and the diagnosis of a class of pathologies of self-regard.

5.1 SELF-OTHER ASYMMETRIES AND THEIR SKEPTICAL INTERPRETATION

If reflective self-consciousness imposes either the assumption or the evasion of responsibilities peculiar to the first-person position, responsibilities that involve the acknowledgment of one's deliberative and not just theoretical role with respect to one's own states of mind, then we should expect that the apprehension of one's own mind will not only be a matter of special privilege and authority, but will also involve its own complexities and uncertainties that are not characteristic of the apprehension of other minds. On this view the privileges of the first-person position are internally related to its special limits and infirmities, and the awareness of one's own mental life presents difficulties which are *not* shared by the corresponding third-person perspective. In this way, the insistence on self-other asymmetries as defining the mental can be detached from the traditional picture of the privileges of self-consciousness.

Philosophical problems concerning the apprehension of the mind of another person have a complex relation to the philosophical discussion of knowledge of one's own mind. Whatever the difficulties one faces in making philosophical sense of the special features of *self*-knowledge, it is usually pictured as the more secure possession when compared with the conceptual difficulties and epistemic risks involved in knowing anything about the mind of another person. Indeed, the contrast between the two perspectives on the "mental facts" is decisive for at least one presentation of the skeptical problem of other minds, where the challenge is to demonstrate how it is possible for me to know the thought or sensation of another person "in the way that *he* knows it,"[1] where this first-person perspective is understood to be privileged, even definitive of what *real* knowledge of a mental life must be. *Self*-knowledge, then, even if not thought of as unproblematic in itself, is cast as a sort of anchor point for our sense of what knowledge of mentality is, and the apprehension of the mind of *another* person may thus only count as knowledge to the extent that it can approximate to this kind of awareness. And the apparent unavoidable dependence of any third-person claims to knowledge on an inference from what that other person says and does, combined with the freedom from such dependence in the first-person case, seems to insure that such an approximation can never be more than a very distant one.

In addition to this more purely epistemic problem, there is a more strictly conceptual problem of other minds that also begins by picturing the first-person position as privileged or defining, and then goes on to ask how or whether an outsider's perspective can hope to capture or reproduce what is available to the insider. This "conceptual" version

---

[1] This is something emphasized in Cavell's (1979) discussions of skepticism concerning other minds.

of solipsism brings doubt to bear prior to raising any question about how an inference from behavior can arrive at knowledge of another person's thought or sensation, and instead asks how I can have so much as the idea of such a thing (let alone sufficient evidence to judge its presence in a given case). On this line of thought, if the very meaning of my use of a term like 'pain' can only refer to the "felt experience" of it, and I can only know about such a thing "from my own case," then I cannot so much as undertake to apply that term to anything in the life of other people. Or if I nonetheless do, then the term will be governed by a strict and unbridgeable ambiguity, referring to a genuine experience in the first-person case, and something quite other (e.g., behavioral patterns, perhaps) in the third-person.[2] Here, again, the first-person position is seen as privileged, but the asymmetry is not presented as the difference between "immediate certainty" on the one side and an insecure inference on the other, but rather as a radical difference in conceptual capacities. In this view, the problem is not that I can never be (really) certain about another person's sensation, but rather that it makes no sense for me to believe *or* disbelieve in another person's thought or experience, for my use of a term like 'pain' expresses no conception at all of such a thing. It would follow from this that there is a whole class of attitudes that simply make no sense to take toward another person; not only are the possibilities of *knowing* or even simply believing in another person's pain or other sensation ruled out, but so are doubting, fearing, or expecting, and any attitude at all toward that *something* in another person for which I have no concept and *can* have none.

A certain form of solipsism, then, pictures us as in principle unable so much as to entertain certain thoughts or adopt certain attitudes toward others, attitudes that would make perfect sense for us to adopt toward ourselves. While this is not the place to engage in any detail with either form of skepticism about other minds, I outline them here in order to insist on a separation of either form of solipsism from the

[2] See Wittgenstein, *Philosophical Investigations*, §§293–302.

more basic fact of self-other asymmetries themselves, the differences in the forms and possibilities of our relations to ourselves and our relations to others. Skepticism of either kind is a particular *interpretation* of these differences (and the expression of a rather restricted type of interest in them), just as skepticism about knowledge of the "external" world is an interpretation of the more basic facts about such things as the situatedness of the epistemic subject, the possibilities of error, and the nature and norms of justification. In both cases (i.e., the peculiarities of the first-person position, or the contingencies and normative requirements of knowledge), these features have a standing and a philosophical importance that is independent of any skeptical conclusions that might be drawn from them. Insisting on the priority of the asymmetries themselves, or these other features of our epistemic situation, does not beg the question against skepticism. But if a skeptical conclusion is warranted or found inescapable, it will be for epistemic reasons that rest on an undistorted description of these facts. The main point, however, regarding either variety of skepticism is that both the self-other asymmetries and the basic features of the perceptual and normative situation of the epistemic subject have an independent philosophical interest that is not exhausted by their role in skeptical or antiskeptical argument. This is made harder to see in the case of the self-other asymmetries by the fact that a skeptical conclusion is often rendered as simply equivalent to a description of these features themselves.

In the earlier chapters I argued that a certain set of asymmetries between self and other are basic to the idea of the person, and that these asymmetries, while irreducible, do not force us to skepticism either about the genuineness or substantiality of self-knowledge or about the possibility of knowing the mind of another. Among the asymmetries taken as basic are such differences as that the claim to credibility of what I say about myself is not always grounded in the evidence about my behavior, whereas any awareness I may have of another person's thought depends on what I can garner from seeing them in action, and that the possibilities of error and correction are not the same in the two cases. The sense in which skepticism of either of the two kinds described is an *interpretation* of these asymmetries is bound up with a privileging of the first-person side of the pair. For, if we begin with a sense of the first-person position as the paradigm for what real awareness of mentality must be and then couple this with a vivid sense of just how different any third-person apprehension must be, it will be natural and all but inevitable to be struck by how far short even the best-grounded awareness of others must fall, when compared to our first-person paradigm.

But if it is the asymmetries themselves that are basic, then their primary significance lies in the fact that they do not, on their own, privilege either side, neither the inside nor the outside perspective. One type of apprehension only "falls short" of the other after it has been assumed that one of them is privileged, and that it is the internal aspiration of the third- (or second-) person position to approximate as closely as possible to the special features of the first-person. Insofar as philosophical interest in the asymmetries has followed the skeptical interpretation of them, then, the problem has been posed in terms of working from the "inside out," that is, taking the "inside" perspective as the paradigm, and trying to see how an "outsider's" perspective could bridge the gap and approximate to the immediacy and certainty of the insider's view (or else, despairing of this, working out the implications of the ersatz "access" we are left with).[3] On the other hand, if we separate the basic fact of the asymmetries from a skeptical interpretation of them, and attend to them philosophically for their own sake, then I think we can see that the picture of "privilege" here is a more ambiguous one, and that the differences between self and other that define the concept of the person involve as much *dis*privileging of the first-

---

[3] That is, the first-person position is treated as a paradigm by those philosophers who do take seriously the phenomena of self-knowledge and its essential differences from the knowledge of others. These days it is perhaps more common for philosophy of mind to be dominated by an exclusively "external" or third-person perspective, which rejects the idea of the asymmetries themselves and sees whatever *knowledge* of oneself there may be, if it is to be worthy of the name, as being grounded in just the same sorts of evidence as is knowledge of anything else.

person position as they are privileging of it. When the asymmetries themselves are taken as basic, we can see that alongside the phenomena that gain expression in the philosophical problem of "privacy" are the phenomena of "counterprivacy,"[4] that is, the various modes of apprehension that seem reserved for relations to *others* and can have only some problematic application to oneself. An investigation of some of these, in their relations to the demands of reflective consciousness, will help to delineate both the motivations for and the limitations of a fully impersonal perspective on the self.

5.2 THE PARTIALITY OF THE IMPERSONAL STANCE

One such impersonal perspective is enunciated by Thomas Nagel in his discussion of the parallels between what is wrong with solipsism (of the conceptual variety outlined earlier) and what is wrong with egoism as a view about the nature of practical reasons.[5] Both views may be said to start from the assumption of the priority of something in the first-person perspective and then raise doubts as to whether what is given from this perspective can have any application (or a sufficient one) to one's thinking about others. Solipsism takes my own experience of states like pain to provide me with all I can know about what the concept applies to, and thus renders doubtful or incoherent the supposition that I could use my concept of pain to conceive of something in the lives of others. Egoism takes my own needs and interests to provide me with all I can know of the immediate compellingness of reasons to act, and thus renders doubtful or incoherent the supposition that another person's need could ever by itself count for me as a motivating reason to act. The basic contours of both views may allow for various

---

[4] The term is taken from Andre Gombay's 1988 paper, "Some Paradoxes of Counter-Privacy," which usefully draws connections between Moore's Paradox and the "Socratic Paradox" in connection with skepticism about *akrasia*. See also Gilbert (1971), which discusses Sartre in this connection.

[5] Nagel (1970) esp. chapter 21.

"secondary constructions" that help approximate to the naive assumption of the possibility of either direct thought about another person's experiences or immediate concern for another's need, but these will always be anchored in the paradigm of the egocentric case.

The conceptual dominance of the egocentric perspective, expressed in either of these forms, is in conflict with a more inclusive perspective, one which Nagel describes as "a conception of oneself as simply a person among others all of whom are included in a single world" (1970, p. 100). And surely this is a thought we would want to be preserved by any account of the first-person. Nagel describes each form of egocentrism as tacitly denying some requirement of rational thought, a requirement that must be acknowledged even within the confines of such a perspective itself. In particular, a "conceptual" solipsism of the sort described earlier, according to which I cannot so much as entertain thoughts about the experiences of others (given the egocentric grounding of those concepts in *my* experiences) would violate the basic principle that "it must be possible to say of other persons anything that one can say of oneself, and in the same sense" (p. 101). Put this way, the requirement amounts to the insistence on the univocality of psychological terms, across first- and third-person contexts, as well as across changes in tense, as argued for here in chapter three (3.1) (and further in chaper four, 4.1 and 4.5).[6] But in Nagel it leads to the development of a stronger principle of Impersonality, which must be handled with some care if the denial of one or another form of egocentrism is not to involve us in the denial of the basic differences themselves, between the first- and third-person perspectives.

At one point, he puts the demands of the Impersonal Standpoint in the following terms: "A complete impersonal description of the world

---

[6] "The impersonal standpoint plays a role in the explication of the idea that one is just a person among others, much like the role played by tenseless statements in an account of what it is to regard the present as just a time among others. Shifts of grammatical person, like shifts of tense, cannot be permitted to alter the sense of what is asserted about the circumstance which is the subject of the statement. They represent only shifts in the point of view from which the observation is being offered" (Nagel 1970, p. 101).

will include a description of the person who is 'I' in the personal description, and will recast in impersonal terms everything that can be said about that individual in the first-person. Thus the impersonal standpoint should be able to accommodate all phenomena describable from the personal standpoint, including facts about the subject himself" (p. 101). A page later he sums it up in the form of a principle: "To regard oneself in every respect as merely a person among others, one must be able to regard oneself in every respect impersonally" (p. 102). This principle is not presented as itself a solution to the problems either of solipsism or egocentrism in practical reasoning, but rather as a description of one of the conditions of any possible solution, a constraint to which, we can agree, proposed solutions must conform. But we've already seen that there is more than one way of understanding the principle as presented, ways that are not simply equivalent to each other. One interpretation is expressed by the semantic principle of univocality across changes of tense or person. Terms that describe some state of mind must be applicable without change of meaning both in the present and in the past tense, and in the first-person and third-person cases. A different interpretation of the principle reads it as a requirement on any thinking about oneself which is to respect the fact that one is "merely a person among others." And this in turn seems to mean that any thought I have about myself must be acknowledged to be a type of thought it would *make sense* to have about another person (which brings it close to the semantic principle), *as well as* that any thought I have about myself must be one that I can translate, without alteration of meaning, into a thought expressed third-personally, as a description of the person who happens to be myself.

I don't think that this last normative demand is equivalent either to the semantic principle of univocality or to the acknowledgment that one is merely a person in the world among others. And that is because, as I've tried to show here, there are requirements of the first-person perspective in thought that do not show up in impersonal descriptions of the person who happens to be myself. To say this much is not to assert the privilege of either the "subjective" or the "impersonal" perspectives, but only to assert that there are distinct rational demands proper to each; and specifically that an observer's stance on oneself is no less limited in its way than is an "egocentric" perspective on the lives of others. And I don't mean to suggest that Nagel's assertion of the Impersonal Principle is intended to deny this. What is wanted, I take it, is an account of the two perspectives that does not assert the dominance of either one of them (as the egocentric perspective is privileged in the two forms of solipsism he relates), but which also does not deny the specifically different demands of each. This may seem obvious enough. But a natural (and not uncommon) way to interpret the Impersonal Principle as presented here is as a denial of any specific requirements of the first-person perspective that would not show up in an impersonal reformulation of its claims, and thus as, in the end, an assertion of the dominance of one perspective over the other, instead of (what I think we want) an assertion at once of their parity and of their differences. For the diagnosis of solipsism from this perspective describes it as *incomplete*, as leaving something out, namely, the full reality of other persons. Whereas the Impersonal Principle itself lays claim to a complete description of the facts, it speaks for a total realism about both the world and the position of the self within it. But in fact each perspective is both complete in itself, in the sense of defining the space of answers to its own questions as well as partial in the demands it takes itself to be subject to.

To avoid such a covert privileging of either perspective, we need to remind ourselves that there are distortions in the dominance of an impersonal perspective on one's thinking that are as serious and as familiar in their own way (though perhaps not under that description) as are the distortions of the dominance of the egocentric perspective, which, as presented by Nagel, gain full philosophical expression in solipsism and rational egoism. In thinking about my own mental life and habits, I may acknowledge that I am one person in the world among others; but I am also the person whose thought about himself makes a constituting difference to the moral and psychological facts themselves. Therefore, the first-person position makes demands with respect to the responsibility for the facts about the mental life in question, demands that do not apply to the apprehension of the lives of others who happen *not* to be me. In various situations of reflection, we face the possibility of conflict between the thinking that is part of the description, assessment, or explanation of one's state, and the thinking that is part of the determination of one's state; between, for example, reflection *about* one's desire and the reflection whose *conclusion* is some desire. This represents a clash of the two perspectives themselves, each authoritative within its own domain, and thus is not to be resolved simply by the assertion of the dominance of the claims of one of them.

From the Impersonal perspective, the akratic gambler is obliged to be empirically realistic about himself; in particular, to acknowledge that he has resolved in the past to quit gambling and has failed to follow through. From this perspective, the question "What am I going to do?" is no different from the question "What is this person (answering to a certain description, with a certain empirical history) going to do?," and here the description and the history lead us to expect that he will return to the gaming tables, despite whatever resolutions he may make now or in the future. In his current condition, his own agent's perspective on the question "What am I going to do?" fails to yield a believable answer, when as a deliberator he produces the answer that he is going to *quit* the gaming tables. A certain "realism" demands that he acknowledge that, in his current condition, his "decision" to quit does *not* fully answer the question of what he is actually going to do. (And yet what *else* is any decision supposed to accomplish?) He must see his current decision and his empirical history as each delivering incompatible answers to the question of what he is going to do. And he may know this about himself as well as any outsider does. Yet, he must also see that he cannot simply dismiss the claims of either perspective. For it is not open to him now simply to abandon the stance of agency (whatever that would mean), and say he just isn't in the business of making decisions or forming intentions anymore. This is

not only because even *that* declaration represe~
part (as resignation, acquiescence), but also be
his future action remains there before him, ar
ceive an answer in the form of his taking one
in the form of opportunities seized or foregone.
am I going to do?" inevitably receives its answer one wa,
in the course of life.

Still, each perspective presents its own demands as unavoidable, requiring an answer in its specific terms. On the one side, the Theoretical perspective tells him to be empirically realistic about himself, and that anything less than this can only be an attempt to make a virtue of his capacity for pretense or wishful thinking. But for all that, it cannot tell him when such "realism" is simply the appearance taken by his acquiescence, or his avoidance of the practical question before him. On the other side, the Deliberative perspective tells him that he is not bound by his empirical history, that he must answer the question of what he will do as a question about what he *is to do*, and that anything less than this can only be a form of evasion. But at the same time, this perspective cannot tell him when his assumption of agency is a mere sham—when, for empirical reasons, he has lost the right to form an intention with respect to this question and expect that to count for anything. Neither perspective *denies* the truths of the other. The assertion from the Deliberative stance that "I am not *bound by* my empirical history" is not in any way a denial that the facts of my history are what they are. It does not deny either the truth of these claims or their relevance to the question at hand; but it does deny their completeness and, in a word, their decisiveness.

Hence, even if both morality and metaphysics insist that we take an objective view of ourselves, and in our deliberations we each consider ourselves as but one person among many, this is not an unambiguous demand. In ethical contexts, the requirement of impersonality can mean various different things, and problems with certain forms of it are not confined to the difficulties concerning the *demands* of morality

he agent, which have been the focus of recent attention by theorists
f "agent-relativity" in ethics.[7] Some earlier writers, such as Sartre, saw
the claim of impersonality in ethics as problematic because it construed
the first-person position of the deliberator as *less* demanding than he
saw it as being.[8] According to him (on one reading, anyway), if I consider myself impersonally, as someone with a certain character and
history, with certain beliefs and desires which then enter into my moral
deliberation along with the character and desires of others, I leave out
of consideration the fact that I am *responsible* for that character and
those desires. But these cannot be for me a set of data for which I must
simply make room in my deliberations, as I may have to accommodate
the empirical fact of other people's beliefs and desires. For in my own
case I remain responsible for their endorsement, justification, and continued role in my life, and this determines whether or not they are to
have any place at all in my deliberations. My reflection on the problem
before me may oblige me to abandon some of the beliefs or desires
that led me into it, the attitudes that made this situation into a problem
for me in the first place, and ordinary rationality involves holding open
the possibility of such revision. The attitudes I bring with me into the
situation may well be said to "frame" the problem for me, but in a given
case I may also be obliged to bring them out of the frame and install
them within the scope of the problem itself, on the negotiating table,
and there my relation to them is unlike anyone else's. Hence, they
cannot enter into my thinking as the fixed beliefs and desires of some
person or other, who happens to be me. Here, then, a certain form of
impersonality is construed not as an oppressive, alien demand on the
self but rather as a form of moral *evasion*.

It should not be surprising if a better understanding of the different
senses of impersonality at stake in these contexts requires attention

---

[7] Since Nagel (1970), some of the initiating discussions are in Parfit (1984), Scheffler
(1982), and Williams (1985).

[8] See Sartre (1956), esp. part 1, chapter 2 ("Bad Faith"), and part 4, chapter 1 ("Being
and Doing: Freedom").

to what is distinctive about first-person discourse generally. However, these considerations (e.g., first-person authority and the like) have normally been discussed in isolation from the broader issues in moral psychology where one might think some of the deeper consequences of such self/other asymmetries would be played out. One general area for such connections to be drawn is in the examination of modes of appraisal that seem reserved for our relations to others, but which may have some sort of problematic or unstable application to oneself. The sources and degrees of tension between first- and third-person cases will be varied. For instance, something deserving the name of *self-deception* may be perfectly possible, even common, but it won't look like the deception of another, or be possible in the same ways. Here the "other-directed" relation of deception will have important application to oneself, but there will nonetheless be conceptual limits on what features (e.g., believing lying testimony) of the deception of others will make sense as first-person possibilities. And, to take another sort of case, pity of oneself may not raise the kind of conceptual difficulties that "lying to oneself" does, but the moral and psychological meaning of self-pity will surely be different from its third-person cousin. And finally, further along the spectrum toward the *exclusively* third-personal, envy and gratitude begin to look exclusively other-directed and to have no first-person possibilities at all.[9] My hope is that the discussion of the preceding chapters, which has attempted to unfold a set of basic and irreducible differences between first- and third-person perspectives, focusing on the central case of belief, will provide a kind of base for investigating some of the more complex areas of our affective lives where we encounter these constraints, and sometimes seek to defeat or deny them. Hence, in the remainder of this chapter I want to

---

[9] Further afield in the philosophical encounter with the idea of "other-directed" attitudes and stances, we might think of Aristotle's concern with whether it is possible for a person to treat *himself* unjustly (1985, Book 5, chapters 9–11), and Wittgenstein's claim that *knowing* that someone is in pain, or knowing what someone is thinking, are possibilities only with respect to *other* people and not with respect to oneself (*PI*, §246 and p. 222).

investigate what the appropriate claims of impersonality with respect to oneself may be, but primarily by looking at certain ways in which the appeal may be misapplied or where acting on it has a self-undermining tendency. Specifically, I will discuss a number of cases where a type of character assessment that seems straightforward when applied to others appears to have something unstable or objectionable about it when applied to oneself. And I will elaborate the thought that a variety of self/other asymmetries are inescapable features of human action and reflection, in ways that complicate and qualify what we can expect from an appeal to impersonality. One example that comes up for extended attention concerns the vicissitudes of reflection on one's own shame, and this should help to broaden the field of self/other asymmetries from the case of simple belief that has anchored so much of the discussion thus far.

5.3 SELF-EFFACEMENT
AND THIRD-PERSON PRIVILEGE

One general set of problems that brings together some of these issues in moral psychology and the epistemology of perspective is found in recent discussions of the possible conflict between what a moral theory may tell us about the moral good, and what it recommends that we *believe* about the moral good. So, for instance, the question of what Derek Parfit calls the possible "self-effacement" of a moral theory[10]— the possibility that it may recommend disbelief in itself as the attitude most conducive to the moral good, by its own lights—has brought attention to such things as the contrast between the reasons for believing some theory to be true and possible reasons for someone being a believer of that theory, and the difference between the reasons a theory has for recommending certain dispositions of character and the judgments of what is good (including judgments of good character)

[10] Parfit (1984), p. 24.

that will be made by people with just such dispositions of character. In considering virtues of character, the moral theorist may sometimes, then, be faced with what, in *Ethics and the Limits of Philosophy*, Bernard Williams refers to as the possible "conflict between the view the theorist has of these dispositions and the view of the world he has from those dispositions."[11] A truly self-effacing moral theory would require a split between one's conception of value and justification, on the one hand, and the types of reason one is actually disposed to appeal to in one's deliberations, on the other. There would then be systematic differences between what another person may believe about my attitudes and dispositions (i.e., that they may be in some way deluded, but still, in another sense, the "right" ones for me to have) and what I myself may believe about them. And within the person, such disunity would thus appear to impose limits on the possibilities for moral self-consciousness.

It is a matter of some debate just what the consequences for the acceptability of a moral theory would be if it were shown to be self-effacing in this sense. But the significance of these self/other asymmetries for the virtues of character is not limited to contexts involving a moral theory that is actually self-effacing. Outside of the context of moral *theorizing*, and within ordinary moral reflection itself, there are situations concerning the virtues of character in which self-consciousness appears to have some kind of destabilizing effect on the virtues or dispositions that are its object. Williams himself suggests just such a difference between first- and third-person possibilities with respect to the virtues of character in the early pages of *Limits*: "[I]t is rarely the case that the description that applies to the agent and to the action is the same as that in terms of which the agent chooses the action. [A] courageous person does not typically choose acts as being courageous, and it is a notorious truth that a modest person does not act under the title of modesty. The benevolent or kindhearted person does benevolent things, but does them does them under other descriptions,

---

[11] Williams (1985), p. 110.

such as 'she needs it,' 'it will cheer him up,' 'it will stop the pain'" (p. 10). He goes on to say how the deliberate *cultivation* of the virtues, while very familiar in its third-person form, "has something suspect about it, of priggishness or self-deception" as a first-personal exercise (p. 10). And he suggests that the reason for this is that the appraising function of the virtue terms has its primary home in their application to *others*, and not in the context of first-person moral reflection.[12]

We should, however, distinguish two quite distinct claims here, one concerning the role of virtue concepts in moral deliberation, and another concerning the deliberate cultivation of the virtues. As to the latter, it's hard to see what should be wrong with someone, say, working to overcome his cowardice and consciously trying to have a bit more courage in certain situations. And if self-deception is supposed to be involved here, it is not at all clear just what it is that the person is supposed to be deceived *about*. In any case, this is different from the former claim that there is something wrong in the idea of having, say, the expression or manifestation of courage or modesty be one's primary motive in action. If there is a defensible criticism of such a motive, it must nonetheless allow for relevant differences between the virtues in this regard. For some are intrinsically tied to the *expression* of certain responses, like those of gratitude or remorse, in which case taking their manifestation as one's direct aim does not seem contrary to their spirit. And there must also be room for historical and cultural

---

[12] This is how I understand his diagnosis of what seems wrong in such cases. The problem, he says, is not that thought is directed at oneself, but that one's thought is, in a sense, not self-directed enough. "Thinking about your possible states in terms of the virtues is not so much to think about your actions, and it is not distinctively to think about the terms in which you could or should think about your actions: it is rather to think about the way in which others might describe or comment on the way in which you think about your actions, and if that represents the essential content of your deliberations, it really does seem a misdirection of the ethical attention" (Williams 1985, p. 11). In the discussion to follow, I try to elucidate the sense in which this self-directed attention partakes of, or models itself upon, an outsider's perspective on one's action and what it expresses. In this way, we can see that what is wrong with the thinking in such cases is indeed, despite appearances, that it is "not first-personal enough."

variation here, when we recall that someone like Achilles, for example, might well be said to "choose acts as being courageous." But after making such allowances, there still do seem to be ordinary situations of reflection where a form of self-consciousness directed upon some aspect of one's character seems incompatible either with the trait itself or with the normal appraisal of it (as it would apply to others). In this way, a kind of "self-effacement" would apply to aspects of moral character as well as to possible moral theories, in a further way limiting the extent to which one can or should model the moral estimation of oneself, in a "person-neutral" way, on the estimation of others.

In considering this possibility, it is important to recall that the virtues and vices of character involve *attitudes* as well as characteristic ways of behaving. Williams's examples of courage and modesty, for instance, involve characteristic patterns of thought and feeling as well as of behavior. In general, a person's attitude toward himself makes a difference to how we feel about him, and an attitude *we* take toward his character may depend on facts about just what attitude *he* takes toward it. Naturally, this is not to say that such attitudes must always match (our attitude toward him corresponding to his own attitude toward himself), and often they will not. A person's attitude of smug self-satisfaction does not normally lead one to feel well satisfied with *him*; and, oddly enough, the apprehension of someone's self-pity, far from inspiring pity in others, will not infrequently drive out whatever genuine pity one might have begun to feel for the person before discovering that he too felt the same way. But is this because we feel here that pity from one person is plenty enough and we can now leave that job in reliable hands? Or do we feel that however justified an attitude of pity toward someone may be, the person himself is for some reason uniquely barred from taking this up, even if he is the only person around in a position to appreciate the pitiable facts of his situation? It may well be true that, in considering myself as but one person among others, I am obliged not to privilege myself in certain ways. But, it might be thought, I ought not to be obliged for that reason to *dis*advantage myself in special ways, either. The call to impersonality, after all, is supposed to be in the service of a kind of evenhandedness in our dealings with people, ourselves included.

This sort of case can be internalized in a way that displays some of the features of self-effacement. We saw that a person's attitude toward himself may inspire a different attitude, perhaps a directly contrary one, in another person. And we can now see the possibility of cases where it is one and the same person responding in these contrary ways. What initially raises questions about such cases is that they need not involve the person's changing his mind, if by that we understand his rejection of the previous attitude, finding it unjustified or unwarranted in some way. Rather, as in the case of responses to someone's self-pity or self-congratulation, this reversal may take place without any sense that the general attitude-type is unjustified or inappropriate as applied to this person; that is, without denying that the person is indeed in some sense to-be-pitied or to-be-congratulated. This of course puts the person himself in an unstable situation. For in spite of the recognition of the value of ordinary moral self-examination, it will appear as if the very awareness of his attitude (and the character it expresses) causes it to be undermined, even if it is no part of his reflection that the original attitude is unjustified. This, in any case, is the possibility that has occurred to a number of writers, and which I mean to explore in the following examples.

5.4 PARADOXES OF SELF-CENSURE

Earlier I quoted Williams as saying that "a modest person does not act under the title of modesty," even when that description truly applies to the agent. Whether or not we agree that modesty might not *sometimes* be a genuine motive for action (or some deliberate *refraining* from some action of self-display at least), this is a different claim from the equally familiar idea that it is part of modesty, insofar as it is a virtue, and hence praiseworthy, not to reflect on itself, in particular not to insist on taking credit for its praiseworthy character (see Driver 1989). Undoubtedly, there is room for some slack and variation in the use of the term and the attitude taken toward the quality it names, but in one central usage the quality is praiseworthy and the praise is carried in the very description of someone as modest. And then, if the quality of modesty is taken to be incompatible with the praise of oneself, this would appear to be a quality that cannot survive reflection on itself, or which is at least qualified by such awareness. Modesty is a special case, of course, and seems designed to illustrate the "self-effacing" character in which Williams is interested. In this case, that feature follows almost immediately from the logic of the trait itself (which is being defined in terms of a certain *un*reflectiveness) and doesn't require that the reflection in question be of any particular character, either "objectified" in some way, or as a misapplication of the Impersonal Principle. Any concept defined in *this* way will reserve itself for the appraisal of others and not oneself, and thus provide occasion for "conflict between a view of some disposition and the view of the world (including oneself) one has from that disposition."

But there are other cases where it is the particular nature of the gaze upon oneself, and the *use* one attempts to make of it, that creates the instability. Samuel Johnson remarks at one point that "all censure of a man's self is oblique praise. It is in order to show how much he can spare,"[13] and at some level we all know what he means. But really, what is the objection here, and why should the first-person case be thought to reverse itself this way? After all, the censure of *another* person does not involve itself in praise in either direction, not of the person judged nor of the person doing the judging. Admittedly, the first-person case may be thought to be importantly different from the censure of others when we feel that there is something praise*worthy* in forthrightly confronting one's own vices and denouncing them, a virtue of clarity and will. But in that case, the man himself may ask,

[13] In Boswell's *Life of Johnson*, April 25, 1778.

"Why then can I not avail myself of this same truth, and help myself to the credit I have just earned in the eyes of others? Doesn't evenhandedness, or objectivity for that matter, demand this?"

Johnson speaks of the censure of oneself as a demonstration of what one can "spare," and this suggests both a situation of public display and a division of the self into (dispensable) parts. What the performance shows is that I am both discerning enough to see my failings, staunch enough to face them *as* failings, censuring them before others, and still able to present myself to the world. The idea of what I can "spare," I take it, is meant to capture the aspect of separation and disavowal in any censure. The part that is named and judged is cast out, delegitimized as a part of the remaining self demanding recognition, while, at the same time, the judging self maintains its rights to invest its words with the authority of that very appraisal. The part named and cast out is what I can "spare" and still present myself to others as a speaking subject, someone whose words are of more than symptomatic value. But we needn't think of this only in the context of public utterance, censure of oneself before witnesses. Such self-criticism is something that can take place in the privacy of one's own mental tribunal, and so can the estimation of what the making of this judgment *demonstrates* about the person in question. Often enough the entire scenario and performance are internal. Nonetheless, something in availing oneself of the perspective of another self is the basis for Johnson's criticism here and for his otherwise unsupported suspicion that such self-censure is undertaken for the ulterior motive of *making* this demonstration of "what one can spare."

Something very much like this same structure lies behind Sartre's insistence on the inherent double-mindedness in any such estimation of oneself: "The man who confesses that he is evil has exchanged his disturbing 'freedom for evil' for an inanimate character of evil; he *is* evil, he clings to himself, he is what he is. But by the same stroke, he escapes from that *thing*, since it is he who contemplates it. . . . In confessing it, I posit my freedom in respect to it; my future is virgin; everything is allowed to me. A person frees himself from himself by the very act by which he makes himself an object for himself" (*Being and Nothingness*, p. 109). Thus I stand here toward my character as toward some fixed, objective, psychological datum, something I can spare from the perspective of this confession. But at the same time, the very act of judgment itself demonstrates that I am not in thrall to this "character," for I can judge it from a standpoint superior in both clarity and freedom. There is a sort of deliverance of myself in the assessment of my character as "just the way I am," for it absolves me of a kind of responsibility for it. At the same time, there is another kind of deliverance involved in feeling that my very act of naming and judgment demonstrates that I am really superior to this given character, not determined by it. Thus, I claim for myself the best of both worlds: I am absolved of responsibility for I am bound to express my "nature," and at the same time I am *not* bound to my nature, for in so judging it I express my freedom and distance with respect to it.

Further, there is an alternative reading of Johnson's word "spare," which would make his observation about self-censure closer to what Sartre says here. For the original reading of the pride Johnson sees in the gesture of self-censure interprets the act as a kind of potlatch of personal worthiness, a display of riches by means of the bonfire of one's own vanities. But from a more severe perspective on the vanity of that very gesture, the point is that the sense of "sparing" in question here is more a matter of saving or rescuing some part of the self than a matter of spending or letting it go. Hence, what is ultimately criticized in Johnson's statement is the fact that it is the judging self that is *spared from* the censure it is making, as if sparing itself the punishment it is meting out to the rest of the self. The meaning of *this* sense of "what is spared" thus runs contrary to the previous one (which was basically: the display of power through one's ability to absorb loss), for there is nothing to *admire* in a judge's exempting himself from the very censure he is imposing elsewhere. On this reading of "showing what he can spare," the man's pride is thus something exposed and undone, rather than something covertly advanced, as in the first reading; and it is only inadvertently, in spite of himself, that his self-censure reveals what he is *willing* (with however little justice) to spare from that judgment.

Where Johnson speaks of the person judging as showing "what he can spare" of the person judged, Sartre speaks of "expressing one's freedom" with respect to the person judged. And the expression of such facts through one's self-censure is in both cases felt to impugn the legitimacy of the original judgment. However, as with Williams's remarks on the role of virtue terms, it seems that while there *is* something unstable or reproachable in the vicinity, it still appears persistently misidentified. For it is not *only* the priggish who may act under the title of some virtue of character, and the censure of one's own self is not *inherently* a calculated act, performed *in order* to show what one can spare. And similarly with Sartre, it ought not to be assumed that any and every act of reflection on one's own character involves making oneself an object for oneself, not in any criticizable sense, anyway. At the least, there ought to be a way for us to distinguish between those cases where such reflection has some such self-undermining quality, and those where it does not. To this end, I will consider a very brief story in some detail, and the suggestion I want to follow is that we can understand what is sometimes paradoxical and sometimes morally dubious in such cases by seeing them as unsuccessful attempts to adopt a stance toward oneself that is only a stable or coherent one when adopted toward some other person. We can thus see how even the legitimate demands of impersonality in reflection can be distorted to serve the ends of a kind of moral narcissism, something that is not selfishness or self-absorption, but the substitution of the perspective of an appraising Other for the first-person perspective of agency.

There's a well-known line from a novel by Kingsley Amis that concerns a married man with family, who at one point in the story spends an evening at a nightclub with another woman he knows from work. As he sneaks back home after the encounter, he describes himself in his guilty reflections as "feeling a tremendous rakehell, and not liking myself much for it, and feeling rather a good chap for not liking myself much for it, and not liking myself at all for feeling rather a good chap."[14] What has gone wrong in this man's reflections? And, more important, what is the implied criticism of himself he makes at the end, when he is "not liking himself at all"? One problem we can see right off is that the chain of reversals of his previous assessment of himself could easily proceed indefinitely, each current exoneration followed by an even harsher condemnation, ad infinitum. At the stage at which we encounter him, he just got himself to feel bad for feeling good about feeling bad; and there seems no reason why he should stop there, especially since with one more step he could be feeling good again. Now, the apparent arbitrariness of his resting point here is not his *founding* problem, of course, but it is not easy to say what that problem is. Rightly or wrongly, he *censures* himself for something at the end. Whatever it is, it is something that occurred in the previous train of thought, something that would make sense of his "not liking himself at all."

Something in the spectator's stance he takes toward his original censure of himself supports the illusion that he can bootstrap himself out of that original judgment. What could be unproblematic if he really were reflecting as an outsider on some other person launches him instead on this chain of reversals. For we can notice right away that there would be nothing odd in this line of thinking if more than one person were involved. Feeling (better) about someone else for their hard (though justified) judgment of themselves needn't lead to the collapse of either of the judgments of the two people. His deflation and remorse may produce an improved opinion of his character in the eyes of others, and this situation may be a perfectly stable one. But for the rakehell in the story himself, there seems to be something wrong in his treating his first judgment of himself as simply a kind of psychological *fact* about himself, like an action that is praiseworthy in much the same way that his original action was blameworthy, a fact about himself that indicates that he's not so bad after all.

[14] Amis (1956), chapter 7, p. 93.

In the first stage of his thought, we find him with the belief that he has acted shamefully, which is distinct from, although obviously in close connection with, the fully experienced *attitude* of being ashamed with himself. He then offers himself an expressive interpretation of his being ashamed according to which it indicates that he's really rather a good chap, after all. The sense in which the expressive interpretation involves his feeling better about himself naturally mitigates his original feeling of shame. At this point, however, he blames himself all the more for the previous train of thought and what he now sees as its shameless exploitation of his attitude. If we could say what exactly was *wrong* with the first stage of thought, up to the adoption of the new attitude of being pleased with himself and his response, then we would have the reason for the rebuking conclusion he reaches at the end. One thing to consider at first is that there's something seriously wrong in using your awareness of some fact as a reason to disbelieve that very fact. However, it might be denied that this is in fact what is going on here. For the new and more favorable attitude toward himself is not strictly speaking the denial of the straight belief that he acted shame-fully; rather, it is only the denial of, or at any rate the supplanting of, the actual experienced *attitude* of shame toward himself, the entire emotional configuration. Now of course this *does* seem cutting it rather close; but there *is* nonetheless an important sense in which the truth of his original belief about the blameworthiness of what he did is not challenged at all in his subsequent reflections. What happens instead is that he realizes that he has the appropriate attitude toward the facts represented in that belief, and this realization causes him to come to a more favorable assessment, not about what he did (that's in the past), but about himself (here, now). Still, although he does not repudiate his original belief, we could speak in terms of the replacement of one attitude by a contrary one, as a *response* to one's awareness of the first attitude, and this would be paradoxical enough. This interpretation obliges us to account for the sense of paradox as something other than a tension among beliefs, and later on we will encounter reasons against construing the situation as a clash of beliefs in the first place.

Nonetheless, the basic paradoxical quality will stand out more clearly if we first consider the situation from the perspective of plain beliefs. In that case, the objection just mentioned would run (in the crudest possible terms): his awareness that he *believes* that he is bad cannot be his reason for no longer believing that he *is* bad. This would involve his adopting a kind of third-person stance toward his own attitudes, in that he takes a belief of his and regards it purely for what his having the belief says or expresses about him. This is what happens when he makes the transition from his belief about his shamefulness to the saving interpretation according to which he's quite a decent sort after all. And in so doing, his attention to the *fact* of his belief eclipses attention to what that belief is about. Thus, his awareness of his belief is not functioning as awareness of the propositional *object* of the belief (his shamefulness), even though he still takes that belief to be *true*. Now, there needn't be anything wrong per se in a person's reflecting on his belief as a psychological fact about himself, something from which certain conclusions about himself may be drawn. What causes concern in the case of the rakehell, however, is the appearance that his attention to the fact that he (truly, and with justification) believes P brings him, through that recognition, to abandon or qualify that very belief. The sense of paradox lies in the fact that he gives up the belief about his shamefulness even though there is no stage in this whole train of thought at which he sees that belief as unjustified. In fact, it is his seeing it as *justified* that supports his giving it up, for the "expressive reading" he gives to his belief, and which leads to commending himself, depends on his understanding his original shame as perfectly appropriate and called for. He has to continue to take the original attitude to be justified and appropriate for his reflection upon it to issue in the contrary attitude.

The rakehell himself naturally makes us doubt the genuineness of his original feeling of shame, since he makes it seem so easy, and so willful, when he rids himself of it. You feel shame, attend to what the fact of your feeling it implies about you, and then you stop feeling (so) ashamed. From the point of view from which we see the shame and the relief from it as absolute, unqualified states, this makes it seem as if no one could ever rationally feel ashamed: since if you do, then rational reflection on the meaning of your feeling will make your shame unnecessary. And all of this can be known in advance. Thus: only someone incapable of shame ought to feel it; or: the only proper object of shame is one's own shamelessness. Shame can seem oddly self-canceling then; the reason for this being that it is an emotion that refers to oneself, and is (often) a "commendable" emotion. It is about the same person who is commended for having it, and yet it seems incompatible with feeling commendable.[15]

It is worth noting at this point that, with regard to any "self-undermining," much depends on one's attitude toward particular attitudes and their types. Nietzsche, for instance, often writes in praise of the attitude of contempt, and it is clear that he thinks of the capacity for this feeling as something admirable, the sign of a strong nature; in other words, something worthy of respect. *Self*-contempt then, is for him an inherently unstable attitude. So he writes that "whoever despises himself still respects himself as one who despises," thus claiming a sort of self-limiting character for this attitude.[16] As with Johnson, the very passing of judgment on oneself is a demonstration of what one can spare. Thus, a kind of *absolute* contempt, without remainder of respect for its object, is not a possible attitude toward oneself. (Incidentally, this is one case where the asymmetries in possible moral attitudes would systematically disadvantage *others* rather than oneself. Only toward another can one feel pure undiluted contempt without any redeeming remainder.) However, Nietzsche does not note that, at best,

---

[15] However, what is wrong here does not depend on construing the attitudes in question in absolute or all-or-nothing terms, for similar objections would apply to the person's attempt to iterate this process until he reduces his degree of shame down to zero. That is, once he has concluded that he's not so bad, it seems he could reflect on the fact of the residual degree of shame he may still feel, and he might conclude that this feeling is itself commendable as well, leading him to feel (even) less ashamed of himself; and so on.

[16] Nietzsche (1886), §78.

this will only be true for those who share his special view of this and other attitudes. A different person, even if self-conscious enough to reflect on the fact of his self-despising, might be additionally ashamed of *that* fact. Hence, his self-reflection would spiral downward, as opposed to Nietzsche's, which has the potential to raise one up out of despising altogether.

So, the recuperation represented in the rakehell's expressive interpretation of his shame depends on his *endorsing* the judgment of shamefulness, being committed to it, and this ladder cannot be kicked away once he reaches the conclusion that he's rather a good chap. No commendation accrues to someone's *un*warranted sense of shame, after all. And this redeeming judgment depends on his continuing to maintain the initial belief that what he did was shameful, for as long as he sees himself in this new and favorable light. For his recognition of this fact about himself, that is, the fact that he *takes* himself to be disgraceful, is not something like a momentary *spur* to his reinterpreting that sense of disgrace as meaning he's really a rather *good* person. Rather, it is his *basis* for believing that about himself; without it, he has no particular reason to believe this at all. Continuing to endorse the original judgment of shamefulness is therefore necessary, and that means that he must continue to see himself and his actions through that belief and not abandon it in favor of something else.[17]

[17] The sense of this as a peculiarly *first-person* phenomenon requires distinguishing it from a similar paradox famous from Pascal. In *Pensées* (1958, §§397 and 416), he writes: "The greatness of man is great in that he knows himself to be miserable. A tree does not know itself to be miserable. It is then being miserable to know oneself to be miserable, but it is also being great to know that one is miserable. He is therefore wretched because he is so; but he is really great because he knows it."

As before, what is paradoxical in this reasoning lies in drawing a conclusion from someone's justified attitude toward himself (man and his wretchedness), which seems incompatible with that very attitude (although it seems clear that it is not Pascal's own point that they are in direct contradiction). In this case, as in the original case of the rakehell, the sense that the original attitude is justified must be maintained in order to reach the estimation that clashes with it. But what is paradoxical in Pascal's inference is not, in fact, an essentially first-person phenomenon. It *does* require that the original attitude be an attitude toward oneself, otherwise there will be no clash between the

However, as before, one might say that, strictly speaking, he satisfies this condition, for he does *not* abandon the belief represented in the original self-censure but only supplants the experienced or felt attitude of shame with another one. So, he is not involved in outright self-contradiction, and it is the difference between the straight *belief* about oneself or one's action, and the unaffected total *attitude* of shame, that provides him with his room to maneuver. For ceasing to be ashamed or to feel ashamed is not the same thing as ceasing to believe that one did something shameful. No one is obliged to continue feeling ashamed of himself forever, after all; but at the same time, he should not give up the original belief about himself without some reason to think it's untrue. And a reason to think it's untrue is what he does not have here. Even giving it up in the sense of *forgetting* it could be blamable if it all took place within a few minutes or a few days. Beliefs are not episodic like emotions; they do not typically run their natural course and then fade out like a burst of anger or relief. There is a temporal dimension to the moral meaning of various attitudes that is difficult, perhaps impossible, to capture in the terms of criticism developed for the evaluation of beliefs as true or false, justified or unjustified.

So then, if he is not using his awareness of some belief of his (which he takes to be justified) as a reason to abandon that very belief, then it looks like he can maintain the expressive interpretation of the merit of his being ashamed without falling immediately into inconsistency. For, on this reading, he *does* maintain the original *belief* about his shamefulness throughout, and does not contradict himself by his later attitude. This interpretation of what he's doing is available to him by

---

original belief and the conclusion drawn from its being believed. But it is just as paradoxical in the *third-person* case to infer from someone else's justified belief that P, to the conclusion that P is not really true. Pascal is indeed including himself in this passage, so it is a first-person expression to that degree, but the paradox is retained when it is read in a third-person manner. He looks at man in his wretchedness, but concludes on the basis of man's awareness of his wretchedness that he is "really great." This is paradoxical whether applied to oneself or to others.

distinguishing beliefs (whose objects are propositions) and general emotional attitudes whose objects are individuals, such things as persons and their acts. This very distinction, however, now threatens his bootstrapping with another difficulty. For we now must ask whether the mere *belief* alone is enough for him to reach any saving conclusion. That is, it is not clear that his simply affirming the proposition that what he did was shameful, without any *feeling* or absorbing attitude of shame, provides any basis for even a limited commendation of him. (Think of the hasty, forced admission, "OK, OK, I screwed up. Happy now?") But if it does not, then it is the same difference that first saved him from inconsistency in maintaining the judgment of character without the actual experience of shame that now prevents him from legitimately reaching the approbation of the expressive interpretation. And this difference concerns the experiential aspect of emotions as opposed to beliefs, and the fact that an emotional attitude constitutes something closer to a total orientation of the self, the inhabiting of a particular perspective.[18]

For suppose that long after some action of his, long after the time for any occurrent feelings of shame about it, he judges as he does here, that what he did was, in fact, shameful. The cool, affectless appraisal of some long distant action of his, of a "past self" whose shameful actions do not shame *him*, would not provide the same reason for commending him, assuming that commendation had any place in our original case. Or at best it would provide much *less* reason for this. And since the bridge from his original sense of disgrace to the new attitude

---

[18] The sense in which a certain moral attitude may involve something like a total perspective on its object is crucial to Hume's account of pride and humility, and relevant to the oscillating quality of the rakehell's reflections. In the *Treatise*, Hume says: "'Tis impossible a man can at the same time be both proud and humble; and where he has different reasons for these passions, as frequently happens, the passions either take place alternately; or if they encounter, the one annihilates the other, as far as its strength goes, and the remainder only of that, which is superior, continues to operate upon the mind" (1740, Book 2, "Of the Passions," part 1, "Of Pride and Humility," section 2).

toward it as expressive of a kind of virtue was a fragile one to begin with, weakening it now by removing from consideration the distinctive aspect of the actual emotional attitude of shame will likely make impossible any passage across to a new attitude toward himself. What matters to the success or legitimacy of the expressive interpretation, it seems, is the shame itself: how it orients the person, the fact that it is something hard to undergo, and what *experiencing* it implies about the quality of the person's attitude toward what he did as well as his attitude toward the future. So, to gather together some of these threads, it looks as though he needs his actual experience of shame, at least initially, to get to whatever esteem he reaches at the end. And he needs the original belief that what he did was shameful *not* just initially but throughout the whole train of thought. So, even if he does not flatly contradict his original judgment about what he did, there is still something wrong with his using the awareness of his proper *feeling* of shame to supplant that very attitude with a contrary one.

To be sure, the temporal and experiential aspect of attitudes such as feeling ashamed may allow room for some gray area here. After all, we say, at some point enough is enough and it's time to get over one's feeling ashamed and move on with one's life. And it may be that there is a time somewhat prior to this point when it is legitimate for the person to reflect on his response as a present psychological phenomenon rather than as an attitude toward his past action, in a way that has the effect of mitigating that very feeling. But, as before, the very temporal distance that allows for such "crediting" of oneself is also what diminishes the moral import of his earlier feeling as an indicator of who he is. There's only so much credit you can take for how you used to feel.

5.5 INCORPORATION AND THE EXPRESSIVE READING

When the person is considered merely as "one person among others," the fact of his shame or shamelessness on some occasion expresses the kind of person he is, and it's the sort of thing we take into account in determining how we feel about him. And indeed, we would be wrong not to do so, wrong not only in the sense of being moralistically harsh, but also more basically in the sense of failing to respect the "total evidence" of the case. For responding to what he did with shame constitutes a new fact, and a perfectly relevant one, and thus is part of the total evidence of who he is. And if the Impersonal Principle means to express a requirement of evenhandedness in our thinking about ourselves and others, then this principle would seem to require that this same "total evidence" be available to the shamed person himself, where its expressive import would be the same for him as it is for anyone else.

The rakehell himself is involved in an "expressive reading" of his own shame, an interpretation of what his proper response of shame indicates about him for an overall assessment of what kind of person this reveals him to be. So we might imagine the rakehell appealing to something like the Impersonal Principle in the following terms. It would certainly make a difference to how we feel about him if he felt no shame at all; so the *presence* of shame is a perfectly relevant new fact that has a legitimate role to play in anyone's overall assessment of him. It would be both unmotivated and unfair for such a fact to be available only to us outsiders, and seen as something the rakehell himself is barred from taking into consideration. Similarly, it would be unmotivated and unfair to allow only the *absence* of proper shame on an occasion to figure in his own estimation, as if the issue of his own shame could only function for him as an aggravating factor and never a mitigating one. That lack of evenhandedness would itself be a breach of the Impersonal Principle. Anything that can be true of others is something that can be true of oneself; and, like a person's shame or shamelessness, it can be expressive or indicative in the same ways. Can't it?

He might also argue that taking his own shame into consideration is demanded by the general epistemic requirement of total evidence for settling any question. When he acted badly, that provides him or anyone else with one set of facts to include in addressing the question of what kind of person he shows himself to be. But now his response of "feeling a tremendous rakehell" constitutes an additional fact, one that demands to be incorporated into the total body of evidence for answering the question of what kind of man he is. Anything less would be epistemically irresponsible, arbitrarily selecting from the total base of evidence. So, it is not only a question of *allowing* him the same "expressive interpretation" that would be permitted to an outsider, but his availing himself of this interpretation now seems to be a matter of basic epistemic responsibility. It can't be, after all, that he is required to ignore some plain fact of the plainest relevance to the question with which he's wrestling.

What consideration of his case shows us is that the Impersonal Principle itself can pull us in different directions. Trying to obey it, we say the rakehell should be allowed all facts and inferences available to an outsider. But if so, then it can look like he has granted himself the capacity to bootstrap himself out of any state like shame, which is both humbling in one way and praiseworthy in another. And that possibility seems to be privileging the subjective self in a way that goes against the very spirit of the Impersonal Principle. This is a problem for self-reflection when it takes as its object what is itself a self-regarding attitude, as shame or guilt are. The possibility of such conflict here stems from the fact that, from the first-person perspective, theoretical reflection (e.g., "What is it that I am feeling here, and what does it indicate about me?") cannot be kept separate from deliberative reflection (e.g., "How am I to feel about myself now?"). And so the facts themselves are altered in the course of his reflecting on them. Hence, at the least, the Impersonal Principle cannot be interpreted to mean that all the attitudes, stances, and conclusions that may be appropriate in the estimation of others can or should be possibilities for *self*-reflection. And often when they *are* legitimate possibilities for both perspectives, they will nonetheless be quite *different* possibilities for the first-person.

Hence, the problem the rakehell is faced with is that for him so much as to raise the question for himself of the expressive import of his feeling ashamed is to alter the facts upon which any such expressive reading must rest. He wants to be permitted to incorporate his current shame into the total evidence base for determining what sort of person this shows him to be. And, as we are imagining this appeal, he presents this insistence as demanded by both ordinary evenhandedness and epistemic responsibility. Yet, for him to incorporate his current shame in his current reflections about himself is not the epistemically innocent (let alone obligatory) move it would be in the hands of another person. For we can look at it this way: if he's asking himself a question which he is appealing to certain evidence to settle, then the sense of this activity presumes both that this question is indeed open for him and that it is one that is properly settled by the evidence (rather than by, e.g., a decision or resolution). If he is appealing to his own shame as evidence for something, we must ask, "Evidence for what?," and the answer is clearly: evidence for what sort of person he has shown him-self to be, evidence for settling the question of how he is to feel about himself. But supposedly he has just answered this question for himself; that's precisely what the shame itself is a response to. He thus would need some *reason* to reopen that question, something grounded in some dissatisfaction with his original *answer* to that question, which is his response of shame. Yet nothing in his reflections displays any rea-son for such dissatisfaction—reasons, that is, that are internal to the justification of a response like shame (as opposed to pragmatic reasons for avoiding its discomforts). Reopening this question requires its own reasons. Just as with decisions generally, we may acknowledge that yes, in principle, any such question *can* be reopened for consideration, or the figures *can* be checked one more time. But that general possibil-ity doesn't make it rational always or at any moment to do so. And even granting some reason to reopen the question, the deeper problem remains of the consequences of reopening it for reaching the expres-sive conclusion he ultimately wants to draw. It is this difficulty that is grounded in the exigencies of the first-person position he is seeking to evade. For the very conclusion he is now attempting to draw is *based on* the fact of his having settled that question, and settled it in a particular way, viz., through his feeling properly ashamed. It is that response which is the very fact his secondary conclusion ("feeling rather a good chap for not liking myself much") is a conclusion *from*.

The particular "expressive value" he wants to exploit here depends on the extent to which his feeling ashamed counts as his settled response to what he did. But in now raising the question for himself of its expressive meaning, he is unsettling that very response because he is thereby reopening the question of how he is to feel about himself. He wants to take *credit* for his feeling ashamed, and invest that credit in a renewed deliberation about how to feel about himself, one whose conclusion will mitigate the very shame on which he is basing his credit. But reopening the question of how he is to feel undoes the creditworthy aspect of his shame as his settled attitude. The credit for this response depended on the degree to which he was *resolved* on the question of how he is to feel about himself. Hence, reopening the question cuts him off from that meaning, and the credit he seeks for it. The epistemic or expressive value of his shame as an indication of his character will vary proportionally with the degree of his identification with it, which is the degree to which he takes himself to have settled the question of how he feels about himself. In this way, the degree to which he takes the question to be in need of an answer, the degree to which he needs the conclusions of the expressive reading of his response, will match the degree to which those very conclusions *diminish* in expressive import.[19]

The tactic of incorporating his current response in his reflections presents itself in the guise of epistemic care or completeness, but for the rakehell to reach that saving bit of evidence (his original shame

---

[19] I think these considerations provide a way of understanding Sartre's phenomenological description of a certain range of character assessment as being "unrealizable" from the first-person perspective, as involving "a meaning out of reach" for the person himself (Sartre 1956, p. 700). See the general discussion of 'unrealizables' beginning on p. 675. This idea is anticipated earlier in the famous section on "The Look": "Such qualities as 'evil', 'jealous', 'sympathetic' or 'antipathetic' and the like are not empty imaginings; when I use them to qualify the Other, I am well aware that I want to touch him in his being. Yet I cannot live them as my own realities. If the Other confers them on me, they are admitted by what I am for-myself; when the Other describes my character,

and its expressive meaning) he must retreat from it, thus compromising its very status as evidence about him. Or, perhaps we should say, he cannot seize on this without compromising its status as the *sort* of redeeming evidence he takes it to be. For in availing himself of the expressive strategy and thus suspending the meaning of his primary shame, he has now constituted a new set of facts about himself, facts that are themselves ripe for an expressive interpretation, but a less flattering one this time. The "tactical" nature of his secondary reflection ("feeling rather a good chap"), the way in which this stopping point is arbitrary and unmotivated from any epistemic point of view, is what he comes to see and what he expresses in the judgment he breaks off with ("not liking myself at all for feeling rather a good chap"). This is what he condemns in himself at the end. What he realizes is that insofar as he may reflect on his current attitude for what it expresses about him, he may do this with respect to the current act of reflection itself, ad infinitum. The dubious reasons he acted on in availing himself of the expressive interpretation in the first place will now count as reasons to undo the conclusion of that very interpretation. And so, what presents itself at first as an inquiry into his character is in fact a continual shifting between two perspectives on the self in order to continually reopen the question, defer closure, keep the answer in suspense for as long as it takes to keep a "redeeming interpretation" in play.

5.6 NOT FIRST-PERSONAL ENOUGH?

Naturally, not every such reflection will involve itself in the sort of reversals that the rakehell's reflections land him in. In good part this is due to the two features of shame that have guided the discussion: that it is itself a "self-regarding attitude," so that first-person reflection on its meaning makes for a difference in the person's total self-regard; and

---

I do not 'recognize' myself and yet I know that 'it is me'. I accept the responsibility for this stranger who is presented to me, but he does not cease to be a stranger" (p. 366).

that, as a condition, shame can be both humbling and praiseworthy, and thus has contrasting "affectual" meanings from the observer's and the agent's perspectives. In principle, *any* response of the person allows these two perspectives, and so, even without the sort of baroque equivocations we've been delineating in this case, various forms of self-regard will find themselves in conflict with the demands of the agent's point of view, even when that same kind of regard would be unobjectionable when applied to another person.

In what I've called a spectator's stance toward oneself, one's attention is shifted from the object of one's intentional state to the state itself, and that state is treated as a psychological phenomenon with various effects and implications for the person. Having the intentional attitude in the first place, however, commits one to viewing the world from that perspective; either that, or else changing one's mind about what it is that the attitude is directed upon. Neither of these requirements applies to our awareness of other people's intentional states. The rakehell as described seems to attempt a relation to his original shame, which does not involve viewing the world through it (in this case, himself and his actions), but instead treats it as an opaque psychological fact about himself that he *has* this attitude, a fact from which he can draw certain conclusions—conclusions which in this case conflict with the original attitude itself. And such a stance may involve a misplaced attention to the self even when this does *not* produce an overturning of the original judgment: the person focuses on the fact or experience of his shame rather than on that which is supposed to be its object. Indeed, normally such focusing of attention on one's own response is a retreat from the more painful attention to the actions and consequences that elicited the response and are its presumed intentional object.

For instance, we can see that, with characteristic stringency, George Eliot tracks down the erring self even when it finds the safe haven of guilty self-absorption. In *Middlemarch*, when Fred Vincy loses the money he had borrowed from the Garths, he is genuinely sorry, though somewhat removed both from his action and its effects:

Curiously enough, his pain in the affair beforehand had consisted almost entirely in the sense that he must seem dishonourable, and sink in the opinion of the Garths: he had not occupied himself with the inconvenience and possible injury that his breach might occasion them, for this exercise of the imagination on other people's needs is not common with hopeful young gentlemen. Indeed we are most of us brought up in the notion that the highest motive for not doing a wrong is something irrespective of the beings who would suffer the wrong. But at this moment he suddenly saw himself as a pitiful rascal who was robbing two women of their savings.

(Chapter 24)

Fred Vincy is assessing the moral significance of what he did by reference to how it may reflect on his character, rather than by reference either to the consequences for others or even to any impersonal deontological considerations. His attention to how he is to be esteemed interferes with reflection on the significance of what he did, a kind of evasion that is made possible by his modeling his thinking about himself on the imagined perspective of another person. To be fair, this is partly because he so loves Mary Garth and values her esteem even more than his own, even in some ways at the expense of his own. She is the witness whose judgment means more to him than anything, and his need here encourages his confusion that he can stand to his own thought and action primarily *as* such a witness.[20] The conversation he has with Mary later, when he has to confess that he lost her mother's savings, beautifully illustrates his confusion between the point of view

---

[20] A few pages earlier, speaking of the role Mary plays in Fred's mental economy, Eliot stresses the "spectatorial" aspect of this role: "Even much stronger mortals than Fred Vincy hold half their rectitude in the mind of the being they love best. 'The theatre of all my actions is fallen'; said an antique personage after his chief friend was dead; and they are fortunate who get a theatre where the audience demands their best. Certainly it would have made a considerable difference to Fred at that time if Mary Garth had had no decided notions as to what was admirable in character" (Eliot, Book 3, chapter 24, p. 178).

he is obliged to take on his own actions, and the outsider's perspective which, however harsh, he wishes to substitute for it.

> "I wouldn't have hurt you so for the world, Mary," he said at last. "You can never forgive me."
>
> "What does it matter whether I forgive you?" said Mary, passionately. "Would that make it any better for my mother to lose the money she has been earning by lessons for four years, that she might send Alfred to Mr Hanmer's? Should you think all that pleasant enough if I forgave you?"
>
> "Say what you like, Mary. I deserve it all."
>
> "I don't want to say anything," said Mary, more quietly; "my anger is of no use."
>
> (Book 3, chapter 25, p. 187)

Fred is weak but wants to be good. In him, this desire takes the form of an attempt to assimilate the external gaze of the "appraising Other," to usurp the role of the being in whom he holds more than half his rectitude. This judgment on himself means more to him than the "outward directed" considerations upon which his remorse should properly be directed, and so he looks upon his own action from the external point of view of this imagined Other. He does not attempt to bootstrap himself out of this remorse, but he does remain stuck in the position of objectified concern with it, knowing that only Mary's redeeming judgment could bring him out of himself. This is something he cannot do for himself—forgiveness requiring a person genuinely other to oneself. Mary herself sees his need and his egocentric helplessness here, and her recognition of her own position as Fred's "appraising Other" creates a trap she is determined to avoid. For she realizes that in addressing him about this matter at all, she is necessarily in the position of appraising him, and that this appraisal, whether good or bad, is what Fred is clinging to. At the same time, she sees vividly that any such judgment at this time is not to the point, and that to deliver it to Fred would be feeding the very self-absorption that created this problem for both of them. Hence, she has to deliver a judgment to him of the form: You must cease now to be concerned in this way with my judgment of you, the moral import of the situation lies elsewhere. And so the conversation ends with her refusal of any expression of her judgment of him or his actions at all: "I don't want to say anything."

We can see something both morally and psychologically amiss, then, when self-reflection on the issue of the virtues of character inhibits or distorts one's moral response to what one has done. And I think we can now see this as the sort of thing Williams has in mind when he says that the trouble with the first-person exercise of cultivating the virtues is that such thought is not self-directed *enough*, focusing instead on "the way in which others might describe or comment on the way in which you think about your actions" (p. 11). Consider another kind of case that involves such a stance; say, the application of virtue terms to oneself when this is undertaken for purposes of prediction. The statement "Given my generous nature, I am likely to loan him the money if he needs it" sounds bizarre not simply in being self-aggrandizing, but because it presents itself as a prediction when it's hard to see how such a statement could be anything other than a declaration of intention. And it is doubly suspicious because, in the first place, the reliance on a more or less probable prediction presents the person as less than fully *committed* to loaning the money, as if the speaker himself needed evidence here to take up the slack of his commitment. And second, it is this very *absence* of full commitment that is expressed by his availing himself of terms of self-*praise* rather than a straightforward declaration of intention that would omit any mention of his own character. It is as though he wants to be congratulated for being at present only halfheartedly inclined to loan the money, but confidently predicting that his better self will prevail, in spite of his current lack of resolve or full endorsement. By contrast, genuine commitment and first-person authority would express itself directly in a nonevidential declaration of intent.

The curious distancing of oneself from one's actions in such a case is paralleled by the sense in the rakehell case of his failure to assume responsibility for his attitudes and dispositions, just at the moment when he turns his attention to the question of what sort of person they show him to be. And this, I think, is where we find the peculiarities in the *appraising* function of virtue terms when applied to oneself, as noted by Williams and others. For both the predictive and appraising functions rest on holding the psychological facts fixed and focusing on them rather than on their objects. Naturally, if the dispositional facts of character are taken to be so fluid and unfixed that it is an entirely open question whether I will (now or ever) act out of my supposed trait of generosity, then ascribing it to me is useless as a prediction and empty as an appraisal. So, the most ordinary apprehension and estimation of another person requires reference to traits or dispositions of *some* stability. But the kernel of truth in Sartre's insistence that reflective consciousness of oneself means "nihilation" of the aspect apprehended, in the sense of "positing one's freedom" with respect to it, acknowledging that one could be otherwise, is that keeping the psychological facts fixed in this way is just what the stance of practical self-reflection does *not* involve. By contrast, Fred Vincy's guilty consciousness of himself blocks his attention to the actual object of his guilt: his actions and the beings who suffered the wrong. His indulgent self-blame, or even his concentration on the general issue of how he is now to be appraised, rests on holding the psychological facts about himself fixed. And fixed they remain, without developing into other world-directed attitudes more appropriate both to the situation and to his original first-order feeling of remorse.

Even if the terms for traits of character are not exclusively reserved for relations with others,[21] there remains the sense in which the stance of agency is subject to different constraints from the stance of appraisal

---

[21] As Sartre (1956), for instance, sometimes suggests: "Character has distinct existence only in the capacity of an object of knowledge for the Other" (part 3, chapter 2, section 2).

of oneself. And yet, of course, we remain subject to the claims of both stances, even when neither of them provides the terms for adjudicating possible conflict between them. The situations of self-reflection discussed here represent one class of cases where a more realistic and detailed moral psychology reveals tensions in interpreting and living up to a commonsense appeal to impersonality. Although it is in many ways a natural and unavoidable appeal (it is not only moral philosophers who may enjoin us to "see ourselves as others see us"), it is also a complex and ambiguous one, subject to conflicting interpretations even within a single reflective consciousness. There are particularly vivid ambiguities in the attempt to accommodate this appeal to some of the basic asymmetries between first-person and third-person perspectives, as outlined in the previous chapters. At the same time, the complexities discussed here do not themselves discredit the claims of impersonality, and genuine concerns about what might be seen as pathologies of "self-objectification" ought not themselves to contribute to obscuring the distinction between the idea that one should judge one's action and character as one would those of any other person, and the idea of conceiving of one's action and character *as* that of another person, or someone who happens to be me. But such phenomena do suggest that we need to pay attention to the fine grain of systematic first-person / third-person differences if we are to be able to draw such distinctions in a principled way. A central aim of this discussion has been to make a start at showing how some of these seemingly remote matters from philosophy of mind have a genuine role to play in accounting for aspects of the structure and phenomenology of moral experience.

The book as a whole has argued that the concept of the person as a reasoning agent is both ineliminable and brings with it a set of basic differences in relating to oneself and relating to others. Among philosophers, these differences have sometimes seemed theoretically suspicious or unmotivated, and in some situations of personal internal conflict they can seem arbitrary, burdensome, or worse. So there are both philosophical and personal attempts either to overcome or evade the asymmetries between the possibilities for self-relations and relations to others, or to assimilate all psychological discourse to either the first- or the third-person case. If the self-other differences discussed here really are integral to the very concept of the person, then I hope to have contributed to our estimation of the cost of such attempts.

Bibliography

Adorno, Theodor. *Minima Moralia*. Translated by E.F.N. Jephcott. New Left Books, 1974 (Suhrkamp Verlag, 1951).

Amis, Kingsley. *That Uncertain Feeling*. Harcourt Brace, 1956.

Anscombe, G.E.M. [1975]. "The First Person." In Anscombe, *Collected Philosophical Papers, vol. 2: Metaphysics and the Philosophy of Mind*. University of Minnesota Press, 1981.

———. [1957]. *Intention*. 2d ed. Cornell University Press, 1976.

Aristotle. *Nicomachean Ethics*. Translated by Terence Irwin. Hackett, 1985.

Armstrong, D. M. *A Materialist Theory of the Mind*. Routledge and Kegan Paul, 1968.

Armstrong, D. M., and Malcolm, Norman. *Consciousness and Causality*. Blackwell, 1984.

Boghossian, Paul. "Content and Self-Knowledge." *Philosophical Topics* 17, no. 1 (1989).

Boswell, James [1791]. *Life of Johnson*. Edited by R. W. Chapman. Oxford University Press, 1953.

Burge, Tyler. "Individualism and Self-Knowledge." *Journal of Philosophy* 85 (1988): 649–63.

———. "Our Entitlement to Self-Knowledge." *Proceedings of the Aristotelian Society* 96 (1996): 91–116.

———. "Reason and the First Person." In Wright, Smith, and Macdonald, eds., 1998.

Cavell, Stanley. *The Claim of Reason*. Oxford University Press, 1979.

Churchland, Paul. *Matter and Consciousness*. MIT Press, 1984.

Davidson, Donald. "Knowing One's Own Mind." In *Proceedings and Addresses of the American Philosophical Association* 60, no. 3 (January 1987).

Dennett, Daniel. *Content and Consciousness*. Routledge and Kegan Paul (London) and Humanities Press (New York), 1969.

———. *Brainstorms*. MIT Press, 1981.

———. [1976]. "Conditions of Personhood." In *Brainstorms*.

———. [1977]. "How to Change your Mind." In *Brainstorms*.

Descartes, René. *The Philosophical Works of Descartes*. Vols. 1 and 2, translated by Elizabeth S. Haldane and G.R.T. Ross. Cambridge University Press, 1911–12 and 1931.

———. (1970), *Philosophical Letters*. Translated and edited by Anthony Kenny. Oxford University Press, 1970.

Driver, Julia. "The Virtues of Ignorance." *Journal of Philosophy* 86 (1989): 373–84.

Ebbs, Gary. "Can We Take Our Words at Face Value?" *Philosophy and Phenomenological Research* 56 (1996): 499–530.

———. *Rule Following and Realism*. Harvard University Press, 1997.

Edgley, Roy. *Reason in Theory and Practice*. Hutchinson (London), 1969.

Eliot, George [1872]. *Middlemarch*. Edited by Gordon Haight. Houghton Mifflin, 1956.

Evans, Gareth. *The Varieties of Reference*. Oxford University Press, 1982.

Falvey, Kevin, and Owens, Joseph. "Externalism, Self-Knowledge, and Skepticism." *Philosophical Review* 103, no. 1 (1994): 107 (31).

Foot, Philippa. "Moral Arguments," In *Virtues and Vices*. University of California Press, 1958. Originally published in *Mind* 67 (1958).

Freud, Sigmund. *The Standard Edition of the Complete Psychological Works of Sigmund Freud*. Edited and translated by James Strachey in collaboration with Anna Freud. Hogarth Press (London), 1966.

———. [1900]. *The Interpretation of Dreams*. In *Standard Edition*, vols. 4 and 5.

———— [1909]. "Notes upon a Case of Obsessional Neurosis." In *Standard Edition*, vol. 10.

————. [1912]. "A Note on the Unconscious in Psychoanalysis." In *Standard Edition*, vol. 14.

————. [1914]. "Remembering, Repeating, and Working-Through." In *Standard Edition*, vol 12.

————. [1915]. "The Unconscious." In *Standard Edition*, vol. 14.

Gibbard, Allan. *Wise Choices, Apt Feelings*. Harvard University Press, 1990.

Gilbert, Margaret. "Vices and Self-Knowledge." *Journal of Philosophy* 68, no. 15 (August 5, 1971).

Gombay, Andre. "Some Paradoxes of Counterprivacy." *Philosophy* 63 (1988).

Grice, H. P. "Intention and Uncertainty." *Proceedings of the British Academy* 57 (1971).

Hampshire, Stuart. *Freedom of the Individual*. Princeton University Press, 1975.

Hampshire, S., and Hart, H.L.A. "Decision, Intention and Certainty." *Mind* 67 (1958)

Holton, Richard. "Intention Detecting." *Philosophical Quarterly* 43, no. 172 (1993): 298–318.

Hume, David [1740]. *A Treatise of Human Nature*. Edited by L. A. Selby-Bigge. Oxford University Press, 1951.

————. [1748]. *An Enquiry Concerning Human Understanding*. Edited by Eric Steinberg. Hackett, 1977.

Hutcheson, Francis [1728]. "An Essay on the Nature and Conduct of the Passions and Affections. With Illustrations on the Moral Sense." In *British Moralists, 1650–1800*, vol. 1, edited by D. D. Raphael. Clarendon (Oxford), 1969.

Johnston, Mark. "Objectivity Refigured: Pragmatism without Verificationism." In *Realism and Reason*, edited by J. Haldane and C. Wright. Clarendon (Oxford), 1991).

Kant, Immanuel [1785]. *Groundwork of the Metaphysics of Morals*. Translated by H. J. Paton. Harper Torchbooks, 1964.

Kenny, Anthony. "Cartesian Privacy." In *Wittgenstein: The Philosophical Investigations*, edited by George Pitcher. Notre Dame University Press, 1968.

Kierkegaard, Søren [1843]. *Either/Or*. Translated by Walter Lowrie. Princeton University Press, 1959.

Korsgaard, Christine. *The Sources of Normativity*. Cambridge University Press, 1996.

La Rochefoucauld [1678]. *Maxims*. Translated by Leonard Tancock. Penguin, 1959.

Locke, John [1690]. *An Essay Concerning Human Understanding.* Edited by
    A. C. Fraser. Dover, 1959.
Ludlow, Peter, and Martin, Norah, eds. *Externalism and Self-Knowledge.* Cen-
    ter for the Study of Language and Information, Stanford University, 1998.
McDowell, John. *Mind and World.* Harvard University Press, 1996.
McGinn, Colin. *The Character of Mind.* Oxford University Press, 1982.
Mellor, D. H. "Conscious Belief." *Proceedings of the Aristotelian Society,* 1977–
    78.
Moran, Richard. "Interpretation Theory and the First-Person." *Philosophical
    Quarterly,* April 1994.
Nagel, Thomas. *The Possibility of Altruism.* Princeton University Press, 1970.
Nietzsche, Friedrich [1886]. *Beyond Good and Evil.* Translated by Walter Kauf-
    mann. Vintage, 1989.
Nisbett, R., and Ross, L. *Human Inference: Strategies and Shortcomings of
    Social Judgement.* Prentice Hall, 1980.
Nisbett, R. E., and Wilson, T. DeC. "Telling More Than We Know: Verbal Re-
    ports on Mental Processes." *Psychological Review* 84 (1977): 231–59.
Parfit, Derek. *Reasons and Persons.* Clarendon (Oxford), 1984.
Pascal, Blaise. *Pensées.* Translated by W. F. Trotter. Dutton, 1958.
Peacocke, Christopher. *A Study of Concepts.* MIT Press. 1992.
———. "Conscious Attitudes and Self-Knowledge." In Wright, Smith, and Mac-
    donald, eds., 1998.
Perry, John. "Frege on Demonstratives." *Philosophical Review* 86 (1977).
———. "The Problem of the Essential Indexical." *Nous* 13 (1979).
Raz, Joseph, ed. *Practical Reasoning.* Oxford University Press, 1978.
Rey, Georges. "Towards a Computational Account of *Akrasia* and Self-Decep-
    tion." In *Perspectives on Self-Deception,* edited by A. O. Rorty and
    B. McLaughlin. University of California Press, 1989.
Rorty, Richard. *Philosophy and the Mirror of Nature.* Princeton University
    Press, 1979.
———. "Contemporary Philosophy of Mind." *Synthese* 53 (1982).
Sartre, Jean-Paul. *Being and Nothingness.* Translated by Hazel Barnes. Wash-
    ington Square Press, Philosophical Library, 1956.
Scanlon, T. M. *What We Owe to Each Other.* Harvard University Press, 1998.
Scheffler, Samuel. *The Rejection of Consequentialism.* Clarendon (Oxford),
    1982.
Searle, John. *Speech Acts: An Essay in the Philosophy of Language.* Cambridge
    University Press, 1969.
———. *The Rediscovery of the Mind.* MIT Press, Bradford, 1992.

Sellars, Wilfred. *Science, Perception and Reality*. Routledge and Kegan Paul, 1963.

————. [1962]. "Philosophy and the Scientific Image of Man." In Sellars 1963.

————. [1956]. "Empiricism and the Philosophy of Mind." In Sellars 1963.

Shoemaker, Sydney. *Self-Knowledge and Self-Identity*. Cornell University Press, 1963.

————. [1968]. "Self-Reference and Self-Awareness." In Shoemaker 1984.

————. *Identity, Cause and Mind: Philosophical Essays*. Cambridge University Press, 1984.

————. "On Knowing One's Own Mind." In *Philosophical Perspectives 2: Epistemology*, edited by James E. Tomberlin, pp. 183–209. Blackwell, 1988.

————. "First-Person Access." In *Philosophical Perspectives 4: Action Theory and Philosophy of Mind*.

————. "Rationality and Self-Consciousness." In *The Opened Curtain: A U.S.-Soviet Philosophy Summit*, edited by K. Lehrer and E. Sosa. Westview Press, 1996.

————. *The First-Person Perspective and Other Essays*. Cambridge University Press, 1996.

Stalnaker, Robert. *Inquiry*. MIT Press, 1984.

Stevens, Wallace. *The Necessary Angel*. Alfred Knopf, 1951.

Stroud, Barry. "Practical Reasoning." In *Reasoning Practically*, edited by Edna Ullmann-Margalit. Oxford University Press, 2000.

Taylor, Charles. "Responsibility for Self." In *The Identities of Persons*, edited by A. O. Rorty. University of California Press, 1976.

————. *Human Agency and Language: Philosophical Papers*. Vol. 1, Cambridge University Press, 1985a.

————. *Philosophy and the Human Sciences: Philosophical Papers*. Vol. 2. Cambridge University Press, 1985b.

————. [1981]. "The Concept of a Person." In Taylor 1985a.

————. [1977a]. "Self-Interpreting Animals." In Taylor 1985a.

————. [1977b]. "What Is Human Agency?" In Taylor 1985a.

Velleman, J. David. *Practical Reflection*. Princeton University Press, 1989.

————. "On the Aim of Belief." In his *The Possibility of Practical Reason*. Clarendon (Oxford), 2000.

Williams, Bernard. *Ethics and the Limits of Philosophy*. Harvard University Press, 1985.

————. *Shame and Necessity*. University of California Press, 1993.

Wilson, George. *The Intentionality of Human Action*. Revised and enlarged edition. Stanford University Press, 1989.

Wilson, Margaret Dauler. *Descartes*. Routledge and Kegan Paul (London), 1978.

Wittgenstein, Ludwig. *Philosophical Investigations*. Translated by G.E.M. Anscombe. Blackwell (Oxford), 1956.

————. *The Blue and the Brown Books*. Blackwell (Oxford), 1958.

————. *Zettel*. Translated by G.E.M. Anscombe. Blackwell (Oxford), 1967.

————. *Remarks on the Philosophy of Psychology*. Vol. 1, translated by G.E.M. Anscombe. Blackwell (Oxford), 1980a.

————. *Remarks on the Philosophy of Psychology*. Vol. 2, translated by C. G. Luckhardt and Maximilian A. E. Aue. Blackwell (Oxford), 1980b.

————. *Last Writings on the Philosophy of Psychology*. Vol. 1, translated by C. G. Luckhardt and Maximilian A. E. Aue. Blackwell (Oxford), 1982.

————. *Last Writings on the Philosophy of Psychology*. Vol. 2, translated by C. G. Luckhardt and Maximilian A. E. Aue. Blackwell (Oxford), 1992.

Wright, Crispin. "On Making Up One's Mind: Wittgenstein on Intention." In *Logic, Philosophy of Science and Epistemology*, edited by Weingartner and Schurz. Proceedings of the 11th International Wittgenstein Symposium, Kirchberg, Vienna, 1986.

————. "Wittgenstein's Rule-Following Considerations and the Central Project of Theoretical Linguistics." In *Reflections on Chomsky*, edited by Alexander George. Blackwell (Oxford), 1989.

————. "Wittgenstein's Later Philosophy of Mind: Sensation, Privacy, and Intention." *Journal of Philosophy*, November 1989.

————. "Self-Knowledge: The Wittgensteinian Legacy." In Wright, Smith, and Macdonald, eds., 1998.

Wright, Crispin, Smith, Barry C., and Macdonald, Cynthia, eds. *Knowing Our Own Minds*. Clarendon (Oxford), 1998.

Index

p. 46.

p. 67.